WHEN STARS LOOK DOWN

By
George Van Tassel
Carlos Allende

SAUCERIAN PUBLISHER

ISBN: 978-1-955087-12-4

© 2022, Saucerian Publisher

Al rights reserved. No part of this publication maybe reproduced, translate, store in a retrieval system, or transmitted in any form or by any means, electronic, mechanical, photocopying, recording or otherwise, without prior written permision from the publisher.

George Van Tassel and the Integratron

Prologue

George Van Tassel was an American author and ufologist once claimed to have been in contact with an extraterrestrial from Venus. He was a controversial figure in the annals of ufology.

Van Tassel was born in Jefferson, Ohio in 1910, and grew up in a fairly prosperous middle-class family. He finished high school in the 10th grade and held a job at a small municipal airport near Cleveland; he also acquired a pilot's license. At age 20, he moved to California, where at first he worked as an automobile mechanic at a garage owned by an uncle. While pumping gas at the garage, he met Frank Critzer, an eccentric loner who claimed to be working a mine somewhere near Giant Rock, a 7-story boulder near Landers, California. Frank Critzer was a German immigrant trying to make a living in the desert as a prospector. During World War II, Critzer was under suspicion as a German spy and was killed during a police siege at the Rock in 1942. Upon receiving news of Critzer's death, Van Tassel applied for a lease of the small abandoned airport near Giant Rock from the Bureau of Land Management, and was eventually given a Federal Government contract to develop and maintain the airstrip.

Van Tassel was an accomplished aircraft mechanic and flight inspector who worked for various firms between 1930 and 1947 before retiring to the desert. In 1947, Van Tassel left Southern California's booming aerospace industry to live in the desert with his family. At first, he lived a simple existence in the rooms Frank Critzer had dug out under Giant Rock. Van Tassel eventually built a new home, a cafe, a gas station, a store, a small airstrip, and a ranch beside the Rock.

He rose to prominence as a key figure of interest in 1953 after claiming that he had been awoken one night by an alien from Venus named Solgonda. The being allegedly invited him aboard its spacecraft where Van Tassel was telepathically gifted the plans for a device called the "Integratron" which was said to be capable of rejuvenating the human body.

Van Tassel began constructing the Integratron in 1954 in "an intersection of powerful geomagnetic forces that, when focused by the unique geometry of the building, will concentrate and amplify the energy required for cell rejuvenation". The construction costs were partly paid for by an annual series of successful UFO conventions, the Giant Rock Spacecraft Conventions, which continued for nearly 25 years. The main structure's construction was complete circa 1959, but Van Tassel continued to work on the device until his sudden death in 1978.

According to Van Tassel, the Integratron's workings rely on the generation of strong "intermittent magnetic fields" resulting in the generation of plasma in the form of a coronal discharge and negative air ionization inside the building. The Integratron is based on the Multiple Wave Oscillator invented by Georges Lakhovsky. The Multiple Wave Oscillator is a combination of a high voltage Tesla coil and a split-ring resonator that generates ultra wideband electromagnetic frequencies. Van Tassel speculated that electromagnetism affects biological cells, and believed that every biological cell has a unique resonant electromagnetic frequency. According to van Tassel, the generation of strong ultra wideband EMF by the Integratron "resonates" with the cell's frequency and "recharges" the cellular structure as if it were an electrical battery. Van Tassel claimed that human cells "rejuvenated" while inside the structure. Van Tassel also claimed the Integratron is intentionally constructed atop a powerful geomagnetic anomaly and its construction is entirely of non-ferromagnetic materials, the equivalent to a modern radome.

Saucerian Publisher was founded with the mission of promoting books in Science Fiction, Paranormal, and the Occult. Our vision is to preserve the legacy of literary history by reprint editions of books which have already been exhausted or are difficult to obtain. Our goal is to help readers, educators and researchers by bringing back original publications that are difficult to find at reasonable price, while preserving the legacy of universal knowledge. This book is an authentic reproduction of the original printed text. Because this book is culturally important, we have made available as part of our commitment to protect, preserve and promote knowledge in the world.

When The Stars Look Down is a collection of selected writings by George Van Tassel over a period of 20 years describing a reality that many of us are not familiar with it. Much of the information presented here is complex and is not easily understood. The subject matters include: Forces and Frequencies, Life And Laws, Static Intelligence, Voices And Visions, Pollution And Blood, Motion And Time, Energy And Tesla, Humans And Man, Free Energy And Progress, Changes And Thoughts, Perception And Mind, Principles And Proof, Secrecy And Space, Lies And Facts, Sightings And Satellites, Contacts And Cycles.

Van Tassel points out that the beginning of all creation has the same meaning as the ending of all creation, for all things have always existed and always will exist. Everything anyone has ever been or will ever be, he is now. This is a truth often overlooked in man's search for understanding. Man forgets God was all there was, and therefore all there is now or will ever be. Van Tassel writes that religion and science are the same things, the only difference being that they are two opposite viewpoints. Just as a wall is a wall regardless of which side one stands on, so are science and religion, life itself. According to Van Tassel, the Bible is an accurate history of events repeating themselves in cycles. He says predictions refer to spaceships throughout the Bible, among them the prophecy that there will be a day when the ships will come to take the ready people, leaving those who are not prepared to face the cataclysmic destruction inevitably approaching.

Original text. This title is the most comprehensive anthology written by Van Tassel and illuminates every dimension of him.

Saucerian Publisher, 2022

*To all those gallant folks
who believe that "thinking
out loud" is good therapy this
book is affectionately dedicated*

TABLE OF CONTENTS

Chapter		Page
	INTRODUCTION	1
	BACKGROUND	2
I	*FORCES AND FREQUENCES*	4
II	*LIFE & LAWS*	13
III	*STATIC INTELLIGENCE*	22
IV	*VOICES & VISIONS*	37
V	*POLLUTION & BLOOD*	53
VI	*MOTION & TIME*	61
VII	*ENERGY & TESLA*	70
VIII	*HUMANS & MAN*	82
IX	*FREE ENERGY & PROGRESS*	111
X	*CHANGES & THOUGHTS*	121
XI	*PERCEPTION & MIND*	131
XII	*PRINCIPLES & PROOF*	142
XIII	*SECRECY & SPACE*	153

XIV	*LIES & FACTS*	162
XV	*SIGHTINGS & SATELLITES*	175
XVI	*CONTACTS & CYCLES*	183
XVII	*PURSUIT & PURPOSE*	197
XIX	*SPACE, ENERGIES & CONCEPT*	206
XX	*VERIFICATION & DATA*	231
	ARTICLES SINCE 1973	234
	HELP GOD MAKE YOU WELL	234
	THE INTEGRATRON	239
	CELL COMMUNICATION	244
	THE PYRAMID PRINCIPLE	249
	BREAKTHROUGH	256
	WORLD POWER GRID	263
	THE BERMUDA TRIANGLE	271

LIST OF ILLUSTRATIONS

The Moon Path	62
Electra-Magnetic Growing	77
Anti-Frost Control	114
The Gassendi Crater	154
Back Side Of The Moon	157
Monguzzi "Saucer" Pictures	171,172
Navy Experimental "Saucer"	173
The "Integratron"	199
The Author, And "Time Machine"	203
Rotation Principle Of The Earth	210
Orbit Principle Of The Earth	214
Orbit Principle Of The Moon	219
The Lines Of Force And People	226

INTRODUCTION

INTRODUCTION

This book is part of the compiled writings of George W. Van Tassel written over a period of 20 years, brought to the reader under one cover.

In presenting this inspired material, it is not expected that everyone will understand it, or accept it. Those readers who have experienced phenomena of some nature in their lives will gather much from it. Some people may grasp a new sense of security from it. It is not an attempt to present a new religion, or science, but rather to expand upon those things that are already accepted. Reality, being so true, is often thrust aside by those who do not see reality close up.

Whatever this book gives you, it is certain that it will not take anything away from those who read it. The effort alone is, many times, the reward of accomplishment. The book itself is sufficient unto itself as a record.

BACKGROUND

BACKGROUND

GEORGE VAN TasseL was born in Jefferson, Ohio, in 1910. He entered the field of aviation in 1927. After three years of experience with early airline work, he came to California and was employed by Douglas Aircraft Company in a variety of responsible positions. He left Douglas in 1941 and became the personal flight inspector for Howard Hughes in flight test of experimental aircraft. In 1943 he left Hughes and became flight safety inspector with Lockheed until 1947, when he held a flight test inspection position on Constellation aircraft. In 1947 he started operation of Giant Rock Airport, 17 miles north of Yucca Valley, California. At the time of printing this book, he has operated Giant Rock Airport for 28 years.

While operating Giant Rock Airport in 1953, he founded a science philosophy organization. In 1958 this organization incorporated as "The Ministry of Universal Wisdom" with a branch, "The College of Universal Wisdom," doing electromagnetic research.

Mr. Van Tassel has appeared on 409 radio and television shows and given 297 lectures in the United States and Canada. He is President of the corporation; has been married 38 years and the father of three daughters, and grandfather of 13 brilliant grandchildren.

He is dedicated to a program of rejuvenation and regeneration of the elderly, and is working on a program to prevent the aging of youth. He is the designer of the "Integratron," a four story high, dome-shaped machine; following up seven years of small research, in a people-size program to double the present life span. This machine is about ready for tests to recharge the cell structure of people, like charging batteries.

BACKGROUND

Designer, author, inventor, lecturer, radio and television personality and airport operator. Being successful in every undertaking throughout his life, qualifies him in experience beyond the level of average acceptance, as an authority on varied subjects.

CHAPTER ONE

FORCES AND FREQUENCES

People who live on this Earth never stop to realize that they are bio-magnetic and electrical absorbers and emitters of energies that are not registered by their five physical senses. The planet is an armature of sperical shape, with a self-energized stratum of fields sur-rounding it and permeating it.

The magnetic field polarized Northerly and Southerly, that swings compass needles, has been known about for centuries. There are other fields in the earth's bulk that are not measurable with a magnetic instrument such as a compass. These fields and currents are the car-riers and distributors of what we will call "life force." This current is not gravity, electrical, or magnetic, and yet is all of these combined, plus a pulsing carrier, or "life force" that conforms polaritywise with uit ot the other three.

Scientific men in the past such as Dr. William J. Kilner of the St. Thomas Hospital in London; Prof. Rohsacher of the University of Vienna; Prof. Regelsberger; Prof. Sauerbruch, and others all found evidence of this fourth force but lacked instruments to prove its poten-tials. This "life force" is only measurable and detectable through "liv-ing" instruments and it is also subject to thought. (Not meaning the brain waves of humans.) Humans do not think. They only respond to thought and "life force" which directs them. Because "life force" has polarity, humans respond with either "good or bad" or "well and sick" results manifested in them.

This "life force" covers a checker-board pattern on the surface of the Earth. Every other square both North and South and East and West is of positive polarity with the squares inbetween being of

CHAPTER ONE FORCES AND FREQUENCES

negative polarity. This life force goes into the Earth's surface in the negative squares and comes out of the surface in the positive polarity squares. If this current could be seen it would look like a serpent or a sine wave, half above and half below the surface going in perpendicular direc-tions horizontally.

These positive and negative squares, starting from the Earth's Equa-tor, measure 32 meters long on each side and diminish in size to zero at the planet's poles.

Each of these squares have poles in their centers approximately 2.45 meters in diameter. These main center poles are surrounded by eight Piae spaced smaller poles of approximately 60 centimenters in diameter.

Here at our research location the squares are about 65 feet on each side at 34° N. Latitude. The main poles exhibit "beam" flows North and South, and East and West.

It was discovered that these squares have definite effects on humans, 'animals, and vegetation, Ants in the most cases seem to like to have their hills at the mainpole of the positive polarity squares. They live *underground* of course. On the *surface* an opposite effect is apparent. People who have their homes in negative polarity squares have the effect of making "one feel at home" in their houses, while the people's houses in the positive polarity squares make one feel "out of place" or in a hurry to live them. Also people, animals and vegetation seem to thrive, be well and alive in the negative polarity squares. Sick people, biting dogs and vegetation that needs constant care seem to be living in the positive polarity square.

These squares also seem to have an effect on T.V. reception in fringe areas, where U.H.F. reception is required. My T.V. antenna at Giant Rock Airport will not receive either the picture or sound if it is moved 30 feet in any direction.

CHAPTER ONE FORCES AND FREQUENCES

Much research must be done and sensitive instruments made to work with "living matter," in order to completely understand this life force. Condensers with alternate insulated layers of *lettuce leaves* and aluminum foil exhibit the strange ability of detecting unseen forces not detected by magnetic or eletrical instruments directly.

I am certain that Hubbard free energy device, demonstrated in Seattle, Washington in the early 1920s, was extracting energy by undergroung coupling with these forces. We have his original mercury filled tubes used in his research.

God (Universal Mind) not only created all forms of life, but it mani-fests the perpetual activity of living. This does not mean, in the limited thinking of an orthodox people on this earth, that it cannot manifest anywhere else in the universe. It does so everywhere.

Everything manifests radiations, from the tiniest particles in atomic structure to stratum of fields in space and spinning galaxies ad infini-tum. Being here, and employing those radiation effects that are bene-ficial to our earthly needs, is the only thing that is important to us.

The earth is a living body, like an electron of our solar system. Its blood is the life giving waters on the surface and underground. Its breathing is in the atmosphere around the surface, in life supporting gases called air. Its nerve system is in the electric charge that conducts radio and television, and climaxes its capacity with lightning bolts. Its brain creates the auroras and swings a compass needle with the subtle force of magnetism. Its breast feeds every living thing, by giving minerals, salts, and the elements to the flesh, feathers, and bone of its offspring.

Life as an essence is not measurable. It is as infinite as space and time. To each his own, and mother earth insists on her children

CHAPTER ONE FORCES AND FREQUENCES

staying in their separate environments, or live in conflict.

Mortal life manifests through cell structure. Cells are the smallest living manifestations of life. The atoms of a cell radiate the life forces of an Infinite Perfect Mind working in the frequencies of a particular requirement for a given effect.

Scientists like to label their life giving forces with names like cosmic rays, electricity, magnetism, atomic energy, and the like; but they cant find the source of these manifestations.

Cells form the structure of people, trees, plants, birds, fish and all. living things. These structures repeat their forms down through time, as other electrical entities are demanding entrance into this physical realm to enjoy or suffer the experiences of life here.

As parts of the atomic structure are only centers of fields of activity, they form together in different densities and polarities to be the matrix of molecular bodies. The molecules join to form cell bodies. Cell bodies unite to manifest people. People occupy the planet like fleas on a dog. Each is dependent on its parent body to manifest here. Protozoa, by the millions, live on the skins of people. The people neither see them, or feel them. Another parasite depends on the protozoa to live. We are all crawling with life manifestations inside and outside.

Now tell me where did humans get the idea they are the greatest of all creations?

This Eternal Life Essence wich permeates and activates all things that life is Pure Intelligence It did not get an education to get smart. It knows how to create a galaxy, a planet, or a rose.

Cells oscillate in different electrical frequencies. They radiate energy according to their ability to assimilate it. Space is eternal life energy in solution. Matter is the structure to manifest it.

CHAPTER ONE FORCES AND FREQUENCES

Medical scientists have proven the heart beats as the result of electrical impulses. Hearing is electrical impulses from the inner ear to the brain. Vision is electrical. Motion is the result of electrical direction both voluntary and involuntary in people. A tree overcomes gravity and raises water from the ground to its uppermost leaves through electrical action of its cell structure.

Cells live in a society of harmonious activity in health or a discord of inharmony in disease.Cells communicate, experience ecstacy or pain, are subject to directed thought and can respond in "good or bad" reactions.

Cells in plants have shown a marked reaction on sensitive electrical instruments when a fellow plant is burned, or injured. The murder of a ,cabbage crop can produce chaotic reactions on a polygraph wired nto a cabbage that didnt get harvested.

Birds fly south to warmer climes before the cold comes, without weather predictions. Animals flee an area before an earthquake. They can sense water miles away. These so-called "dumb" creatures tune in to the part of God that knows their requirements. We label this "instinct." Humans like to believe, by separating everything in a mass of words and labels, that this makes one an intellect, if he knows more of the separations than other people. God has been brainwashed out of people as the source of life and intelligence.

Try thinking to your plants and friends, and include God in the action. You're all related in the world of cell structure.

The essence of life is not only being made manifest in you, but you are submerged and encompassed in it.

Thoughts, words, and actions are each of different densities. Each of these three forces are manifested by, and from, individual levels.

Thought is the prime force and is neutral Thought can be used

CHAPTER ONE FORCES AND FREQUENCES

either for creative effects, or destructive results.

Words are the effect of thoughts, whether they be good or bad. They are the sound manifestation of thoughts. Actions are the manifested results of either thoughts, or words.

Words are in the range of our physical hearing. They are the means by which thoughts are conveyed between people with sound. Various languages convey the same meaning by different sounds.

Actions are the manifested workings of sounds conveyed through hearing, or thoughts conveyed through thinking.

My words are conveyed to your mind, by placing the thoughts I have, within the range of your vision in written words that are symbols of the sounds.

Not long ago the printing you are now reading was not within the-range of your vision. This paper was blank paper. You couldn't see anything on it until the ink symbolized my thoughts in contrast to the blank paper. Had you been within range of my voice I could have transmitted my thoughts to you through sound.

Thoughts are not ordinarily seen, nor is sound; so I brought them out of their densities so you could see them in print. I have made it possible for you to see the thoughts in my mind by placing them on these pages.

I have materialized my thoughts to your vision. You may not believe what I have written, but you must admit it is here where you can see it.

There have been many arguments, discussions, and efforts to prove that things, and people, not seen in our life level, can be materialized. The Bible tells many times about "angels" appearing before people apparently out of thin air.

CHAPTER ONE FORCES AND FREQUENCES

I have just proven that I can materialize my thoughts on this paper where you can see them in the symbols of the sounds that you could also hear.

To believe in the Bible of Christianity, with the concept that "angels" appeared in olden times, and cannot appear in our time; is certainly bullheaded orthodoxy. This is primarily done by some "Christians" who or not want "angels" to interfere with their selfish ways and pleasures.

Much had been said about the space people of today materializing and de -materializingon several occasions. I can truthfully say that I have seen and talked with one of them that instantly disappeared to my vision; but I could still feel him when I touched where I had just seen him.

Just as orthodoxy places limits on people's thinking, so does your physical sense of sight place limits on your seeing. Your eyes can only see within the range of the visible spectrum; about 4000 to 7800 angstroms in wave length measurement.

You cannot see the air, yet you breathe it. You can see water in its fluid density and its vaporous density, but when the steam is absorbed in the air, you cannot see it.

Vibrations from about 20 to nearly 20,000 cycles a second can be heard with the ears. Vibrations below our hearing level are called "infrasonic" and those above it "ultrasonic."

Because the five lower senses all have limits, people's thinking has become narrowed into a groove that will not allow them to accept anything that is not within their limitations.

Many spiritualist mediums can materialize people from beyond the door of death. Do not let yourself be confused, however, with these people generated through the ectoplasm of another person, are from the transition or earthbound level, or are created from the

CHAPTER ONE FORCES AND FREQUENCES

mind of the medium.

This is not to be scoffed at, as the power to create from the mind is a great one indeed. *None* of the space people from other levels of life are ever materialized through a medium. It is not possible to bring through ectoplasmic means, anyone from beyond the earth's force field.

Every element crystalizes in its own pure form due to its individual frequency. A quartz crystal will always be the same in form no matter where it is found. All other crystals also follow a pattern of formation that is established in different densities of vibration.

In order to progress to the finer frequencies of life in other levels, you must first know where you stand in this level. The Creative Spirit so designed His light universe that nothing can exceed its individual vibratory qualifications.

Your individual record is being made daily by the way you live. Everything you think, say or do is recorded in your aura. In the life following this one, you will only be able to progress to the highest level in which your light record will vibrate. No one is going to judge you, but yourselt,and you will be faced with the result of the records you established here.

You must conform in the way you live to the laws of the universe. *The civil laws and social standards of this little earth do not mean a thing.* The densities are established by different vibratory frecuencies of light. You can qualify to "jump grades" by the way you live here now.

Because the unseen Creator made unseen forces for mankind to use FREE; and the minds that operate within the limits of profit, dividends, and control don't want you to use your part unless they can SELL it to you. Yet they go to church to make you believe that they believe in God, the Supreme Good.

CHAPTER ONE FORCES AND FREQUENCES

Everything that is unseen is not accepted by the narrow minds of many, unless it can be brought into the seen, or materialized. You can't see your thoughts, but someone will make money on them if you materialize them into words, or writing.

The Goverment is financing the research, by private firms, into the unseen force of magnetism. All they can study and record is its materialized effects. But the Government does not finance research into thought, which is also an unseen force!

If scientists, authority, and clergy, knew as much about thought, as they know about material effects from its by-products, then they would know some of the correct answers.

CHAPTER TWO LIFE & LAWS

CHAPTER TWO

LIFE & LAWS

Easter in the Christian world is symbolic of the resurrection of Christ. Down through history, long before the time of Jesus, the ancient pagan rituals observed a period of resurrection. Usually they con-ducted some kind of fertility rites, or sex orgy at the time.

Sex was once the basic religious philosophy in phallic worship. The re-birth or propagation of the species, is continuous in all living things.

In biology and science the same thing is observed in the microscopic world; a cyclic period of reproduction relative to each germ, cell, or protoplasm.

Humanity in its Easter bonnet and new frock exhibition of its self importance, reproduces in fabrics and foam rubber the demand to be noticed each year.

Nativity, in its expression of the resurrection, demonstrated the rebirth cycles annually with off-spring to propagate itself.

Today Easter is another of the economic world's ways of giving itself a periodic "shot in the arm" to carry it over to the next religious holiday.

The Christ, called Jesus, was trying to demonstrate to an ignorant people that life was continued even after death, so called. His return, after three days, was a physical manifestation to prove what he came on the earth to accomplish.

People today spend endless hours, if they are going on a trip, to

CHAPTER TWO LIFE & LAWS

prepare for their journey, or vacation. Yet in their short life span here they make almost no preparation spiritually to be equipped for the great journey into the hereafter. Those who leave their preparation up to the priest, or preacher, are going to find out when they pass trough the open door, labeled death, that these emissaries of the church didn't have any connections with anybody beyond *here*.

The spirit confined in the mobile coffin of the carcass here, in the ever constricting pressure of aging, will arrive at the hereafter with no luggage, and greatly confused.

If this life is manifested in reality by spiritual effort to conform to the Golden Rule, one can be welcomed at the hereafter station in state. Some of the money-loving, war mongers are going to be met by many of the cannon fodder kids who found out what it was all about when they got out of here. It won't be pleasant for these "hawks."

Some individuals can resurrect the physical body here by saturating it with spiritual effort in daily meditation, and exhibit youth in their aged body up until their dying day.

The distorted revision of the Bible, in our time, and the ecumenical changing of rules of the church to conform to Caesar's modern requirements is further evidence of boot licking in high places.

Each spring the resurrection takes place in nature about Easter time, when all things manifest new life in blossoms, fruit and progeny. In the human level each Easter time finds us a little further away from the Creative Spirit, and a little closer to the destructive, mammonistic, chaotic end.

There is no resurrection in the economic level. Only deterioration by greed is manifested. From gold to silver, to paper, to credit cards, each stage stealing more from the value of stability, is leading to an economic collapse.

CHAPTER TWO LIFE & LAWS

The resurrection of peace is only empty words from the mouths of hypocrites in authority, who increase the destructive stockpile of arm-aments by catering to the military-industrial complex for puppet positions in political office. There are no more diplomats trying to solve the problems of international disagreement; only horse trader appointees each trying to get the best of a bargain for their economic masters.

Resurrection of the spirit comes only through the Golden Rule effort. If race treated race like they want to be treated, there would be no racial troubles, in spite of the perpetual agitation by the agents of dissention.

Resurrection does not come from the mouth of the clergy — it comes from the love in the heart. Human relations cannot be solved by physical sounds registered from mouths to ears. There are only empty noises that end with their beginning, and cannot be registered in many languages and dialects.

Laws cannot resurrect order out of insurrection. Laws only provide a whip to punish the violator. Legislatures do not consider whether their new laws conform to Nature or God.

Humanity looking at itself reflected, cannot wash its face by scrubbing the image in the mirror. Neither can it raise itself to spiritual resurrection in the flesh by submitting to the ideology that might makes right.

The spirit eternal, submerged in the flesh in this physical environment, is crying for resurrection now, here, to express its ability to bring an end to the madness on this beautiful planet. It does not want to live here only to be rejected and wait until that day of physical death so that it can be free.

Let the spirit of Creation be resurrected no daily, in every act, by rejecting the world of hate, war, and greed.

CHAPTER TWO LIFE & LAWS

Give and ye shall receive. Effort alone produces results and the reward is in satisfaction which no other feeling can duplicate.

The Easter Lily cries for Humanity to Resurrect itself!

"And they asked him, saying, Master, but when shall these things rode sign will there be when these things come to pass?" (St. Luke 21-7).

The Christ answered, "when there are wars and commotions." No one war but wars, several or many at the same time. Katanga, Algeria, Morroco, Viet Nam, Yemen, etc.

"Nations again Nation," "Earthquakes in diverse places," Missouri, Massachusetts, Georgia, Alabama and many other places where earthquakes are not common — diverse places.

"Famines and Pestilences." India, China, Russia and many other countries are now starving by the millions. There are diseases that the doctors admit they do not know what they are. Radiation sickness with practically every rain, or snow.

"And ye shall be hated of all men for my name's sake." The minority of atheists getting court rulings against the majority in school prayers, in eliminating God from expressions in documents, pledges, etc. The elimination of swearing on the Bible in courts and efforts to stop Christmas plays, etc.

"And when ye shall see Jerusalem compassed with armies, Then know that the desolution thereof is nigh." The city of Jerusalem is compassed with armies and the New JerUSAlem is compassed with armies and infiltrated with traitors and enemies in high places.

"But woe unto them that are with child, and to them that give suck, in those days". This is in reference to the radiation effects of fallout which scientist have stated will last the next 30 years, In Iowa this

CHAPTER TWO LIFE & LAWS

year the ears of corn are from 1/4 to 1/3 larger than ever before, as a result of radioactive rains. In some Pacific Islands, rats grow three times larger due to radioactive fallout, Children being born in litters; triplets, quadruplets, and quintuplets are becoming commonplace. In some highly radiated areas the size of children being born is making Caesarean section necessary because the babies are so large they cannot be breached by normal birth — "woe unto them that are with child" in an increasing radioactive time.

"And there shall be signs in the Sun, and in the moon, and in the stars; and upon the Earth distress of Nations, with perplexity; and sea and the waves roaring;"

Astronomical scientists recently announced that the Sun's poles had reversed their polarity. The Moon's orbit is increasingly becoming more erratic, and certainly "distress of nations" is apparent to everyone. I recently talked at length with a sea captain of thirty-five years sailing experience. He said there are unusual tides at sea that were never known before; with swells running the middle of the oceans up to 50 -feet and higher at time.

"Mens hearts failing them for fear." It is known that heart failure is now of the greatest killers and is on the increase.

All of the above references are from St. Luke, Chapter 24, and Revelation, Chapter 18.

The scientists admit 53,000 children in Utah alone have exceeded the critical dosage in radiation from 28 to 136 times.

This is foretold for the latter days in St. Matthew 24-21; "For then shall be great tribulation, such as was not since the biginning of the world to this time, no, nor ever shall be."

The suppression of God for political reasons, the Military crisis, the economic crisis ($306,000,000,000.00 debt), the geophysical

CHAPTER TWO LIFE & LAWS

crisis, the social crisis, the effort of materialistic, wealthy leaders to solve the needs of the masses by taking taxes out of one of their pockets and handing it back in doles and contracts. The virtual end of free enter-prise. The wealthy people catering to decisions of authority that will eventually backfire. These things portend the end of this civilization as anyone with common sense can see, that this cannot go on much longer under the present conditions.

Religion has always professed the intangible Deity. Science deals with many invisible intangible things such as electricity, magnetism, atomic particles, gases, gravity and space.

Most religions today are the philosophy carried down to us over the centuries. Many rituals used by the churches now, originated with the witch doctors of pagan tribes centuries ago.

Today the people need to understand their religion in a manner that fits the time of an atomic and space age. The church has failed to bring the ancient writings up to date. With increased knowledge and scientific ability, it is possible to explain many of the mysteries and miracles of the past.

Some of the churches are changing their dogma to more closely fit the accelerating changes of today, but mostly they are merging together to relieve the economic pressure of inflation and overhead.

Those who survive the chaos facing the world today will be mostly people who are not religious, or scientific in their training. The political and military people who survive could write a history of what happened after it was over, but their training would only permit their writings to explain events from political and military views.

None of Christ's disciples wrote about what happened in His time, except Paul. The most ignorant tribes of savages on the earth today have their stories of Noah and the flood, and Jonah and the whale. They never heard of the Bible, or the dogma of the world's

CHAPTER TWO LIFE & LAWS

predominant religions. Neither can they read, or write. In spite of these failings they can discuss with each other what the see in a motion picture brought to them through science. It is a strange paradox that the more people are educated, the more gullible they are to propaganda that appeals to their inflated ego.

Religion like life insurance, doesn't promise you anything until after you are dead. Science is accelerating so fast that the people cannot be brought up to date fast enough in a technological sense. The church cannot interpret the old records of religion, in a modern way to fit the times, because their preachers, priests, and rabbis, have no scientific training in most cases. This makes it impossible for the church to give answers to questions asked by people in today's thinking. Science has a duty, to religion, to help them explain things in today's terminology. Religion must bring the verities of dogma up to date, or close their doors.

God made space, atoms, electricity, magnetism, and all other intangible invisible things before humanity had science. Science has advanced the use of these creations faster in the last 50 years than in all of the preceding thousands of years.

Yet the ignorant materialists in science propound the theory of human evolution without considering that the atomic elements are each the same in perfect order wherever they are found. Solar systems work by cyclic ordered principles, and the known universe is in perfect order — that could not exist except by creation from an Infinite Boundless Intelligence that knows all of the principles that science has not discovered yet.

Electricity and magnetism were here in Caesar's time. Gravity existed on the planet since the planet was formed, long before egotostical men of degrees decided they are smarter than God. When science discovers each principle of nature, they take on the attitude that science created it. Science could not produce transportation, communication, or heat and refrigeration, without God's rubber trees, gases, oils, iron ores, and other products taken

CHAPTER TWO LIFE & LAWS

from the earth that were not made by scientists. When science realizes that they couldn't do anything, with all of their _brains and degrees of education, without a Supreme Intelligence making the materials and energies they use, then the scientists will have religion.

When religion recognizes that it could not propagate its God to people without sciences making printing presses, paper and writing equipment; and today, radio, television, telephones, photography, and motion pictures, then it must reciprocate to science for its part in manifesting God's works in an endless production of God's raw materials into parts, assemblies, and working equipment.

Each is lost in this latter time without the other. Science is the religion of manifesting God's principles through materialism. Religion is the: science of manifesting God through teaching of the intangible spirit. In today's thinking these things are chemical *matter* and spirit *energy*. These are the dual opposites of the same thing. *Intangible electricity* is everywhere, but without the *matter* of wire, coils, and cores, it cannot be manifest for use by science.

Science today knows the heart produces a magnetic field; an electric current is measurable in the blood stream. The body has electric capacity which can be demonstrated by the increase in reception on your car radio by touching the antenna. Every action of the voluntary muscle system depends upon electric impulses from the brain through the nervous system. Without the electrical function of the eternal spirit of you in the matter body, it would not respond, or perform any motion. Motion in matter can only exist when energy moves it.

God is the infinity of an endless electrical universe that thought atoms, solar systems and galaxies into being. Humans are thought forms of God's creation of individual forms of life. When "God created man in His image" He didn't mean we looked like Him. He meant we had the power through imagination to create like Him He meant we have the power through imagination to create like

CHAPTER TWO LIFE & LAWS

him through thought. e designer of anything pictures the design in the mind and through *thought*. This designer of anything pictures the design in the mind and through *though* puts it in blueprint form on paper, from which it is made as a tangible physical product. This is a product of science.

Religion is the effort of trying to understand this invisible energy from which the thought came. If the intangible invisible thought produces a tangible physical thing, this is accepted as science.

If *tangible physical things* reverse this process, to understand this *Intangible Infinite Mind, this is Religion. Both* are valid opposites of each other, but it is time to stop being opposites to each other. Unless this is realized, religion cannot survive in an advanced scientific age. If science does not accept the moral responsibility it professes so ardently, it will destroy itself, without religion in its acts. We have a scientific computerized hydrogen bomb planet because science became as materialized as the matter of their science. They forgot the God of their image to create and are manifesting the Devil of their ability to destroy.

Religion failed to keep pace with the changes in human thinking and the division widened, with science, until today they are not accepted as two hemisphere of the same sphere. Religion cannot be accepted by the space age people when it teaches the Fatherhood of God and it cannot manifest the brotherhood of man.

Both Science and Religion have gone beyond their limits as established by God in giving man "dominion over all things," for they are demonstrating the dominion over man; and God never gave man dominion over his fellow man.

So now the God created law of reciprocation is going to destroy them both, because religion didn't perform its function far enough, and science went too far beyond its limits to create, and swallowed its own tail.

CHAPTER THREE STATIC INTELLIGENCE

CHAPTER THREE

STATIC INTELLIGENCE

An ion is a particle of matter carrying a static electrical charge. A planet is a composition of many particles of matter. It also carries a static electrical charge. Our planet, surrounded by its atmosphere, is basically a condensed chunk of energy surrounded by a thin film of gases with water on the surface and in the atmosphere. The rotation of our planet on its axis generates a magnetic field. Ions carrying static charges answer to the same laws of polarity as magnetism.

People on this planet must breathe oxygen in order to live. Our atmosphere contains oxygen. Oxygen is para-magnetic. In otherwords it is attracted, or repelled, by magnetic and static electrical charges. The atmosphere is held to the surface of the planet by the static charge of the planet's mass, The planet's magnetic field is about 98% below the planet's surface and about 2% in the atmosphere.

The planet's breathable atmosphere is about six miles thick. On a planet such as ours we are increasing the amount of particles of matter in our atmosphere through industry (smoke), automobiles (exhaust), and fumes of chemicals from refineries.

The combination of these particles, plus moisture in the atmosphere, in cities has now been labeled "smog." Smog spreads throughout the atmosphere to all points on the planet in different degrees.

When the atmosphere containing untold billions of particles of matter is excited by magnetic disturbances, electrical fluctuations,

CHAPTER THREE STATIC INTELLIGENCE

or friction through winds, static and magnetic charges accumulate in these floating particles. When a particle accumulates a charge to its potential capacity it condenses moisture around it. This is what forms a cloud. Clouds usually form over mountains are continuously emitting flux from the planet's static charge. When a cloud reaches its full capacity of static charge it discharges to the nearest ground surface or cloud near, as lighting

The book called the Bible (from the Greek word Biblos, meaning a record) gives many references to clouds and lighting and coronas referred to as "divine fire".

In the times when the records of the Bible were written, few men could write. Donkeys, horses, camels and chariots were the best form of transportation. Nothing was known of electricity, magnetism, ions, radio, T.V., biology, geography, or geophysics. The known world was a small place — flat, not spherical — occupied by ignorant, superstitious people. The few scribes of that time recorded the events to the best of their limited thinking. Authorities of governments ruled by torture and force. The priesthood ruled through fear and superstition. Every nomena we can explain today was an act of God, or Satan. The Sun was believed to orbit around the Earth. Ignorance, fear of the unknown, and superstition, ruled the thinking of the people of that time. Rituals warded off evil, or appeased God.

Today people still cling to this ancient ritual in an atomic age, with & round world thoroughly mapped and photographed and orbitted by men in space capsules.

The rich people hold positions of authority now as they did then. The poor still struggle for survival. The authorities finance "friendly" foreign nations for political favor, or bribery, while their own people go hungry and without employment.

So many aspects of society have not maintained pace with the scientific advancement. Excessive taxes are still with us.

CHAPTER THREE STATIC INTELLIGENCE

Emotional instability still exists. People are still ignorant. Rituals are still practiced to get you to heaven, or condemn you to hell.

Why do people persist in following ritual, custom and dogma full of fear? Afraid to live and afraid to die What a dilemma!

When the Bible, or any other record continues to be a source of mystery, superstition, or misunderstanding between people, it has ceased to serve the enlightened purpose for which it was written, Do the modern churches promote faith, or condone mammon and hypocrisy? Do the teachers practice what they preach?

The Bible says "the Sun shall no longer give forth her light," in the latter days. We know today ionization of the atmosphere causes a cloud to condense. We also know the electrical and magnetic effects in our atmosphere as a result of atomic, or nuclear explosions. They cause the atmosphere to ionize, forming more clouds and heavier rains that are radioactive, or emitting detrimental emanations in the electromagnetic spectrum in excess of the ability of the body capacitor to store — without burning out with cancer or leukemia.

The only thing that could cause the "Sun to no longer give forth her light" would be a cloud layer surrounding the planet, caused by a sudden, or continuous increase of ionization of the atmosphere by atomic tests, or nuclear war. Venus has this condition.

Politicians cannot solve the problems of humanity. Neither can the church. The only solution can come from the people. The people must expand their thinking. The must find out about life and death. The people must build in themselves an awareness of consciousness to follow de laws of nature and spiritual enlightenment. They must not be afraid of anything.

The Bible says "death shall be overcome." This is our prime effort here — to charge this body mass. To use the right and left hands of God — Electricity and Magnetism. To give to humanity a purpose

CHAPTER THREE STATIC INTELLIGENCE

in living besides eating, sleeping and reproducing in ignorance.

"And the Lord spake unto Moses, saying, According to all that I shew thee; after the *pattern of the tabernacle*, and the pattern of all the instruments thereof, even so shall ye make." (Exodus 25: 1 and 9).

Back in time Moses built a tabernacle, according to the pattern, or blueprint; and according to the schematic diagram, or *electronic hook-up of the instruments* to make it operate.

Recording of these facts back in the days when the people had no knowledge of electricity, magnetism, or technology, is amazing. When one considers that scribes in that time recorded events to the best of their ability, without knowing anything about what they were writing, it is fantastic that these records in the Bible have come down to us so accurately. In the time of Moses, according to the Holy Book, the Lord above in the sky dropped food from heaven to the Israelites, parted the waters of a sea, and instructed Moses in what to do, in personal contacts, "And the Lord spoke unto Moses face to face, as a man speaketh unto his friend." Exodus 33:11.

Chapter 37 of Exodus1 and 2 tells of the wood construction being covered with gold "within and without." Today we know this makes an electrostatic condenser.

Moses said "I do not do these things of my own mind." Nicola who discovered alternating electricity, steam turbines, and the mMany controls of electrical power, said, "I am convinced that I an automaton, controlled by some external power" The Bible says "in the latter days all things shall be revealed."

Anyone who has not seen modern miracles; who has not experienced outside assistance; who has not been inspired and directed by external help, probably will not understand the things being written here.

CHAPTER THREE STATIC INTELLIGENCE

"For the Lord's portion is his people; Jacob is the lot of his inheritance, He found him in a desert land, and in a waste holwing wilder-ness; *he led him about, he instructed him*, he kept him-as the apple of his eye." Deuteronomy 32: 9 and 10.

"And on the day that the tabernacle was reared up the *cloud covered the tabernacle,* namely the tent of the testimony: and at even there was upon the tabernacle as it were the appearance of fire, until the morning," Numbers 9:15.

Our present science knows *an electrostatic charge produ*ces a cloud by ionization and a corona in the dark, which could be described as "fire" by anyone who didn't know electrical terms.

"See that ye refuse not him that speaketh. For if they escaped not who refused him that spake on earth, much more shall not we escape, if we turn away from him that speaketh from heaven:" Hebrews 12:25.

How many people have heard voices today? How many people have recovered from some terminal disease which human agency cannot explain? How many people have had things fall into place in experiences beyond human planning? Is the Bible fantasy, fiction, or fact? If it were fantasy it would have long ago been lost in the years. If it were fiction, it would have faded in the haze of time. If it is factual in its context, it will last through the ages, which it has. The works of God did not stop with the writing and printing of the events in the Bible. The things that it tells are happening today in many ways. Those who don't believe this, are lost in the darkness of ignorance.

People today, in the time of television, air transportation, and men in orbit around the world, should be able to comprehend that this age of destruction is beyond human solution. Then where is the intelligent help coming from to bring order out of chaos?

CHAPTER THREE STATIC INTELLIGENCE

"And when he had spoken these things, while they beheld, he was taken up; and *a cloud received him* out of their sight. And while they "looked stedfastly toward heaven as he went up, behold, two men stood by them in white apparel; which also said, Ye men of Galilee, why stand ye gazing up into heaven? this same Jesus which is taken up from you into heaven, shall so come in like manner as ye have seen him go into heaven." Acts 1:9, 10 and 11.

The Lord that instructed Moses came in a cloud. Was the Lord in the time of Moses, the same Lord later called Jesus? Or was there more than one Lord? The Bible also mentions "a Lord of the harvest."

Can one accept, *that life* being eternal, the son of Man (which Jesus was called) was also active in the time of Moses? Can people today, without present scientific know how, believe that Jesus was picked up bodily on an antigravity beam and taken into a cloud ionized by the electrostatic field around a space ship?

Jesus said "Ye are from beneath; I am from above; Ye are of this world; *I am not of this world.*" St. John 8:23. He didn't say where he *was from. He is calle e son of Man" many times in the Bible. Man was the species God created "with dominion over all things." This would include space travel, antigravity, telepathy, faith healing, and all other things explained as miracles. Humans, in the Bible, are called "men," not "Man."

Assuming humanity is composed mostly of "fallen angels," with a few species of the race of Man among us, it is easy to understand why the hierarchy of destruction on earth is reluctant to admit there are "signs in the sky."

The mountain smoked from burning brush in the time of Moses. Patches of burned areas have been seen in many places today. The Lord spoke to Moses "face to face" in his time. People have spoken "face to face" with visitors out of the sky in our time. Moses was given a pattern to build a tabernacle by someone

CHAPTER THREE STATIC INTELLIGENCE

called a Lord in his time. It ionized a cloud around it. We have been given a "pattern" to build a structure that is an electro-static generator, in our time. It will also create a corona, "or fire" by night, and ionize a cloud in humid weather, in the day time.

And all the people saw the thunderings, and the lightnings, and the noise of the trumpet, and the mountain smoking; and when the people saw it, they removed, and stood afar off. (Exodus, 20:18).

You can imagine the consternation of the people in Moses' time, when a chariot was the best form of transportation, and few of the people ever owned a donkey. They saw it (a spacecraft) come out of the sky (heavens) and hover over Mount Sinai. The *lightnings* (force . field of static electricity) causing the grass and brush to burn and the *mountain* to smoke. The sound, or *noise*, as of a trumpet — could be very easily explained as the humming, pulsating sound which a space-craft makes while hovering.

There have been many cases of "burned areas" where spacecraft have been seen hovering in our days. There have also been instances where airplane pilots, forced down in remote areas, have been taken for a god, because the natives had learned from their legends that god , Was in the heaven above.

Today people accept aircraft speeds, rocket speeds, and instant radio communications and television pictures through our atmosphere. In these days when minds should be receptive to the rapid changes taking place, a few people are ridiculed because they have said they talked to the people from a spaceship, or went aboard, or even rode in the craft.

The Bible records this happening to Moses way back in the donkey days. It is written in Exodus, 20:92: And the Lord said unto Moses, Thus thou shalt say unto the children of Israel, *Ye have seen that I have talked with you from heaven."*

People profess the Bible as a Holy Book, yet they do not accept it

CHAPTER THREE STATIC INTELLIGENCE

as a history of events that are now being reenacted in their very presence, enforcing through repetition the spiritual development of nations.

Numbers, chapter 14:27, 28, reads: "How long shall I bear with this 'evil congregation, which murmur against me? I have heard the murmurings of the children of Israel, which they murmur against me. Say unto them, As truly as I live, saith the Lord, *as ye have spoken in mine ears, so will I do to you.*"

It is evident enough that, in nearly every case, where any of the persons who have contacted the space people and were brought before the public (as on television or platform work), that every effort was made to make them appear both ridiculous and ludicrous. Persecutions practised today are only a repetition of those of the old Biblical days.

The United States is the New Jerusalem of our time. The same clique is working from within its boundaries and from outside, trying to overthrow its God given rights. They shall fail because they are known to our friends from the spacecraft.

None of the persons contacted by the space people had any part in. inciting the meeting. It *happened to all of them* at the inducement of the people of in spaccarft.

Moses was in the same awkward situation as related in the book of Numbers, 16:28: "And Moses said, Hereby ye shall know that the Lord hath sent me to do all these works; for *I have not done them of mine own mind."*

In Deuteronomy, Chapter 18:18, it says: "I will raise them up a prophet from among their brethren, like unto thee, and *I will put my words in his mouth;* and he shall speak unto them all that I shall command him."

It should be quite evident by now that many strange things are

CHAPTER THREE STATIC INTELLIGENCE

happening in this time of "wars for peace." Everyone should read the story of Moses in the Bible. It is being reenacted now if you are aware of the times.

Back in the time of Moses, people didn't know what electricity was. Neither did they know what magnetism, or ionization, was.

They referred to natural electrical phenomena like lightning, as "divine fire."

If they saw a large cigar-shaped spaceship in the sky they called it a "flying roll." If it ionized the atmosphere around it in the daylight, causing moisture to collect around the electro-static field, they referred to it as "a cloud by day."

If the electro-static charge created a corona around the ship in the darkness they called it a "pillar of fire."

If someone in the ship surrounded by a cloud spoke to people on the ground, either through a photon beam activating by galvanic action, from the inner ear to the brain, or through a loud speaker amplifier system through the outer ear drum, the people of Moses tine called it "a voice from a cloud."

Clouds don't speak to people. Unless there is someone in the cloud with a device capable of speaking to people on the ground, a voice could not come from a cloud.

And it came to pass, as Moses entered into the tabernacle, *the cloudy pillar descended,* and stood at the door of the tabernacle, and the Lord talked with Moses.

And all the people saw the cloudy pillar stand at the tabernacle door: and the people rose up and worshipped, every man in his tent door.

And the Lord spake unto Moses face to face, as a man speaketh

CHAPTER THREE STATIC INTELLIGENCE

unto his friend." Exodus 33:8-11.

This indicates the people saw a man who came from the cloudy pillar in broad daylight speaking to Moses.

I have heard several people in the present time criticize some of us "for making a religion out of the flying saucer incidents." Well hurray! This only proves their ignorance. I for one am not "making a religion" out of anything. I am only trying to explain in this time what caused the superstitious people of another time to record those events to the best of their knowledge — when they did not understand the faintest scientific thing about what caused a cloud, or a corona of "fire." I am only trying to explain phenomena that occurred then, in the present understanding of modern electrical science now. I am trying to prove scientifically that religion is a reality, instead of an intangible, superstitious myth.

I am not changing anything that religious books say. I am only explaining what caused the phenomena that was not understood by thé people then. One does not have to have degrees, or robes, to be intelligent.

When the exodus of the people out of Egypt took place, according to the Biblical record in Exodus 13:21-22, this cloud by day, and pillar of fire by night, went *before* the people, leading them.

Whether the sea the followers of Moses crossed was the Red Sea, according to the Bible, or the Sea of Reeds, according to the modern interpretation of "experts," doesn't really matter. The thing that matters is that from the ship in the cloud "the Lord" parted the waters.

This takes some pretty advanced equipment, that oür modern science cannot duplicate today, in order to part waters and hold them Back.

The cloud was called thé Shechinah by the jews, According to

CHAPTER THREE STATIC INTELLIGENCE

other records not in the Bible, there was not *one* cloud and pillar of fire, but seven of them. In "The Baraitha" (a book of the tabernacle), it states: Son a cloud covered the tent of the congregation, and the glory of the Lord filled the Tabernacle. And that was one of the clouds of glory, which served the Israelites in the wilderness *forty years*. One on the *right hand*, and one on the *left,* and one *before them*, and one *behind* them. And one over them, and a cloud dwelling in their midst (and the cloud, the Shechinah which was *in the ten*), and the pillar of cloud which moved before them, making *low* before them the *high* places, and making *high* before them the low places, and *killing serpents and scorpion*s, and *burning thorns and briars*, and guiding them in the straight way."

Now don't forget that a cloud *filled the tent*, which was the Tabernacle.

Our "Integratron" is a Tabernacle in this same respect. When our ectro-static fields are generated, and the relative humidity of the air i is high enough, the "Integratron" will also ionize a *cloud in our midst.*

It takes a pretty potent antigravity beam from a ship to level the way before the Israelites. And any high voltage electrostatic field will kill serpents and scorpions, and burn thorns and briars.

The old records show. that Tabernacle was subject to though. This means that a "time field" - was generated in it the same as we are going to do in the "Integratron.

The ancient writing on this states: "There is a legend to the effect that any who chanced to enter the Holy of Holies unclean were destroyed by *a bolt of Divine fire* from the *mercy seat*. If the High Priest had but *one selfish thought*, he would be struck dead. As no one knows when an unworthy though may flash through his mind, precautions had to be taken in case the High Priest should be struck dead while in the presence of Jehovah. The other priests could not

CHAPTER THREE STATIC INTELLIGENCE

enter the sanctuary, therefore when their leader receive the commands of the Lord, they tied a chain around one of his feet so that if he were struck down while behind the veil they could drag his body out".

Recall in this article the ancient records spoke of *a bolt of Divine* from the Mercy seat, like a bolt of lightning, or a large electro-"static discharge. It is evident that the ark referred to in the tabernacle was recorded in a time when electricity was unknown and today is called an *arc* in electrical terminology.

The Tabernacle of Moses also had recording instruments to tell what was going on in its operation. In Exodus 25:9, when Moses was being informed how to make the tabernacle it says: "According to all that I shew thee, after the pattern of the tabernacle, and the pattern of all the *instruments* thereof even so shall ye make it."

That the Tabernacle of Moises was an electric-static generator is evident if its construction is interpreted in the electrical terms of today.

In Exodus 40:38 it states: "For the cloud of the Lord was upon the tabernacle by day, and fire was on it by night, in the sight of all the house of Israel, throughout all their journeys."

Ionization of a cloud is the effect of an accumulated continuous electro-static charge. *Fire at night* is the corona given off from any body arged with a continuous flow of high frequency electricity.

We are building a permanent tabernacle, similar to the portable one Moses built in the last civilization on this Earth. We were given instructions on how to construct it in the same manner that Moses was instructed,by a man that came out of the sky,who may have also carried the title of the Lord.

Here all of us are, riding around on a ship in space we call the

CHAPTER THREE STATIC INTELLIGENCE

Earth. We aren't even inside of our space ship. We are stuck onto its surface by an *invisible* force called gravity. We breathe invisible gases we call air. This even runs out at about five miles up, so our ocean of air isn't much compared with the mass of the water oceans.

We create *unseeen* electricity by cutting unseen magnetic lines of force. We use this unseen force for power and lighting purposes.

We worship an *unseen* God. We function through an unseen spirit.

Our planet orbits around the Sun and is rotated on its axis by unseen forces. Galaxies 100,000,000 light years in diameter rotate in space powered by an invisible principle. Energy in all of its original states *cannot be seen.*

Still people go around saying, "I won't believe something unless I can see it."

In an eight inch known spectrum our vision covers about 1/8th of an inch. This is about 1/64th of the known frequencies, or from about 4000 to 7800 Angstroms on the Angstrom scale.

Our hearing is limited from about 20 to 16,000 cycles per second. This is a smaller fraction of the vibratory scale even then the visible limits. We don't see the vibrations we hear, either.

Our sense of touch doesn't function until we come in contact with something.

Our sense of smell also detects odors we can't *see*, or hear.

We get ptomaine poisoning from food that our sense of taste cannot determine is poisonous to us.

Everyone of our five physical senses has limits and are subject to failure within their small limits.

CHAPTER THREE STATIC INTELLIGENCE

Surrounding us, and throughtout our physical bodies unto infinity is a pure, unfaling sense of perfect Universal Mind. Most people acept this *Unseen Force* either, or use It when they can, because Jt cannot be seen.

Mostly this Unseen, Perfect, Infinity of Perfect Intelligence is resting now, as It did in the seventh day of creation; waiting for people to use m unlimited knowing.

People on the Earth are afraid of this potent, unseen force except as a fist aid kit when they hurt, or are afraid they are going to die — then they pray for comfort and relief, expecting miracles to save them. They expect this force to respond in minutes after being ignored for years.

The law of riprocation responds only to those who give to get. See if your fire will burn without first supplying fuel for it. Show u us anything that produces something without first putting something into it.

This Supreme Intelligence doesn't have degrees from a college. It doesn't care whether the government recognizes It or not.

It is stillness, resting, waiting for manifestation through individual creatures It has made.

You could take all the brains in the world and put them in one vessel and all you would have is a big pot of meat.

Brains are not intelligent. They are only receivers of thoughts and transmitters of motion. *Thoughts* are also *unseen, unheard, untouched, untasted and unsmelled.*

Everything physicall manifest on Earth is the result of an unseen thought. Whether it be a chair, a bolt, or a skycraper, it existed in the Unseen, Perfect, Intelligence before some engineer put it down

CHAPTER THREE STATIC INTELLIGENCE

on paper, and then it was made.

We do not believe that each development must be achieved through trial and error, and correction, in an endless chain of small improvements.

The principles of radio existed in Caesar's time. A steamship could have been made in Alexander's time. Everything we know about now, existed then in principle.

Using this Supreme Intelligence doesn't require degrees, or recognition by some authority. It only requires application and effort to use It. It knows everything about all principles that trial and error methods will not "discover" for a hundred years.

Why wait a hundred years to have something we can use *now*. The Bible states that death will be overcome. This means death of the physical body as the spirit is already eternal.

People build machines to ride in. Machines to dig with. Machines to bring pictures into your livng room. Untold numbers of machines to work principles that have always existed, and will work wherever they are applied.

Nikola Tesla, the greatest genius in history, stated after years of analysis of himself "that he was an automaton run by an external force."

If we all served as automatons of the Creator we would all create. Creators cannot destroy. By the same token destroyers cannot create.

Everyone should read the life story of Nikola Tesla. You can get it in your library or book store. "The Prodigal Genius" by O'Neil.

CHAPTER FOUR

VOICES & VISIONS

The people of Japan consider the event of the coming of the spaceships as a sacred thing. In their ancient records the Japanese people called a spaceship a "Shinta." Out of this came the Shinto religion of Japan. In the records of their "pagodas," or temples, they record that the original yellow people came out of space and established a colony on the earth.

Up until World War Two the emperor of Japan was looked upon as a deity. This was because the emperor was a direct descendant of the original leader of the colony of their people who came out of space.

The Japanese were known as the people of "the rising Sun." Their flag bears the symbol of the Sun. The yellow people originated from the tribe of Japheth. Thence the slang term of calling them "Japs." "

The American Indian's legends tell of Ewatah, an ancient wise man, literally a Christ to them, who taught them many things. American translation of Ewatah became Hiawatha. Many Indians were named Hiawatha after him, it being considered a sacred name, just as many people have been named Jesus for a first time. |

The Indian legend tells of of people who came through "a hole i sky" in "fire canoes" and taught them. When the white man first came to America they found potatoes tobaco and corn were grew up by the indians. The rest of the world had never know these plants. The indians explained that that these items had been brought to them by the people in the "fire canoes" and they were

CHAPTER FOUR VOICES & VISIONS

taught how to grow and cultivate them.

The Inca people were brought to a highly educated level by following instructions from the "Incas" who came out of the sky in ships. Many giant size symbols still remain, as built on the ground by the people for guiding and welcome signs in South America; so the Gods would know where they were welcome. '

The Christian Religion in its time of origin recorded people coming out of the sky in "Flaming Chariots" The records over time, by the scribes of that time, tell of people getting out of ships, or speaking from clouds, which were ionized air created, by the electro-static corona around the ships.

Greek legend tells of how the people of that time made Gods of the people who descended in their midst. One was named "Mercury" and pictured with wings on his heels. This legend tells of this man being able to deliver a written message to a distant town and be back in a small fraction of the time required by the Greeks to go to the same town and back by horse. Mercury, the fluid metal, being the most elusive and almost impossible thing to hold led them to name this man, who used an anti-gravity belt to fly through the air, the God of Mercury.

There have been several instances in our time, of pilots of aircraft crashing, or landing by parachute, among natives who did not know people could fly. Becauses they came out of the sky they were looked upon as deities, or Gods.

The most isolated tribes of savages on the earth all have their version of Jonah and the Whale. Most of the savages in unexplored areas, when they were first explored, had their own version of Easter and Christmas. In the motion picture "Mondo Cane," a tribe of aborigines is pictured with a full size model of an airplane on top of a mountain; and the worship there waiting for their God to return out of the sky.

CHAPTER FOUR VOICES & VISIONS

Jesus said, according to the New Testament, "I am not of this world". It also says, "He knew their thoughts," revealing that he could read minds, or perform mental telepathy. The people from some of the spaceships communicate mentally.

These people came out of the sky to talk to Moses, Joseph, Lot, and many others. They either communicated with them mentally, or "from a cloud" by a loudspeaker, or public address system. Today, when we know people can fly, we have radio, television and public address systems, and we can understand an advanced species of Man using these things; it should not be difficult to accept that all religions system from "up there" and were instigated by the people from other places to make the human race raise themselves by moral and spiritual understanding.

The Bible also says "All things will be revealed in the latter days." Many people have heard their names called loud and clear when there was no one around within calling distance. Today we have established an authority of psychiatrists who assume to know all about other people's mental processes. Most of them don't even know about their own mental frustrations, emotions, and egotistic desires to be recognized as authorities of something. They would catalog "spiritual inspiration," "mother " or "voices people hear," as mental abberations due to some malfunction of the brain.

People accept the Bible as a Holy Book. The Churches profess it was "the inspired word of God." They would have you believe that God ceased to inspire people after the books of the Bible were composed. The "angels" that came out of the sky in the Biblical times were messengers from God. Today they are considered by the Church hierarchy and Political authority as "hallucinations".Anyone who doesn't accept a "greater society," of people from "up there" better throw their Bible out the window and quit being hypocrites.

Every religion on the Earth is based on people coming from out of the skies.

CHAPTER FOUR VOICES & VISIONS

"Set your affection on things *above*, not on things on the earth.

For *ye are dead,* and your life is hid with Christ in God." Colossians 3:2 and 3.

In the contrast between heaven and hell, the churches lead you to believe heaven is an estate after death here. Since Christians generally look forward, with faith, that there is something better than this life, they hope they can get into heaven through the church since the individual doesn't know where heaven is. They assume that the church does know, because they are always professing about it. Naturally the preachers and priests won't tell you hell is here because this is where they are too.

Verily, verily, I say unto thee, except a man be *born again*, he can not see the kingdom of God." St. John 3:3.

Just suppose one looked at the opposite side of the door marked birth on side, and found the other side of this physical environment is marked *death.* Then one could believe when you get out of here you are born again into life. This would then make reincarnation an actually because if you didn't pass the grade and qualify to stay "over there", you would come squaking back, crying like the devil, after your re-entry here, because yo didn't make it again. It seems one of the most used expressions here is the devilish demand for someone to "go to hell."

Religions over times past have all contended that heaven is "up." Hell is defined in the Bible as, "a place of the dead, or of punishment."

For if God spared not the angels that sinned, but cast them down to Hell, and *delivered* them into chains of darkness, to be reserved unto judgment." 2 Peter 2:4.

Now this *says* that God cast down *angels* into hell, not humans;

CHAPTER FOUR VOICES & VISIONS

and *delivered* them into chains of darkness. Babies are delivered here, and they are born in the darkness of no memory of their past, into a chain of events that are against them until they "get the hell out of here," to quote another favorite human expression.

But these, as natural brute beasts, made to be taken and destroyed, speak evil of the things that they understand not; and shall utterly perish in their own corruption." 2 Peter 2:12.

Could anything better discribe humans generally throughout history? Brute beasts made to be drafted and destroyed in wars. Always condemning others and ridiculing the things they do not understand; and the only living things on the earth that contaminate their own drinking water, and air, and shall perish in their own corrupt greedy system of society.

"While they promise them liberty, they themselves are the servants of corruption: for whom a man is overcome, of the same he is brought in bondage." 2 Peter 2:19.

This describes the human political world, where millionaire politicians promise the poor, the minority people, and the sickly and aged, liberty from their conditions if the "un-millionaires" pay for it, and let them run the show in the corruption of graft and bureaucracy.

Hell is supposed to contain "hellfire and brimstone." Well we have that here too in atomic and hydrogen bombs. Hell is supposed to be a place where misery is inflicted on the inhabitants. Every law passed here by the people in authority through history has been to limit you, ar S you, or burden you for being a little devil instead of a big evil.

The Bible says "the meek shall inherit the earth" and if you're addled enough to get committed to a mental institution you won't have all these troubles, and be cared for too.

CHAPTER FOUR VOICES & VISIONS

"For even when we were with you, this we commanded you, that if any would not work, neiher should he eat." 2 Thessalonian 3:10.

Satan's policy here is feed them all with money provided by someone else who does work, and run the show with people who never learned how to work. This "rob Peter to pay Paul" policy never has worked in history. Well this only makes hell more hellish.

"But Jesus said unto him, "Follow me; and let the dead bury their dead,." St. Matthew 8:22.

Now if this is hell, and you are already dead, then this makes some sense, because all Jesus was saying was let the vertical dead bury the *horizontal* dead.

"A good name is better than precious ointment; and the day of death than the day of birth." Ecclesiastes 7:1

Here again the Bible indicates that the day of death is a release, or exit, from a bad condition, while birth is an entry that is not good.

Heaven is described in the Bible as a "firmament, or the abode of God." "For as the heaven is high above the earth, so great is his mercy toward that fear him." Psam 103:11.

"I knew a man in Christ above fourteen years ago, (whether in the body, I cannot tell; or whether out of the body, I cannot tell: God knoweth;) such as one caught up to the *third* heaven." Corinthians 12:2.

This would indicate heaven has grades, or levels, into which people go according to their qualification.

"For a fire is kindled in mine anger, and shall burn unto the lowest hell." Deuteronomy 32:22.

CHAPTER FOUR VOICES & VISIONS

The *lowest* hell shows there are other, or higher, levels of hell also. Where is the dividing boundary between the highest hell and the lowest heaven?

And *no* man hath ascended up to heaven, but he that *came down* from heaven, even the Son of man which is in heaven." St. John 3:13.

The idea seems to be that *everyone* here came *down* from up there either because they fell from their high estate since the creation, or volunteered to come *down* to help people to get out of here. People on our earth have not *evolved* from the amoeba up to humans, they have descended from the original creation of man with "dominion over all things," to the human destructive critter with dominion over nothing. They are pawns of every devilish influence on a satanic planet that kills, and corrupts.and contaminates.

"For I came *down* from heaven, not to do mine own will, but the will of him that sent me" St. John 6:38.

And he said unto them, Ye are from *beneath*; I am from *above*: Ye are of this word; I am *not of this word*." St. John 8:23.

Here again Jesus said the world was beneath and he came down from heaven which was above.

The Bible does not indicate there is any "in-between" level. It does not describe any place lower than the earthly existence. Everything is here that is attributed to hell. One thing about it, if we can establish where we are in the scheme of things, we can start going in the right direction if we want to.

Materialism, ego, and corruption on our planet, indicate this is hell. Has anyone seen any evidence of an effort to make the Golden Rule law, punishable when violated?

Does anyone say "to heaven with you?" Are people awarded

CHAPTER FOUR VOICES & VISIONS

medals more for killing, than for anything else? Are power politics open and elean, or hidden and dirty? Does the church profess God here, or up there?

You draw your own conclusions, but in order to have a heaven on earth, it will take someone from *up there* who knows what it should be like.

Two women shall be grinding together; *the one shall be taken*, and the other left.

Two men shall be in the field; the *one shall be taken*, and the other one left. (St. Luke 17:35, 36).

Either you have faith in the prophecy of the Bible, or you must reject the whole book. The Bible is an accurate history of events that repeat themselves in cyclic repetition.

The above paragraphs say a division of humankind will be made. *One shall be taken and one shall be left.* Who is to make the decision? Who will do this judging of humanity to see who will be taken and who will be left?

Each person will have written their own ticket. Each individual will have already judged himself. There will be no one accepted b last minute decision.

The time is very close for the ones who qualify to be taken.

Every day that passes you, individually, are establishing your right to be taken by the way you live. You are manifesting your choice by your actions and thinking.

Each person ads increase to their vibratory body aura by conforming to the laws of the universe. Your aura, or frecuency of the body force field will determine wether you are taken, or left.

CHAPTER FOUR VOICES & VISIONS

A definite vibration will be established in the force field surrounding each spacecraft that will pick up people, your body aura, or force conforms with, or exceeds, the established level of the spacecraft force field, then you can enter the ships.

Remember *you* are *now* qualifying, or disqualifying *youself* to be taken aboard. None can qualify another Jesus can't "save" you.

This sounds kind of fantastic in our everyday living conditions. God works His ways in mysterious fashion. By your own way of thinking and living, you write your own ticket for the ascension.

Some narrow-minded sects of religious fanatics have established that only 144,000 people will be saved. Of course *they* are part of the chosen few. 'Those who will be taken, and those who will be *saved*, are two separate conditions.

The next thing one asks is, "where will the people who are picked up | be taken?" This is answered in St. Luke 17:37. "And they answered and said unto him, Where, Lord? And he said unto them, Wheresoever the *body* is, thither will the eagles be gathered together."

Naturally the eagles gather together in the sky. This was said in a parable at that time, because the people in the Biblical days didn't know what it was to fly in the skies. It was not meant for the people of those days. It was said for the people of *our time*.

The space people (angels) explained that the people who have been aboard their craft in these times were not taken aboard because they were better than anyone else. They explained that these people were taken aboard for t*heir own test purposes* to see how different types of people would react. Each one who has been so honored was readily accessible (in a remote place).They were of cooperative minds, and each represented a different type of the earth's people.

CHAPTER FOUR VOICES & VISIONS

This mass pickup of people will take place very soon, prior to planet's rebalancing on new poles. This catacysm will wipe out the destructive mammon lovers who will *be left on the surface*.

After the earth has re-stablishing on its new poles, and continents and oceans have been changed, wiping out this human legislated, lawcontroled, materialistic minded, "siva-lization;" then the people who have been taken up in the air will be landed back on the surface.

What happens afer the people are landed back on the earth is told in Isatiah 65:17.26.

And when he has spoken these things, while they beheld, *he was taken up*; and *a cloud received him out of their sight."* (The Acts 1:9).

The people actually saw the man Jesus taken up on the transistor beam. This beam is used by the spacepeople to nullify gravity. "And while they looked steadfastly *toward heaven as he went up,* behold, two men stood by them in white apparel: Which also said, Ye men of Galilee, why stand ye gazing up into heaven? *This same Jesus, which is taken up from you* into heaven, *shall so come in like manner* as ye have seen him go into heaven." (Acts, 1:10, 11).

Most Christians who profess the Bible, as their holy book, do not understand what it says. They think because nothing has happened in their lifetime, that these things are written for some other people in some distant future. — This is not so!

The man called Jesus is about to return. How can one make such a statement? How can one know when the time is to be?

The Bible says, there will be signs in the heaven (God's people in spacecraft are being sighted daily many times all over the world.

The spacepeople are angels of God. They can manifest visible in

CHAPTER FOUR VOICES & VISIONS

human form (Read the foot notes[1]).

The spacecraft and their people are only one of the signs of the time of the return of Jesus.

Second Peter, Chapter 3, Verse 3 says: Knowing this first, *that there shall come in the last days scoffers,* walking after their own lusts.

Can it be more evident that the time is near? Air Force Intelligence has been scoffing to the public through the newspapers, making a flat denial that there are spacecraft in our atmosphere. This is an

---

1 . Footnotes on page 1291-92 of the The Scofield reference Bible Angel, Summary: Angel, "messenger," is used of God, of men, and of an order of created spiritual beings whose chief attributes are strength and wisdom (2 Sam. 14. 20; Psa. 103. 20; 104. 4). In the O.T. the expression 'the angel of the LORD" (sometimes "of God") usually implies the presence of Deity in angelic form (Gen.16. 1-13; 21, 17-19; 22. 11-16; 31. 11-13; Ex. 3. 2-4; Jud. 2.1; 6. 12-16; 13. 3-22). See Mal. 3. 1, note. The word angel i iS used of men in Lk. 7. 24; Jas. 2. 25; Rev. 1. 20; 2. 1, 8, 12, 18; 3.1, 7,14. In Rev. 8. 3-5 Christ 1s evidently meant. Sometimes angel is used of the spirit of man (Mt. 18. 10; Acts 12.15). Though angels are spirits (Psa. 104. 4; Heb. 1. 14), power is given them to become visible in the semblance of human form (Gen. 19. 4, cf. v. 5; Ex. 3. 2; Num. 22. 22-31; Jud. 2. 1; 6. 11, 22; 13. 3, 6; 1 Chr. 21. 16, 20; Mt. 1. 20; Lk. 1. 26; John 20. 12; Acts 7. 30; 12. 7, 8, etc.). The word is always used in the masculine gender, though sex, in the human sense, is never ascribed to angels (Mt. 22. 30; Mk. 12. 25). They are exceedingly numerous (Mt. 26. 53; Heb. 12. 22; Rev. 5. 11; Psa. 68. 17). Their power is inconceivable (2 Ki. 19. 35). Their place is about the throne of God (Rev. 5. 11; 7. 11). Their relation to the believer is that of "ministering spirits, sent forth to minister for them who shall be heirs of salvation," and this ministry has reference largely to the physical safety and well- being of believers (1 Ki. 19. 5; Psa. 34. 7; 91. 11; Dan. 6. 22; Mt. 2. 13, 19; 4. 11; Lk. 22. 43; Acts 5. 19; 12. 7-10). From Heb. 1. 14, with Mt. 18. 10; Psa. 91. 11, it would seem that this care for the heirs of salvation begins in infancy and continues through life. The angels observe us (1 Cor. 4. 9; Eph. 3. 10; Eccl. 5. 6), a fact which should influence conduct. They receive departing saints (Lk. 16. 22). Man is made "a little lower than the angels," and in incarnation Christ took 'for a little' (time) this lower place (Psa. 8. 4, 5; Heb. 2. 6, 9) that He might lift the believer into His own sphere above angels (Heb. 2. 9, 10). The angels are to accompany Christ in His second advent (Mt. 25. 31). To them will be committed the preparation of the judgment of the nations (see Mt. 13. 30, 39, 41, 42; 25. 32, note). The kingdom- age is not to be subject to angels, but to Christ and those for whom He was made a little lower than the angels (Heb. 2. 5). An archangel, Michael, is mentioned as having a particular relation to Israel and to the resurrections (Dan. 10. 13, 21; 12. 1, 2; Jude 9; 1 Thes. 4. 16). The only other angel whose name is revealed, Gabriel, was employed in the most distinguished services (Dan. 8. 16; 9. 21; Lk. 1. 19, 26). Fallen angels. Two classes of these are mentioned: (1) "The angels which kept not their first estate [place], but left their own habitation," are "chained under darkness," awaiting judgment (2 Pet. 2. 4; Jude 6: 1 Cor. 6. 3: John 5. 22). See Gen. 6. 4, note. (2) The angels who have Satan (Gen. 3. 1; Rev. 20. 10, note) as leader. The origin of these is nowhere explicitly revealed. They may be identical with the demons (Mt. 7. 22, note). For Satan and his angels everlasting fire is prepared (Mt. 25. 41; Rev. 20. 10).

CHAPTER FOUR VOICES & VISIONS

outright lie to the people by a branch of the government. They have material proof that they are real.

First Thessalonians tells us in Chapter 5, Verse 3: "For when they shall say, *Peace* and *Safety*; then sudden destruction cometh upon them, as travail upon a woman with child; and they shall not escape."

While the diplomats talk peace and safety the militarists of the world reveal their lusts for power in a race for weapons of destruction.

"*They* are of the world: therefore speak they of the world, and the world heareth them. We are of God; *he that knoweth God heareth us;* he that is not of God heareth not us. Hereby know we the spirit of truth, and the spirit of error." (1st John, 4:5, 6).

Experts by the dozens, bearing the marks of earthling-authority, have had their say about the spacecraft. They give various opinions based on earthly science that spacecraft are hallucinations, inversions, jets, balloons, sea gulls or spots before the eyes. Little do they reali that only about one percent of the sightings «are being reported-to em, People who believed in spacecraft used to be in the minority. . Now more than half of the people believe in the spacecraft whether they have seen one or not.

One top investigator of "unidentified flying objects" who discounted them while he was witht the military forces, is telling the opposite now.

Revelations, Chapter 21, Verses 5 to 16 inclusive, tell in what manner Jesus will return. Verse 16 gives the dimensions of the ship he will return in. The spacepeople call this ship a "star craft." It is 1500 miles square. It is named (Shanchea) and it is the positively charged "moon" orbiting around the Earth now.

Too big? You can't believe it? You are riding on a spaceship 7500

CHAPTER FOUR VOICES & VISIONS

miles in diameter and the Earth is a small globe compared to some of the large planets. Expand your mind — you are living in an endless Universe and have lived on many other planets before you came here.

Second Peter, Chapter 3, Verse 17, says: "Ye therefore, beloved, *seeing ye know these things before,* beware lest ye also, being led away with the error of the wicked, fall from your own steadfastness."

Jesus was seen after his resurrection by his disciples and others.

"After that, he was seen of above five hundred brethren at once; of . whom the greater part remain unto this present, but some are fallen asleep. (1 Corinthians, 15:6).

Many recognize that a great change is upon us. Earthlings are playing with the death force of atomic energy. More evidence that the return of Jesus is near, is recorded in Second Peter, Chapter 3, Verse 10 which says: "But the day of the Lord will come as a thief in the night; in which the heavens shall pass away with a great noise, and the elements shall melt with fervent heat, the earth also and the works that are therein shall be burned up." Could atomic explosives be more accurately described than "the elements," (uranium, plutonium, hydrogen and lithium), *melt with fervent heat.*

If the passengers of an airline saw the crew throwing grenades out of a window, upon the wings, of the plane; the crew would be com titted to an asylum upon landing.

The "crews in authority" are as insane, when they explode kilotons of bombs upon the Earth; which is the ship we are riding through space.

"And he that sat upon the throne said, Behold, I make all things new. And he said unto me, Write: for these words are true and

CHAPTER FOUR VOICES & VISIONS

faithful." (Rev., 21:5).

Write the things *which thou hast seen*, and the things which are, and the things *which shall be hereafter.* (Rev., 1:19).

The "New Jerusalem" referred to in the Bible, quoted in Rev., 21:10, is not really new. It is the positive polarity "moon" that has been orbiting around the earth for many thousands of years.

This satelite, called "Shanchea" by the spacepeople, is a spacecraft.

Their name for the earth is "Shan". "Chea" means child in their langauge of the Solex-Mal, or Solar Tongue. Therefor the name of this ship is "Earthchild" in English. This same craft was called "The Star of Bethlehem" nineteen hundred and sixty years ago at the birth of the child called Jesus and still is- in the Bible.

This positive polarity spaceship is square.

No, I'm not crazy. Columbus said the earth was round and you can plainly see that its flat. Do not be fooled by what you see. The earth is round and the Sun is square. You only see the negative forcefield ütound the Sun, not the body inside the force-field.

This is not new information. It has been before the eyes of earthlings hundreds of years in print; though it was not recognized. Rev.21:16, tells you: "And the city lieth foursquare, and the length is as large as the breadth; and he measured the city with the reed, twelve thousand furlongs. The length and the breadth and the height of it are equal."

The reason it was called "The Star of Bethlehem" was because when it is activated under control — it looks like a star to physical vision. The last time its power units were activated was when the man Jesus was "born." This "positive star body" generates a negative force-field around it, to protect it when it is in motion as a ship.

CHAPTER FOUR VOICES & VISIONS

The name "Bethlehem" tells you that "Beth" is used today as "Beta" meaning negative. "Le" is used today as "lea," meaning a meadow. "Hem" can be understood by any woman — as the thing that goes around the bottom of a dress. "Star of Beta-le hem" means — a positive body, with a negative force-field, around it, over a meadow. That is where Jesus was born — in a manger, in a meadow.

The population of Shanchea is given in Rev., 5:11: "And I beheld, and I heard the voice of many angels round about the throne and the beasts and the elders: and the number of them was *ten thousand times ten thousand, and thousands of thousands."*

The seven sealed books in Chapter 5, 6 and 7 of Revelations are as follows. First seal — Colonization. Second seal — War. Third seal — Money system. Fourth seal — Money control. Fifth seal — Salvation. Sixth seal — Cataclysm. Seventh seal — Spacepeople tabulating mind intent of earthlings in order to determine whom will be "taken up". The earth is now in the beginning sate of the Sixth seal.

Shanchea will be the craft that will bring the man called Jesus back. When it is seen approaching the surface with its irridescent force-field; and the occupants broadcasting over every radio and television loud-speaker, whether the sets are turned on or off; that will be the day.

When Jesus was asked if he was the son of God, he said in St. Mark, 14:62, "I am: and ye shall see the Son of man *sitting on the right hand of power*; and coming in the clouds of heaven." "The right hand of power,"again expressed positive polarity.

The great pyramid of Gizeh was used to generate positive polarity power; and it is also square.

Ezekiel, Chapter 1:26 to 28 further describes Shanchea, "as the

CHAPTER FOUR VOICES & VISIONS

appearance of a *sapphire stone*; as the appearance of fire *round about within it*;"and "as the appearance of the bow (irridescent rainbow force-field) that is in the cloud in the day of rain, so was the appearnce of the brightness around about."

Ezekiel also said, when describing the wheels within wheels, Chapter 1:17. "When they went, they went upon their *four sides:* and they *turned not* when they went.

"And he saith unto me, Seal not the sayings of the prohecy of this book: for the time is at hand." (Rev., 22:10).

CHAPTER FIVE POLLUTION & BLOOD

CHAPTER FIVE

POLLUTION & BLOOD

"The earth also is defiled under the inhabitants thereof; because they have transgressed the laws, changed the ordinance, broken the everlasting covenant." Isaiah, 24:5.

In the last 60 years, material sciences, industrial effort, and financial investment, have accomplished more progress than in the history of this civilization and all the past combined.

In the desire to perpetuate political prestige, profit in a viscious competitive business world, and military supremacy in an environment of overkill capacity, the people have forgotten their spiritual foundation, They have ignored natural law and lost the long range perception of tomorrow's effects for today's acts.

"As ye sow, so shall ye reap," is a truth, not only in agriculture, but in all things. We follow laws of breeding for faster race horses, more milk production, meatier turkeys, more eggs from chickens, and many more improved and profitable ventures. Then we nullify the knowl-edge that all this works, by killing off our physically fit young people in four wars, and breed up four successive generations of youth from people that were not physically qualified to fight. Now we need a law to upbreed a generation from our prime physical youth, to fill a so called "generation gap" of misfits, created by the down breeding. Instead, we are breeding down in disease, and orphaned children, and further increasing the generation gap.

This is the result of political ignorance, parental apathy, and bureaucratic mismanagement. If we drafted the best qualified of

CHAPTER FIVE POLLUTION & BLOOD

our elders to run the government, and quit appointing stooges for political pay-off, this county could be the America that was respected by the rest of the world up until 40 years ago.

Television in its great potential brings us pictures from space, and many worldwide wonders, then it becomes the "boobtube" in hypocrisy of "don't smoke" commercials followed by cigarette advertise-ments. Some of the idiotic commercials only show the level of the mental dopes who make them. Kiddie cartoons are one scene after another of blow-up, bang, and kill.

We pay a 10% surtax foisted on the people "to stop inflation," and everything has gone up in price since it started. Has anyone yet seen Congress repeal any of the laws that don't work since Prohibition?

Detergents, and industrial wastes have killed most of the fish in the Great Lakes and some major rivers. But then we must have our clothes "cleaner than clean" — whatever that is. Now we have enzymes in all of the "whiter than white" and pre soak cleaners. Did anyone in biochemistry, or government agencies ever figure out what these enzymes will do to *anything* organic in lakes, and rivers? Wildlife is already on the decline in many areas from D.D.T. sprays.

As profit increases, so does nationwide pollution increase. As bureaucracy increases, so does graft, cover-up, and the cost of living.

Then comes the ultimate mistake in ignorance. The profiteers, the bureaucrats, the know-it-alls with degrees, all combined for their individual reasons to conduct atmospheric atomic and nuclear bomb tests. Toys for the military and scientific playboys, with a hundred-million suckers financing their wild fiasco.

After over a hundred meetings in Geneva, Switzerland, to arrive at an atmospheric bomb test agreement, with no results, suddenly

CHAPTER FIVE POLLUTION & BLOOD

President Kennedy and Khrushchev arrive at an overnight agreement and sign a bomb test ban treaty. Why? Because it finally got through to them too late, that the fallout from past atomic and nuclear bomb tests were exceeding the critical level for human safety in many areas. The A.E.C. says the fallout from past atmosphereic bomb tests will increase until 1975. It isn't the earthquakes that will get you, it's this silent, unseen curse from atomic fallout.

A recent analysis of wildlife in Northern California shows the bones of animals loaded with Strontium 90. The areas of the country that get the most rain, and snow, are where the most fallout is. If the bones of animals have the accumulation of radioactive debris, so do the bones of people. The A.E.C. says the safest place to live is where there is the least precipitation. Here our average rainfall per year is three and one half inches. What is it in your area?

U. Thant, Secretary General of the United Nations, says we have no more than 10 years to solve our political, economic, military, and social problems throughout the world. If anyone thinks this is possible they should examine themselves in a mirror,

A Congress of scientific pollution experts, meeting recently, said that if our present rate of pollution of air, water, and land, continues there will not be a living thing on the Earth in 35 years.

We have long contended over the years, in the "Proceedings," that the "spirit" of religion and the "matter" of science are merged, Medical science has now discovered and verified our contention. In an article printed in the Los Angeles Times of November 26, 1967, on page 15 of Section D, the following data was revealed.

Under the heading "New Finding of Energy May Aid Heart Patients," doctors doing research at the University of Maryland revealed the following findings and we quote from this article.

CHAPTER FIVE POLLUTION & BLOOD

Discovery of an at present *unidentified electric power supply in the blood stream* of a living animal could revolutionize the design of the electronic pacemakers implanted in certain patients to regulate and stimulate the heart beat.

The discovery was made by a team of research scientists from the University of Maryland.

Their preliminary experiments indicated that sufficient energy was produced from this source to provide the power for a pacemaker.

The leaders of the team, Dr. Adam Cowley of the school of medicine and Dr. Mostafa Tallat of the mechanical engineering department believed the new source of energy could provide a permanent, reliable power supply.

Pacemakers at present in use, usually run on small batteries inserted near the patients heart. These need periodic replacement — and a surgical operation to do it.

Commenting on their discovery, Dr. Cowley said "battery systems are just not adequate. They are supposed to be good for five years, but most do not last two years and are unreliable even before then."

In a statement released by the University of Maryland, Dr. Cowley said that finding sufficient *energy within the body* itself would be a "great asset to medicine," not only for pacemakers but also for "future electrical devices in the body."

In the healthy human heart, a sheaf of nerves and muscle sends out a tiny electrical impulse which stimulates the powerful heart muscles, squeezing oxygen-laden blood throughout the body.

More than 10,000 Americans today owe their lives to artificial pacemakers which help supply that tiny, all important impulse.

CHAPTER FIVE POLLUTION & BLOOD

Dr. Cowley, Dr. Tallet and their team achieved their results by placing one electrode in a dogs heart and a second electrode outside the heart, in various combinations.

"In each case, a sustained power level *two to four times that needed to power a pacemaker* resulted," the university statements on the experiments said.

Although they were not sure precisely how the electric power was produced, Dr. Cowley and Dr. Tallat believed they have found a *"truly biological electrical power supply."*

Italicized words in the quoted article are ours. First Corinthians 15:44 says, "It is sown a natural body; it is raised a spiritual body. There is a natural body, and a spiritual body."

Medical science is finding out that this physical biological body is powered by the *electrical spirit body*. When the electrical spirit body departs from the chemical physical body, the matter body dies. The electrical spirit body is eternal because you can't kill electricity.

The physical body rejection of organ and heart transplants is the result of the *spirit* body rejecting a part that it didn't assimilate to itself in the spirit electrical frequency and vibration of the person.

People are electrically, or spiritually as different as their fingerprints, Matter and energy are opposite poles of the same thing. Matter can be converted into energy and energy can produce matter. The energy electric spirit body assimilates the matter physical biological body from the earth through food, water and air.

The legs of dead frogs can be activated by electrical currents to its nerve ends. This same principle is used in the heart pacemakers. You are electrically powered by the spirit which is you. Every sensing in the physical body is electrical. There are spiritual, or

CHAPTER FIVE POLLUTION & BLOOD

electrical senses beyond the five misnamed physical senses of sight, taste, touch, smell, and hearing. There is the sense of feeling. This sense normally makes one blush when they are embarrassed. This is the sense that makes you know that you are the sense of being. This sense can be expanded through silence, or meditation, and practice in this respect will make you more intuitive. Extra sensory perception, called E.S.P., is not extra in any respect. It is only more developed in some people than in others.

A sense of time also exists in the spirit electrical individual. This makes it possible for some people, using this time sense, to awaken at a given time without an alarm clock. The spirit knows the time and awakens the physical body by reversing its polarity from the back to the front of the brain. This too has been demonstrated by science with sleep machines.

The limits of the physical body are the limits of physical matter environment. The *spirit,* or electrical body *has no limits*, that is why it is infinite and eternal.

We hope science continues to discover the unlimited extent of religion, and that religion finally recognizes through science that it can measure and record the eternal forces of life in the flesh.

You are a walking battery. Your body is composed of millions of cells; these cells are composed of millions of atoms. Atoms are centers of positive and negative centers of activity, which are spinning fields. You are a mass of condensed energy, of which you probably only use less than one percent.

Iones are charged particles of positive, or negative polarity. When you breathe you take in about 22,000 cubic inches of air a day. A cubic centimeter of normal air carries an average from 200 to 1,000 ions of both polarities. Air pollution may increase this to as high as 6000 ions in scubic centimeter. Positive ions in air make you tense and irritable. Negative ions make yon.relaxed and tranquil.

CHAPTER FIVE POLLUTION & BLOOD

Positive ions are detrimental, and negative ions are beneficial. The sooner science can accept the fact that human bodies are only the-matter polarity of the anti-matter opposite polarity of spirit, then the sooner health will be restored to a sick humanity.

Dr. Leon Lederman, Professor of Physics at Columbia University stated, "It is not possible now to disprove the grand speculation that these antiworlds are populated by thinking creatures."

The ion content of the air changes with density, temperature and barometric pressure, as well as humidity.

Asthma patients have felt so much relief in the presence of a negative ion emitter that they don't want to leave the room.

Dr. Kornblueh, in Philadelphia, studied brain wave patterns and found that negative ions tranquilized people in severe pain. Pain is now relieved in many major hospitals by placing the suffering patients in rooms charged with negative ions. Dr. Robert McGowan of Northeastern Hospital in Philadelphia says, "Negative ions make burns dry out faster, heal faster, and with less scarring. They also reduce the need for skin grafting."

Cilia normally whip around in a motion of about 900 beats a minute in normal air. Negative ions increase this beat to about 1200 a minute and positive ions slow it down to 600 a minute or less. This is an electrical effect.

As magnetic storms occur on the Sun, the Earth is affected and research shows an increase in suicides and nervous and mental disorders during these periods.

Electrostatic potentials are associated with all living things. Vegetation shows regeneration rates that are proportional to direct current induced in it. Malignant tumors in mice gradually disappear if direct current is applied periodically. People go to

CHAPTER FIVE POLLUTION & BLOOD

sleep electrically. The polarity reverses in the head. The front of the head has a negative polarity potential and a positive polarity in the rear. The polarity reversal brings on sleeep.

Numbness is not only a lack of circulation, it is a lack of neuron electrical flow. The senses are all electrical to the brain and depend upon the movement and charge of ions.

Joseph Molitorisz, research engineer, says "I am inclined to believe in an era when electrical stimulation of living systems may replace much of the chemical treatments." Molitorisz, with the Department of Agriculture in Riverside, California, has controlled growth and production electrically in orange trees. He found he could also draw water through cut twigs electrically.

This is how a tree defies gravity in moving sap up through it. It is a living ion antenna emitting ions from every leaf and extracting them from the earth.

The old idea that no one can live on another planet because there is no oxygen there, is out of the window.

The gas, or air, is not what effects you as such. The respiratory tract is lined with millions of microscopic little hairs like small antenna, called cilia. These minute antenna extract the static charge of ions in the air and charge the blood cells like batteries. The blood as such is a saline conductor electrically and is para-magnetic.

The electro-magnetic energy, or "spirit," of man is infinite in its com-posite form, or field. The blood in its para-magnetic ability to absorb ions of energy, transmits this energy throughout the body. Since blood is subject to thought, as established by Dr. Littlefield in his book, "Man, Mineral, and Masters," it is possible to create levitation of the body by concentrated thought, or electromagnetic fields.

CHAPTER SIX

MOTION & TIME

Matter-energy, being magnetic-electrical condensation of Space in polarity opposition, manifests its confinement in a perpetual jail called Gravity. Universal desire for a state of rest in the static solution of Space, makes time the measurement of the duration of the sentence intposed by a judge called motion. The quarantine of the structure of one environment, in fields of its own mass, is essential to the order of the universe.

A planet submits to contamination of its body, by the parasites that live on it, until the point of interchange between energy and matter react as a death sentence to protect the galactic society.

Motion is the result of the linear breathing of Universal Being manifesting as the perpendicular cross of electric and magnetic energies that spin galaxies, solar systems, and atoms.

Galaxies spin, solar systems spin, planets spin, and while you are moving, in space, in these three major motions on the planet; you are a moving body occupied by moving cells composed of billions of atoms that are also spinning.

The moon appears to rise in the East and set in the West, relative to the horizons, when we view it from the Earth. If you were in space looking perpendicular to the Earth's orbit around the Sun, the Moon would appear to follow a wave motion relative to the Earth's orbit track as shown in figure 1.

CHAPTER SIX MOTION & TIME

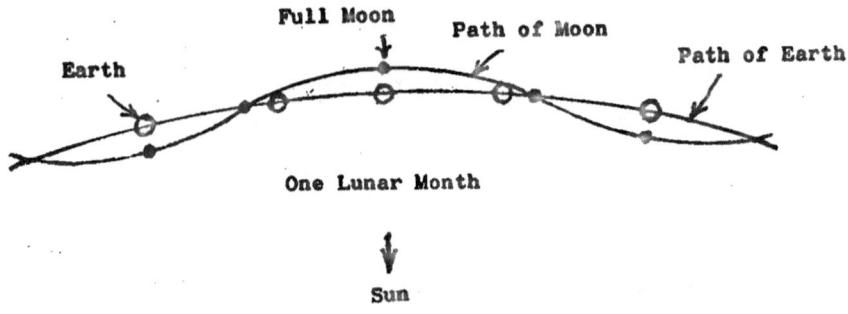

From the surface of the Moon you would see the Sun rise once every 28 Earth days. Everything appears different from different points of view.

These motions are brought out to show that things are not always what they appear to be.

Metal cones positioned at critical points in magnetic fields have produced 100% pure silica out of the energy of space. This occurred because the frequency of the fields was in the electromagnetic zone of silica in the spectrum. Other pure elements could have been produced as they are all in solution in the total energy of space. Sound recorded during this experiment showed a sign wave on the oscilloscope that was curved above the line and square below it.

Space propulsion will ultimately be the resonance of vibrations on a diaphram in the rear of spaceships that is in discord with the harmony of space. This will result in speeds in multiples of the speed of light. Acceleration will not be felt because the people in the spaceship will be inside of their electrostatic magnetic fields surrounding the craft.

The center of activity in fields has no motion. This is the only point of view from which true records can evolve.

Antigravity can be produced in any mass of matter by arranging

CHAPTER SIX MOTION & TIME

the poles of the atomic fields in linear polarity as the molecules are ar-ranged to produce magnetism in a magnet. In this event it will be easier to levitate the Empire State building in New York than it would be to raise the pen with which I am writing, because the Empire State building has more mass than the pen. Antigravity is proportionately relative to the charge of the mass of a body, in contrast to the charge of a planet's mass.

A bumble bee does not fly by the air reactions of its wings, or aerodynamic flight. Its wings produce an electrostatic accumulation in polarity bands around its body and it rises by electrostatic magnetic insulation from gravity at the same time controlling direction of flight by the wings in the air.

Every principle that can ever be used, already exists in nature, in one manifestation or another, of an Infinite Mind that created galaxies, planets, people, bees, and atoms.

Prana, or breath, the circulation of atoms of air in multiples of activity, can produce antigravity, or levitation. This can be demonstrated by five people breathing in unison creating the charge, and partially removing the confinement of gravity. Set a heavy person on a chair with two people standing on each side. All five bend at the waist expelling air from the lungs at the same time in this downward bow. Then all straighten up at the same time inhaling fully. Do this seven consecutive times. Then the two front people standing on each side of the person on the chair, place one index finger under each knee of the person on the chair; and the other two people, standing behind those two, place their index finger under the armpits of the subject on the chair. This is done on the seventh down bend exhalation. As all five straighten up for the seventh time, the four can lift a 200 pound man off the chair above their heads,with no apparent effort.

Motions within motions in the activty of solar systems to atoms bring about gravity as a result of all structure being disoriented in its countless fields. Once the center poles of activity of activity of

CHAPTER SIX MOTION & TIME

the fields are all oriented perpendicular radially from the center of the planet, at any place on its surface, antigravity will result. A toroid coil with a caduceus winding will separate the positive and negative fields. With the positive polarity field up, the order of oriented fields want to get away from the random matrix of disoriented fields in their discordant relations in the earth's mass.

Antigravity is harmonics of orderly energy trying to escape from the confusion of matter.

Time is an absolute in space even as space is an absolute of energy in solution. Time does not exist in the center of energy fields. Time only exists in the periphery of fields, the orbit of planets, a day of rotation relative to the Sun, or a period of satellite orbit around a planet. Motion is the only reference to time.

Matter is the mass of disoriented energy rejected by the oriented order of space and confined in forms because of its instability.

People are about to discover that the materialism of disorder can only destroy itself, when it discards the order of intelligence of the Creative Spirit, or stable static energy.

Higher education can only load the brain with a record of known things. It cannot offer a course of a in inspiration, or a course of intelligence.

Motion, in time, is relative to the limits of the body in motion. If this were not true, nature would have destroyed the universe a long time ago.

The eternal qualities are the still, motionless matrix of time, space and being. Things in motion change and things that change are not eternal in any one pattern of form.

CHAPTER SIX MOTION & TIME

"T" is the symbol of time.
"S" is the symbol of space.
"B" is the symbol of being.

This is the Cadeusus, or the triune of "T", "B" and "S."

Division of eternal things is what creates opposites.

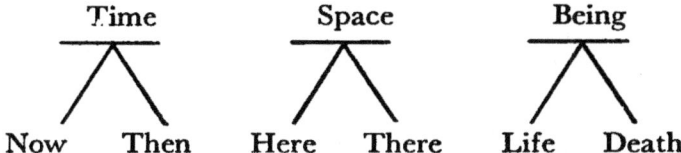

Cycles are repetitions of the divisions. All divisions of opposites reach a fulcrum pinnacle of stillness, at times. Everything in the universe comes under one, or the other, of the three aspects of infinity. That which can bring these three aspects into one is in perfect balance.

Each of the opposites cycles an interchange within itself like a swinging pendulum.

Here becomes there as soon as you cross the street, and there becomes here. As you register your own changes in time, tomorrow becomes today as the Earth revolves on its axis, and today was tomorrow yesterday.

Life and death also interchange, so that being may manifest through the action. This in itself is proof that you have always been and always will be. It is odd when you hear someone who professes belief in an after life refer to someone dying with this remark: Well that's the end of him."

CHAPTER SIX MOTION & TIME

The old expression, "Time heals all things" is as erroneous as saying "the Sun comes up, or sets." The ability to forget, in time, may heal something such as sorrow. *Forgiveness is forgetness.*

Time cannot be a dimension, as Einstein tried to prove, because everything in motion in time will never repeat itself again exactly as it was before.
Be-ing is to manifest substance in form to conform to the requirements of an environment you are in at the moment. Death is the requirement of change from living in one environment to living in a different environment.

If you could be *not,* then you could not be *now,* because now was then before you arrived here from there. You *are* all the time, even when your body sleeps. The real you never sleeps, although it rests at the peak of the fulcrum in the interchange between the opposites of life and death.

Flesh is only matter you assimilate as a requirement of this dense Earthly condition. Flesh moves only because your real body moves. Your matter body of flesh is not going to walk, or talk, after you out of it. *Death* can only manifest in matter. This is the interchange that permits it to return to what it was before you assimilated it in form.

That portion of space which is you, will always be in time somewhere. Expressing *life here now* is really *death there then,* when you observe from the opposite side of things.

The trinity of time, space, and being are the deity called God.

Space is energy in a static state. Matter is energy in a condensed state. The energy in matter is not static. Every atom of its matrix is in motion. It is in constant change through erosion, corrosion, and the decay of its atomic structure.

CHAPTER SIX MOTION & TIME

Space is the static essence of pure intelligence and is the Infinite Creative Mind that knows all and everything. Discoveries, inventions, and all new things are derived from this Absolute Mind. No function, act, or principle, can be employed by mankind, that was not already operating by some natural law somewhere throughout time. This static conductor of thought is the absolute time that occupies every atom, olecule, cell, and individual that manifests separate levels of action rom the stillness of mind.

The Creative Spirit isn't dead. Anyone who professes this has rejected back to the animal state of unconsciousness and caused the spirit within to become dormant. They have rejected the very essence that makes them man.

Ignorance demands something they can see, or sense with the five animal senses, in order to accept God. Thus they must have effigies, a mian on a cross, or statues, to comprehend their God. They cannot comprehend that the Infinite Spirit is manifesting in every atom and cell of their physical bodies.

Atoms are the first level of creation and are perfect in their order. An atom of hydrogen is identical with every other atom of hydrogen. Its mass, its atomic weight, its position in the society of the elements, its boiling point, its melting point, its electron structure, and oxidation state and density, are exact. Could this have been the product of evolution? If so from where did it come to achieve such identical order in its makeup?

Hydrogen functions for its purposes, within its created limits, because it cannot manifest anything except that which it was created for.

Humans are an assimilated mass of billions of billions of atoms in their physical matrix. They are what they are, because this environment on this particular planet requires that they be that way, in order to manifest here.

CHAPTER SIX MOTION & TIME

One adult human is composed of approximately 300 trillion cells. each cell is a living entity unto itself and performs all of its activities within its limits. It knows what to do because that perfect Absolute Mind runs it. It takes about 250 cells, end to end to reach one inch. The combined cell structure of one adult human, placed end to end would go around the world, at the equator, over 200 times. Can the activities of these trillions of cells in one human body, each performing its job in harmony and order with all of the others, be accidental, or evolutionary? This alone, in its function of one human physical body, proves a mind control beyond brain understanding.

Then when one realizes that *each* of these trillions of cells is composed of genes, chromosomes, and other parts, each performing their functions within the cell, one begins to grasp the order and ability of the perfect Mind; of an Infinite God in manifesting one human being.

Those humans who are with God, allow Him to run them in their complex makeup. Those who are *not* with God are dreaming up new additives, or taking them to try to make the body work differently with makeshift human ideas that are not part of natural human assimilation.

This Perfect Mind that makes all of these things, and keeps them working, will respond from Its static state if one activates a response from It. You will not get a response from this Perfect Mind by bowing, kneeling, praying, or begging for help whenever the occasion demands it. You will only get a response by continually admiring It, loving It and respecting It in supplication and reverence.

Do all *things* in *moderation* is God's command and law. Treat others as you like to be treated. Have courtesy and respect for that part of God manifesting in everyone you come in contact with, if you would have God respond in you when you need Him.

CHAPTER SIX MOTION & TIME

The laws this Perfect Mind made in atoms, solar systems, and people cannot respond in violation of Its own laws. One has to build up a deposit of response, under God's law of reciprocation, or He cannot give anything back to you. If you, as a matrix of trillions of God's cell creations, recognize this order and activity and think love and *admiration* and *appreciation* to them for their daily work in making you function, you will be surprised at your well being.

You are in God and God is in you. If you find God in yourself, and others, you do not need to seek the Infinite Incomprehensible God out there, in space.

In the space you occupy, you are the most important assembly of complex structure, that can manifest God where you are.

Each person is the center of the Universe unto themselves. From within them God sees everything from their individual point of view | and understands and responds according to their actions. God is not an "Indian giver," and he gave man the right of free choice. Use it accordingly.

CHAPTER SEVEN ENERGY & TESLA

CHAPTER SEVEN

ENERGY & TESLA

Fohat — Mind — Life Force — Eloptic Energy — Thought Force — E.S.P., and other names, have tried to express what little is understand-able about an effect that manifests through all living things.

Even those few who do understand it, would want to attribute its universal essence to the Creative Spirit which makes all life eternal.

We have discovered that electricity and magnetism are the right and left hands of God, so to speak. Without electromagnetic energies a Sun, or Planet, or a Solar System; an atom, or structures of the atom, living bodies, ants, or people, flowers, birds, or fish, *nothing can be* without these invisible forces of electricity and magnetism. In polarity response they both interchange with each other and one cannot exist without the other.

The mysterious energy that makes electricity and magnetism work, is perpendicular to both the electric and magnetic patterns, and establishes a third plane of reference which we call a "time zone." This "zone" is not detectable, or measurable, with standard electric or magnetic instruments. It responds to thought and can orient the magnetic pattern out of perpendicularity to the electric pattern. If the magnetic field exceeds 87° and coincides to the electric wave pattern, disintegration results in matter and it becomes energy. This occurs with no sound, or heat, or explosion, but will be accompanied by brilliant light emissions. Teleportation can be accomplished by this effect. Pure elements of matter can be created out of energy in the spectrum frequency of any element with

CHAPTER SEVEN ENERGY & TESLA

controlled polarity reversal in the electric flow.

To our understanding this "zone" is Universal Mind which creates reciprocal actions between electric and magnetic effects. This "zone" being responsive to thought, makes it possible to understand how all matter from galaxies, to people and atoms, can be created by a Universal Mind, or Cosmic God, which is everywhere. This could explain the old expression, "never let your one hand know what the other hand is doing," because the other hand would set up an equal and opposite effect. This also would explain how a Supreme Infinite Intelligence could create matter and the physical universe out of the unseen energy. Mind had to come before matter, otherwise how can one explain the order of celestial bodies in unlimited magnitude down to the complete order in atoms. Should one feel that they are infringing on God to try and understand his creations?

Should one feel that it is "off bounds" to try to find Out how the perfect laws of the universe operate life in matter? There is no "tree of knowledge." Knowledge is in finding out what makes a tree a tree. Wasn't man supposed to have "dominion over all things"? Wasn't man given a "right of free choice" by God?

Three-hundred-trillion cells in one adult human body perform an interchange of biological electrical functions in such order that only a perfect Universal Spirit could direct their activities; No human study of effects in physical structure will ever reveal the causes of these effects, unless one works through the spirit in dedication to a beneficent purpose for mankind.

This Other Energy" is the conductor of cell communication between all living things. Cleve Baxter's research proves the communication but it doesn't explain how it works. Cells do not have ears, but they do respond to thought.

The Hieronymus device proved that communication from cell structure in the astronauts in Apolla 8 and 11 had no loss in power

CHAPTER SEVEN ENERGY & TESLA

from the earth to the moon. Hieronymus also proved plants would grow in total darkness by bringing "This Other Energy" into the darkness from metal plates exposed to sunlight through wires connected to metal plates over the seeds. Light does not travel through wires.

Franz Anton Mesmer, who was born in 1734, called "This Other Energy" "animal magnetism." Dr. D'Eslon, Mesmer's chief pupil, formulated the laws of animal magnetism as follows:

"1. Animal magnetism is a universal, continuous fluid, constituting an absolute plenum in nature, and the medium of all mutual influence between interstellar bodies and between the earth and animal bodies.

2. It is the most subtle fluid in nature, capable of flux and of reflux of ebb and flow, and of receiving, propagating and continuing all kinds motion.

3. The human body has poles and other properties analogous to the magnet.

4. The action and virtue of animal magnetism may be communicated from one body to another, whether animate or inanimate.

5. It operates at a great distance, without the intervention of any body.

6. It is increased and reflected by mirrors, communicated, propagated, and increased by sound," and maybe accumulated, concentrated tansported." Is this "increase by sound" thr reason for singing hymns in the churches?

"This Other Energy" was called "The Mumia" by Paracelsus. "The Odic Force" by Reichenbach, "The Nervous Ether" by Richardson,

CHAPTER SEVEN ENERGY & TESLA

"The X Force" by Eeman, "The Prana" by Indian Gurus, and is "Life Force" itself.

Forms has a lot to do with the manifestation of "This Other Energy." Cones produce a cohesive transmission of this energy for miles. Minerals crystalize in their individual forms because "This Other Energy requires exact order. Pyramids oriented in the planes of North, South,East and West, relative th their faces, will produce vortices and strange reactions in their center . An egg out on its shell, in a saucer beneath a pyramid will have the albumen harden in less than a week, while another egg in a saucer outside the pyramid remains liquid.

If a circle of seven pyramids could be located equally spaced in a vacant areas surrounding the Los Angeles Basin, the smog could be eliminated, This would require seven masts 600 feeth high and the top, or longest, guy wires would have to be on a 52° plane on all sides equivalent to the great pyramid of Gizeh in Egypt. The only disadvantage of this would be malfunction of some aircraft instruments if they flew over the masts. On the other hand they wouldn't cost anything to operate except the cost of their construction. We have tested pyramids made of welding rods at all four corners and they work as well in experiments as if the sides were filled in as with cardboard pyramids.

So much could be accomplished with the use of "This Other Energy" if the orthodoxy of educated scientists would investigate and accept those principles of nature that operate in life itself. No one seems to bo able to break through that wall of selfinflicted ego that keeps science within the profit structure of a defunct economy, while humanity goes down to its own destruction in a chemical and radiation disaster.

It seems that today, the people who know how to do things are stopped in their tracks, by laws and opinions from authorities who don't know how to do things. Maybe this is the destiny of a planet that reaches for the Moon, when it needs something to divert the

CHAPTER SEVEN ENERGY & TESLA

peoples thinking about the mess it has made on the earth, A hungry child cannot understand this philosophy. Disease, and poverty, and war are manmade results of wrong thinking over the years. "This Other Energy" can only respond, and reciprocate, according to the fixed laws of the universe, Education can only give from the past. The present must operate on inspiration and faith, or the future is lost.

A past civilization knew how to use "This Other Energy" to levitate anything including themselves. It manifested in the Kings Chamber of Great Pyramid to revive dead V.I.P.s in three days, or mummify their bodies if they failed to come back to life. This activity took 28 days or one magnetic month. This is the reason the Kings Chamber was built off center in the pyramid in order to be in the proper area of the energy generated.

Modern science, in their two-dimensional electro-magnetic science, cannot accept the fact that a handful of people, today, understand this third plane of refererence.

Dr. Hendrick's cell theraphy, in Swizerland, proved that organ cells, injected into the body, would only go to the same kind or organ in the body and fortify it.

People are as diferent as their fingerprint and "This Other Energy" makes them all live. How long are the authorities going to ignore the basic philosophy of life, known only to a few people, when it could add multiplicity to present life spans?

Over 30% more is being spent now, for weapons of war, than was being spent four years ago. This 30% spent in the right direction could have already unlocked so much more of the secrets of life and we could have already been on the road to 150 year life spans without aging.

Those few of us who understand "This Other Energy" continue to plod on at a snails pace, determined in our direction, to break trail

CHAPTER SEVEN ENERGY & TESLA

for a heaven on earth in the future.

Tests conducted with vegetables growing in a garden, show remarkable results when they are grown under electro-magnetic-stimuli. They've found that up to 30% more seeds will germinate after they have been in the ground for 24 hours. Growth of the crop to the time of harvest, is accelerated by several weeks. In some growing areas this makes it possible to plant the second crop sooner, thereby avoiding early freezes; as about 6 weeks can be gained on both the plantings to the time of the second harvesting.

Leaf vegetables and above the ground vegetables will be nearh twice the size of normal vegetables that are grown in uncharged soil. Root vegetables, like carrots, parsnips, etc., will not only be larger, but will have more flavor. Ball-shaped vegetable will not react as well as pointed root and pointed leaf vegetables. This includes head lettuce, cabbage, turnips and potatoes, among others. This is because their spherical shape accumulates the charge instead of permitting flow of current to keep passing through them.

A device to perform this activity can be made as follows. Get a straight length (21 feet) of 3/4" diameter galvanized water pipe. Take a a 3/4" standard coupling and weld a four-foot cross of ½" pipe on one end of it. The cross is to be horizontal to the ground when the coupling is screwed on to the top of the pipe mast. Solder eleven spikes onto each arm of the cross — from center. These will be spaced 2 inches apart from the ends coming in, and cach 9 inches long. These spikes are made from #10 copper wire and all point straight up. Tho top ends shuld be sharpened to a point by hammering, or grinding before they are e soldered on to the cross arms.

Solder 12 wires around the base of the mast, 18 inches up from the bottom end. This can be #14 bare copper wire, each equal in length to your garden radius. Screw the spiked cross onto the top of the mast. Connect four guy wires to the top of the mast at the center of the cross. Put an insulator on each guy wire six feet down from

CHAPTER SEVEN ENERGY & TESLA

their connection at the top of the mast. Add ten more feet of guy wire to each of these insulators, and put another insulator on each of *these* wires. Drive four pipe stakes, at an angle to the ground, 15 feet from the mast and equally spaced about it. Fasten four guy wires to the stakes, each long enough to connect to the bottom insulators.

Dig a small hole for the mast. This hole should be big enough for a wide mouth large glass peanut butter jar. Be sure the *top* of this jar is above the ground level, Put a smaller glass jar in the peanut butter jar, and another smaller one in it; until the jar inside is just big enough to fit around the pipe mast. Slide the jars on the pipe mast lower end, set the mast up and attach the stake guy wires to the four lower insulators, Adjust the guy wires so the mast is vertical, but not tight enough to bend the pipe mast.

Now dig twelve, equally spaced, radial ditches out from the mast to the size of your garden, They are not to exceed 200 feet from the mast, These ditches should be deeper than the working depth of hoe or cultivator. Extend the twelve wires out and down these ditches and cover them up, after placing a stake at the outer end of each wire; so you can always tell where the wires are.

Now plant your rows radially from the mast in your round garden. Do not plant directly over the wires, as roots may entangle them, Rows should never be closer than four feet to each other on the inner end, Plant what you like best parallel to the wires.

This device works by activating the natural electric charge in the atmosphere and the earth. These charges being in unbalance (between. the solid earth and the gaseous air) try to balance, thereby creating an electric flux in the mast and wires. The current in the wires produces a magnetic field around them, and brings about a gentle magnetic vortex perpendicular to the ground. This in turn creates accelerated ion and electric activity in the plants, and roots, which are in the vertical line of electric flux, Each vegetable,

CHAPTER SEVEN ENERGY & TESLA

then becomes a miniature atomic accelerator, and thus increases its own growth and current flow..

This device employs natural electric and magnetic principles and costs nothing to operate. It will stimulate growth over an acre of ground.

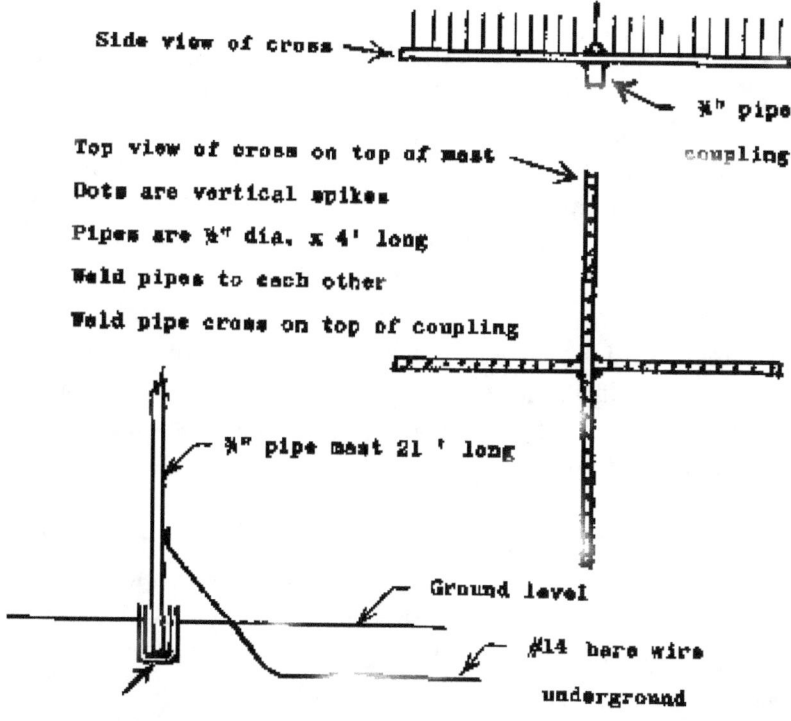

The greatest genius of all time is practically unknow in the annals of American history. Marconi, Edison, Bell, the Wright brothers, and Fulton, are known for their contributions to the scientific and industrial world by nearly everyone.

Nikola Tesla was born at Smiljan, Yugoslavia, on July 10, 1856,

CHAPTER SEVEN ENERGY & TESLA

He was the inventor of alternating current generators and motors, the polyphase system of the transmission of power, and the four tuned circuit system which is the basis of radio transmission. He radio controlled a ship model in 1898, By this he laid the basis of all radio telemechanics, Tesla was 18 years old when Guglielmo Marconi was born in Marzabotto, Italy in 1874, Tesla preceded Marconis radio discoveries by several years.

Tesla held 25 patents on electrical motors and generators from 1886, 9 patents on the transmission of electrical power, 6 patents on electric lighting, 17 patents for controllers and high frequency apparatus, 12 patents in radio technics, 5 patents for turbines, and 11 other patents on various devices. Nikola Tesla was the father of alternating current which made it possible to transmit power over great distances and run the industries of today.

In 1891 Tesla said "There is no subject more captivating, more worthy of study, than nature, To understand this great mechanism, to discover the forces which are active, and the laws which govern them, is the highest aim of the intellect of man."

Tesla said, "The superstitious belief of the ancients, if it existed at all, cannot be taken as a reliable proof of the ignorance, but just how much they knew. can only be conjectured, A curious fact is that the ray or tope fish was used by them in electrotherapy. The records, though scanty, are of a nature to fill us with conviction that a few initiated, at , at least, had a deeper knowledge of amber phenomena. To mention one, Moses was undoubtedly a practical and skillful electrician far in advance of his time. The Bible describes precisely and minutely arrangements constituting a machine in which electricity was generated by friction of air against silk curtains and stored in a box like a condenser. It is very pausible to assume that the sons of Aaron were killed by a hilgh tension discharge, and that the vestal fires of the Romans were electrical. The beltd drive musth have been known to engineers of that epoch, and it is difficult to see how the abundant evolution of static electricity could have escaped their notice. Under favorable

CHAPTER SEVEN ENERGY & TESLA

atmospheric conditions a belt may be transformeid into dynamic generator capable of producing many striking actions. I have lighted incandescent lamps, operated motors and performed numerous other equally interesting experiments with electricity drawn from belts and stored in tin cans."

These last two sentences describe exactly the static generator for which Van De Graaf was later given credit for developing and discovering. Tesla again was excluded fromt he scientific history and another person was given the credit.

Tesla's reference to Moses tabernacle, as an "electro-static generator," is describing our "Integratron" closely as to principle of operation. It regenerated the body also, as Moses died at one hundred and twenty years of age, and it says in Deuteronomy 34:7 "his eye was not dim, nor his natural force abated."

This is even as our modern life saving technique called "mouth to mouth resusitation" was described in tho Bible in Second Kings 4:34, where Elisha went to a child that was pronounced dead; "And he went up, and lay upon the child, and put his mouth upon his month, and his eyes upon his eve, and his hands upon his hands: and he stretched himself upon the child; and the flesh of the child waxed warm." We still have the eye to eye, and hand to hand, contact to learn. It may be the hand to hand contact is like using jumpers from one battery to another to assist it, and the eye to eye could be a form of mental autosuggestion employed.

Sixty years ago Tesla said, "I believe that the telautomatic aerial torpedo will make the large siege gun, on which so much dependence placed at present, obsolete."

He was right again, as today we have intercontinental ballistic missiles control by electronics, which he called teleautomatics.

In his reference to "a revolution will be brought about through the adoption of electrical agricultural apparatus," again this

CHAPTER SEVEN ENERGY & TESLA

information has been neglected, or avoided for commercial reasons.

In experiments conducted at the government agricultural station at Amherst, Massachusetts, in 1900, it was established that atmospheric electricity conducted to vegetable gardens would enhance the growth, and crop, by at least 30%. Why has this never been used? Why does the government hide everything it discovers? Why discover something if it is not going to be used?

After printing the Electro-Magnetic Gardening article in the last "Proceedings" we received a letter from one of our readers, well up in years, who said his father and his grandfather both used to stick a wire in the ground extending into the air vertically by each plant to make them grow bigger and faster. This was years ago in Germany.

Why does the government bureau of Health, Education and Welfare, state the country is 50,000 doctors short of what is needed in the medical profession? It isn't because we need more doctors, it's because we need less disease. This is an admission that illnesses are gaining on the medical care of them. Then why not to employ Tesla's electro-therapeutic discoveries?. Dr. Ruth Drewn, Abrams, Hicronymus, and many others as well as the old violet ray machine, all of which prove beneficial in so many cases, could be used.

Nikola Tesla was financed By J. P. Morgan, George Westinghouse, and several others, who all benefited from their association with him.

Tesla used himself as a guinea pig in many of his experiments. He said "Soon my efforts were centered upon producing in a small space the most intensive inductive action, and by gradual improvements in the apparatus, I obtained results of a surprising character. For instance, when the end of a heavy bar of iron was

CHAPTER SEVEN ENERGY & TESLA

thrust within a loop power fully energized, a few moments were sufficient to raise the bar toa high temperature. Even lumps of other metals were heated as rapidly as though they were placed in a furnace. When a continuous band formed of a sheet of tin was thrust into the loop, the metal was fused instantly, the action being comparable to an explosion, and no wonder, for the frictional losses accumulated in it at the rate of possibly ten horse-power. Masses of poorly conducting material behaved similarly, and when a high exhausted bulb was pushed into the loop, the glass was heated in a few seconds nearly to the point of melting.

When I first observed these astonishing actions, I was interested to study their effects upon living tissues. As may be presumed, I proceed with all the necessary caution, as well I might, for I had evidence that in a turn of only a few inches in diameter an electromotive force of more than ten-thousand volts was produced, and such high pressure would be more than sufficient to generate destructive currents in the tissue. This appeared all the more certain as bodies of comparatively poor conductivity were rapidly heated and partially destroyed. One may imagine my astonishment when I found that I could thrust my hand, or any other part of my body within the loop and hold it there with impunity. The only plausible explanation I have so far found is that the tissues are condensers."

This conforms to Dr. Georges Lakhovskys findings "that the cell-organic unit in all living beings, is nothing but an electro-magetic resonator, capable of emitting and absorbing radiation of a very high frequency."

The human body is matter manifested. All spirit is matter, and all matter is spirit, each manifesting in opposite polarity under different conditions.

Nikola Tesla's inventions are the basic foundation of all electrical power, and without his discoveries, the scientific advances of today would have been impossible.

CHAPTER EIGHT HUMANS & MAN

CHAPTER EIGHT

HUMANS & MAN

"In the beginning God created the heaven and the earth" (Gen. 1:1). This creation was a part of the continuously evolving creation throughout the Universe. Each instant that passes new things are made, new phases of life unfold, to live in ever progressing cycles of rebirth.

As related above God made heaven before earth. In these heavens of ; the sky He had already created man. On many planets, of many other "solar systems and on other planets in this solar system man was developed through thousands of years, before the earth was habitable.

Man was created (Gen. 1:27), he did not evolve from the lower animal.

However he was not created on the earth. Man was created throughout millions of solar systems, to serve as the instrument of God's doing. Anyone who contends that this planet is the only one occupied by intelligent life forms, does not accept God in His infinite completeness. Their narrow mind has placed a limit on His ability to perform his creations, to one planet.

Adam was not a single man. The Adamic race of man were the first people to inhabit the earth. This is confirmed in Gen.1:27)where the face of man in the original creation are described as "male and female." In (Gen. 1:28)the scripture relates how "God blessed them." This is plural, not *him,* but *them,* more than one. And God said unto them (the Adamic race, both male and female) "be fruitful, and multiply." This before Eve is ever mentioned.

CHAPTER EIGHT HUMANS & MAN

So the Adamic race is established on on earth, while badly misinterpreted in the first chapter of Genesis.

Then God finished His work of creation in regard to man. He had also finished the creation of the *heavens* and the *earth* (Gen. 2:1) and all the host of *them*. This means all the beings who occupied the *earth and* the *heavens*. So God "ended His work" and rested (Gen. 2:2,3).

Can this be? God ended His work, and still no mention of Eve. Yes that is accurate, the Bible is right on God's beginning of His creations.

Then comes the summary of his creation. This is where people are led into confusion. This summary was originated by a "brain". For the first time, God is left out of the picture and we have a "Lord God" (Heb, Jehova Elohim). This character was one of the Adamic race who was in the colony that had been landed here by spacecraft. The men of the Adamic race did not bring their women with them when they first landed on earth. This summary of the creation of man by God is an excuse written to explain away the fact tha people of earth today are crossbreeds.

The Lord God brings Eve into the picture — not the Creator. The Lord God were lonesome (Gen. 2:18) so the relator names everything, to further confuse you. Then the Lord God pops Eve out of a rib after one of their people fell into deep sleep (Gen 2:21,22).

God brings about the creation of people through birth everywhere in the Universe, not by making women out of ribs.

The race of Eve were the highest form of lower animal life on this planet. They were not apes, but they were also not the race of man, created by God.

So comes the story story of Adam, Eve and the apple (Gen 3: 1-

CHAPTER EIGHT HUMANS & MAN

14). This son of the Adamic race of man blamed the woman and the woman blamed the serpent. The serpent didn't have anyone to blame.

One of the true species of man, as God created the Adamic race, mated with an animal. There is no violation of God's law in man mating with woman after his own kind. The spacecraft people have wives and childred. Adam's violation of the law was not in "eating the people;" it was eating the wrong apple.

God created every creature after its own kind (Gen 1: 11-13 and 21-23), but one of the race of man mated with an animal of the earth and crossed blood.

This is where man became hu-man. Eve gave birth to Cain and Abel. She didn't know who was the Creator was so she said, "I have gotten a man from the Lord" (Gen 4:1), thinking the Lord was the Adamic man who was her mate.

When Cain killed Abel he revealed the animal nature of his mother. He started the practice of murder, that has expanded to a point where people now vaporize thousands with bombs.

That is why the people of the earth are call humans. The Adamic sons of God knew the tiger as a killer among beasts. Their name for tiger was Hu This has been brought up through the centuries as simbolized here from the ancient records.

虎 **Hu** **Tiger**

Most of the people on earth today are crossbreed of the true Adamic Sons of God, as originally created, and the animal of the race of Eve. That is why you have an earthly, dense animal body and an inner body of created reality, as God made you.

The true created man and women of the Adamic race of Man, have

CHAPTER EIGHT HUMANS & MAN

been watching the people on earth for thousands of years.

This "siva-lization" of hu-umans has expanded the science of destruction to the point of crisis. The nations having atomic bombs have enough to wipe out all living things on the earth. The animal of Eve is in power. In the United States the President is trying to regain control of atomic energy. Our elected branches of Administrative Government realize that the beast is loose. Some of the eminent physicists are beginning to turn about.

The Adamic race of Man have brought nullifier ships into earth's thin film of breathable atmosphere. We call them green firebals. They | have nullified concentrations of atomic radiation that were in our atmosphere. They feel responsible for the fact that one of their people Started this destructive cycle on the earth. God may have to "shorten the days" and bring the man called Jesus back before schedule, in . order to awaken the people. You have a choice to make. You either accept the Creator's Adamic constructive part of you, or you recognize the physical human's destructive influence of the Eve ancestry.

The *field* is the *world*; the good seed are the children of the kingdom; but the tares are the children of the wicked one.

The enemy that sowed them is the devil; the harvest is the end of the world; and the reapers are the angels (Space People). St. Matthew | 13:38,39).

It stands to reason that the spacepeople are not going to reap the weeds (tares). Even humans gather the weeds only to burn them.

You must understand; that to spacepeople who colonized the earth to begin with, that the earth is a field where they "planted a crop" of people.

They use the planets like humans use the land. Men plant various crops, but they segregate them; they do not plant wheat, oats, corn,

CHAPTER EIGHT HUMANS & MAN

barley and rye in the same field. This would cross the crops and make harvesting each separately impossible.

A race horse owner does not breed his thoroughbred mare with a plow horse. An oak tree does not mate with an elm tree.

Wheat is pure seed stock grown as wheat. Tares are the result of crossed seed. This applies to the seed of humans as well as anything else.

The spacepeople originally landed (planted) three species of man on earth. The Ham (black), Shem (white), and Japheth (yellow). These are all true seed as long as they are not mixed.

The Black people, and the yellow people, are as true a race of humans as the white people, as long as they do not oss seed by intermating. *This is the "original sin"*.

All of the "angels" are not white, They are pure seed of their own color, however., *"The Son of man* shall send forth his angels, and they shall gather *out of his kingdom* all things that offend, and them which do iniquity." St. Matthew 13: 41.

The "Son of Man" are the people of the Adamic race of true seed. Humans are the crossbreed descendants of the Adamic race of Man and the animal race of Eve.

This original sin of the Adamic colony, that was first planted (landed), on this field (the earth), is further crossed by the intermating between the true races. This has brought about an increase in the tares. Cossbreeding of the word tares has even taken place by making a diagonal line through the letter R. This has created a new monster called taxes. `

"And *they* shall gather *out of his kingdom* all things that offend, and them which do iniquity."

CHAPTER EIGHT HUMANS & MAN

What is meant here by *out of his kingdom*? Have you not often heard of the places of natural beauty being referred to as, "God's Country"? The farms, the forests, the deserts, and places where people go on their vacations, in order to escape for a moment from the human cauldron of siva-lization in the cities?

The spacepeople are gathering out of these places who don't belong there, in *his kingdom*. This is evidenced by these people, who place mammon above God. rushing to the cities because they can "make more money there."

The money-mad people are being influenced mentally to follow their professed god mammon.

On the other hand, many people are fed-up with the money mad crowd, and are being influenced to go back to God's Country.

This migration is the separation of the wheat from the tares. Those who do iniquity, by seeking more and more money, have separated oer from the people who are seeking more and more "kingdom of God."

"So shall it be at the end of the world: the angels shall come forth, and sever the wicked from among the just. And shall cast them in the *furnace* of fire: there shall be wailing and gnashing of teeth." (St. Matthew 13: 49, 50).

What is this *furnace of fire*? Can it be atomized cities?

"And except those days should be shortened, *there shall no flesh be saved*: but for the *elects* sake those days *shall be shortened.*" (St. Matthew 24: 22).

This paragraph explains why the spacecraft are being seen by millions of people, in such great mumbers.

The spacepeople would have normally made their appearance in

CHAPTER EIGHT HUMANS & MAN

the future, at the time the earth changes on its poles. They have made their appearance sooner, or "shortened the days" in order to see to it that all flesh is not destroyed by the radiation of atomic experiments, or atomic | and hydrogen bomb warfare.

The "elect" are those who elect themselves by choosing "his kingdom" instead of mammon's satanic roost.

The efforts of the forces of darkness, through the actions of humans, are apparent on every side.

Everything is valued in monetary terms. Not for the service it performs. No consideration is taken by the legislators, as to whether the legislated laws conflict with the laws of nature, or God.

Be grateful that the days have been shortened by the "angels" in the spacecraft. Their appearance in the sky has verified the Bible as no other thing could do.

The agents of satan in the flesh, have authority under their thumb. The "free press" has been ordered not to carry the spacecraft stories, except locally. The greatest event in recorded history is being hidden from the masses. Fortunately nothing can interfere with the sapcecraft appearances in the sky.

"So likewise ye, when you shall see all these things, know that it is near, even at the doors." St. Matthew 24:33.

Verily, verily, I say unto you, the hour is coming, *and now is*, when *the dead shall hear* the voice of the Son of God: and *they that hear shall live.*

Of course we know dead bodies cannot hear. So what is implied here where it states, "the dead shall hear the voice of the Son of God?"

CHAPTER EIGHT HUMANS & MAN

You must remember that the man Jesus said many times, "It is not I who speak but the Father who speaks through me," Of course the spirit of God is speaking from realms of perfection, from a universal point of view, not from the surface of Earth.

The first birth a on this planet, is through the parent instruments of your conception.

The second birth is when you leave this limited condition on Earth and are reborn into your true state.

Death is the confinement to this planets surface, not the condition of transition that brings the second birth.

In the mobile coffin of the physical body, you can hear voices and receive thoughts that are not your own.

You are *reflecting* the real everlasting you in this level. You can't die here; you are already dead! You died before in order to get here.

Jesus said, "For I came *down* from heaven, not to do mine own will, but the will of him that sent me." He didn't say *up*, he said *down*. People talk of going down to hell. That is because the consciousness remember having been up before.

There is no hell more confining, or limiting, than the dense physical body here. Everyone makes their hell wherever they are. Of course here you have laws, and a social system, and ordinances, and rackets to keep you little devils in line, while the devils agents have loopholes in the laws, for their convenience so they can be more comfortable in this hell where Satan rules supreme. The footnote number 2, at the bottom in the Scoffield Bible says, "In the sense of the *present world system* the ethically bad sense of the word refers to the "order," "arrangement," under which Satan has organized the world of unbelieving mankind upon his cosmic

CHAPTER EIGHT HUMANS & MAN

principles of force, greed, selfishness, ambition, and pleasure. The world system is imposing and powerful with armies and fleets; is often outwardly religious, scientific, cultured, and elegant; but, seething with national and commercial rivalries and ambitions, is upheld in any real crisis *only by armed force, and is dominated by Satanic principles.*"

Yes; it says this in the Bible. It isn't in the Holy script but it is just as true.

Jesus *came down* to demonstrate the principles by which you must live in order to *go up*. Yes, humanity on this planet are "The dead who shall hear," if they listen.

Of course the present world system does not function by constitutions, or laws of God. It functions by National Emergency Laws, by crooked politics and by who has got the most of what.

Nobody in "Gods country" own anything. The boys up front have put it all in hock for you, so the parents all have to work, to break even, while their children become juvenile delinquents.

On top of that they are hatching up the "hellfire and brimstone" by piling up Hydrogen Bombs while you foot the bill. Bombs to "insure" peace. Who ever heard of weapons of destruction bringing peace?

The radioactivity from this country's stockpile alone would eliminate the citizens of America if they were dropped on any portion of the Earth. When the race for "supremacy in bombs" is finished, what do we do; settle our differences with cream puffs at 10 yards?

The Satanic influences are bein g followed by the makers of these "hellfire" devices, and the authorities, who break you, to make them.

CHAPTER EIGHT HUMANS & MAN

We are not inferring that this country alone is guilty of being in the control of Satanic forces. All countries who manufacture mass murder weapons are guilty before God.

"And *no man hath* ascended up to heaven, but he that came down from heaven, even the *Son of ma*n which is in heaven. (St. John 3-13).

Every person who has had a contact with the "angels" in the spaceships has received the same information from them. "Atomic energy is a death force whether used for war, or commercially."

You are in a hell of someone elses making. The Satanic forces are going to make sure it's hell for you. They cannot *hear*!

"And when *they found not his body*, they came, saying, that they had | also seen a vision of angels, which said that *he was alive*." (St. Luke | 24-23). This tells you that you are *alive after* the transition. That's what | Jesus came down here to prove. You are *dead now*!

"Jesus answered and said unto him, Verily, verily, I say unto thee, Except a man be *born again*, he cannot see the kingdom of God." (St. John 3-3).

This is only one grade in the school of life and you can't polish God's apple to pass to the next grade. He doesn't care how many times you take this grade over to pass it. He has forever.

Rebirth into this into this grade again, because you flunked it, does not constitute the second birth. The second birth is only possible when you have passed the grade here.

According to the Holy Scriptures, Ezekiel was commissioned to reveal information to the people as it was given to him.

"And thou shalt speak *My* words unto them, whether they will

CHAPTER EIGHT HUMANS & MAN

hear, or whether they will forbear; for they are most rebellious." (Ezekiel 2:7). |

Our commission at the Ministry of Universal Wisdom is also to reveal information relative to the Universal Laws as it is given unto us. In these times the people are still rebellious, because they are not anxious or willing to *Know*; when they can coast through life conditioned by dogma and custom into believing that belief is the one essential of their salvation. Truly, "Faith without work works are *dead.*"

The Old Testament of the Christian Bible and the Holy Book of Scriptures of the Jewish faith both derive from the same source. Both are an accurate record of what occurred in the greater civilization that was On the Earth *before* this present one.

It is remarkable that records so old as these have been carried down to the people of today as accurately as they have been. People of today still do not interpret these ancient records as anything but something *Holy*. Holiness is recognized by accomplishment.

When Ezekiel "fell upon his face" to worship the Lord, the Lord told him to "stand upon thy feet." That is what the people of today are going to have to do to prevent being stepped upon and trampled into slavery.

Ezekiel followed the instructions he was given, otherwise you wouldn't be reading about him today in any of the "Holy" books. He was told that the people were rebellious; meaning too ignorant to listen and reason.

Charles Lindberg wouldn't have completed his solo flight to Paris if he hadn't listened to "the voice" that instructed him on how to correct his course when he was lost over the middle of the Atlantic Ocean. He gives full credit to this fact in his autobiography, which makes him the great man that he is today. Washington, Lincoln,

CHAPTER EIGHT HUMANS & MAN

Edison, and many other great men were only recognized as great because they too followed instructions given to them by "a voice."

Michael Faraday recognized scientific principles in the books of the Old Testament. "The voice" gave him the key to interpret them.

Wisdom does not wear a title. Intelligence does not advertise itself.

Wisdom is the developed ability to know when to listen to intelligence speaking and when to put the instructions into action. Rebellious people are those who refuse to listen to "the voice," and are afraid to act upon what they hear. These are the ones who profess faith by their mouth without works by their hand. These people always have advice *for someone else* to do something.

Faraday duplicated "Ezekiel's Temple." Since then it has become known as "Faraday's Cabinet." The principle is being used today in scientific research. The only reason the present results are not satisfactory is because the "Faraday Cabinet" now being used was not constructed to the *correct form*.

In (Ezekiel 41:6) it says, "And the side chambers were one over another, *three and thirty times*." This is thirty three layers of alternating metal and insulation. Faraday had this part right, and of course he used a different type of insulation between the layers of metal. According to (Ezekiel 41:16-21) "there was a *veneering* of wood round about, and from the ground up to the windows; and *the windows were covered*; to the space above the door, even unto the *inner house*, and without, and on all the wall round about *within and without, by measure,*. And it was made with *cherubim* and *palm tree*; and a palm tree was *between* cherub and cherub, and every cherub *had two faces*; so that there was the *face of a man* toward the palm tree *on the one side,*

and *the face of a young lion* toward the palm tree on the other side; thus was it made *through all the house round about*. From the ground unto above the door were cherubim and palm trees made;

CHAPTER EIGHT HUMANS & MAN

and so on the wall of the temple. As for the temple, the jambs were *squared*; and the *face* of the sanctuary had an *appearance* such as is the appearance. (Ezekiel 41:23-25) goes on to explain the doors. "And the temple and the sanctuary had two doors. And the doors had two leaves apiece, *two turning leaves; two leaves* for the *one door* and *two leaves* for the *other.* And there were made on them, on the doors of the temple, cherubim and *palm trees, like as were made upon the walls."*

Ezekiel described Cherubim as winged beings (something that flew through the air }. He also described them as being like coals of fire. (Brightly burning and hot to the touch).

To ignorant people the present anti-gravity ships being tested by the Air Force and Navy, as well as in England and Russia, the field (corona) of orange colored electro-static effect would answer the description of cherubim. Something that flies and glows and if approached while the corona were operating would leave the evidence of a hot coal in the sense that it would char anybody to a crisp as it discharged through their body. This is because "Ezekiel's Temple" was a very large condenser.

Palm wood is a very porous wood similar to Joshua Tree wood. There are many more good insulators available for use today.

Ezekiel said to make thirty-three layers of cherubim and palm wood. This was all round about top, bottom and all four sides. This should be done with one layer of metal covering the bottom and all four walls. Then the layer of insulation. The next layer of metal should cover the top and all four walls.

Ezekiel described these layers as alternately positively and negatively charged. He said one cherub had "the face of a man." This didn't mean the features looked like a man's face. It meant that it was the positive polarity layer of metal. If you stand back and look at a man with his arms straight out, like you would look at the face of a building, you would see a t cross. This is carried down to

CHAPTER EIGHT HUMANS & MAN

us today as the positive, male, projective, polarity symbol .

✝

He said the other layer of cherub (glowing from the corona) had the face of a young lion. The key to this statement is also very simple. Apparently in the various translations, or interpretations throughout time, some scribe didn't know what a young line was so it was changed to a young lion.

A young tree, child, or anything else is always *shorter* than an old one, so a young lion meant a young *line*, thus — ; still the symbol of negative polarity.

Cherub is a word that came about at the time of the "confusion of the tongues." From the "Man Tongue" or "Solex Mal" or "Mother Tongue" "C" meant conscious; "her" meant receptive; "u" meant you, and "b" meant being. Thus cherub is a receptive, conscious, being.

This is very likely why Ezekiel described a cherub as a being, although it can be anything that exists or has being; animal, mineral, or vegetable.

"Faraday's Cabinet" which he copied from "Ezekiel's Temple" does not work satisfactorily today because he missed two pertinent points when he used his key to interpret the verses. *Form means everything* when one is working with the unseen forces of the lines of primary energy. "

Faraday's Cabinet" is a square oblong condenser. "Ezekiel's Temple" was an *inverted pyramid* condenser.

In (Ezekiel 41:7) it says, "And the side chambers were broader as they wound about *higher and higher.*"

In Ezekiel 41:6 it tells of the "cornices," "that they might have hold therein." In the *inverted pyramid* these were *hand holds* so one

CHAPTER EIGHT HUMANS & MAN

wouldn't slide down.

The other key was in (Ezekiel 41:21) where he described the temple with the jambs squared, like the base of a pyramid.

The doors also were built in layers of metal and insulation and when closed, or inserted, made contact with the rest of the structure's metals by the *"two leaves, turning leaves,"* on each door. These were like knife switches. When the door was in place one set of *leaves* made contact between the positive plates in the structure and the door and the other set made contact with the negative plates in the temple and the door.

At this point you may be wondering why Ezekiel built this inverted pyramid temple. The answer is for the same reason that people meditate and others spend their entire lives in sanctuaries or monasteries; so that they can commune with God.

It was in the "arc of Noe," that the animals were brought to Earth in an arc (not ark) by Noah. Arc, in the dictionary, is described as; "the portion of a circle (or flight) described by the sun, or *any other heavenly body in its apparent passage through the heavens."*

The spacepeople landed the various animals that could survive in the second density germination temperature. Naturally they were brought in pairs in the arc, (or spaceship). The space people know about the birds and the bees.

Of course there was a flood in the arc of Noe. The Bible is correct when it said all the water was in the firmament, (in the first density). That was why the vegetation was so thick in the first density. The moisture would condense and water the vegetation at night and rise as fog in the daytime.

When the Earth flipped on it's poles in the arc of Noe, the rotational speed changed and the new temperature of the Earth being less, the waters condensed and fell from the atmosphere and

CHAPTER EIGHT HUMANS & MAN

flooded the land. The Bible says the waters were only fifteen cubits deep (310 feet) in Genesis, 7:20.

So the story, in the Bible, of the ark and animal cargo, is a badly twisted version of a man and a boat. The fallacy of this is evident when the size of the Bible ark is given as 300 cubits long, 50 cubits wide and 30 cubits high, (about 620 feet, by 110 feet wide and barely over 60 feet high).

Imagine caging a pair of each kind of living thing in an area that large. And don't forget they had to be caught, they were wild and sufficient food carried to feed them for 40 days.

Then the story gets further off. They confused the accurate ancient records with another arc. This was when the Bible story puts Noah's sons in the same boat.

The animals were landed in the arc of Noe, between the first and second densities. Three hundred and twelve thousand years later Ham and Shem and Japheth were landed on Earth, between the second and third densities, in the arc of Spae.

Noah's "sons" were not individuals either. The race of Ham were the black people. The race of Shem were white people, and the race of Japeth were the yellow people.

The various tribes that descended from these three original colors of people, that were colonized on Earth by the space people, is listed in (Genesis, Chapter 10).

Each race is pure in its own color. And the universal law reads "each seed after its own kind." In all the creations, on the Earth, each flower, tree, animal and all of nature follows this law — except humans who were given the right to choose. Humans were given the intelligence to raise themselves; yet humans are the only creatures that violate this law.

CHAPTER EIGHT HUMANS & MAN

That is one of the big reasons why the world is in such a confused mess today. The highest court of this land has sanctioned the violation of Gods law, "each after his own kind." All the governments are training men to kill in direct violation of the law, "Thou shalt not kill."

The Lord told Jonah to go and preach against the wickedness of the city of Nineveh. This contact with a "lord" scared Jonah so much that he tried to get away and hide, like some people have done these pres-ent days when they were contacted by superior beings, or "lords," from the heavens.

In the process of escaping by ship to Tarshish, the superstitious sailors tossed Jonah overboard, because they assumed he had angered the Lord and was directly responsible for the terrible storm the ship was then experiencing.

"Now the Lord *had prepared a great fish* to swallow up Jonah." 1:17. To the ignorant people who recorded this event, and who knew nothing of submarines or cylindrical-shaped space ships that could go beneath the water, as well as through space, this was indeed a miracle.

They knew then, as we know now, that no man could survive in the belly of a "great fish" or whale for three days and three nights.

"And the Lord spake unto the fish, and it vomited out Jonah upon the *dry land*." (Jonah 2:10).

Naturally in the time this was recorded there were no mechanized forms of transportation. The people of that time knew nothing of space, that man could fly, or any of the many amazing things we have today. Their only concept of anything that existed in the water that could swallow a man was a "great fish," or a whale.

You will notice in (Jonah 1:17) that "the Lord *had prepared* a great fish." They could have recognized that this "great fish" was

CHAPTER EIGHT HUMANS & MAN

manufac-tured like a ship, and wasn't anything like a fish except that it went in and under the water. The point is — they credited the Lord with *preparing* it.

The record says Jonah was released out of it on dry land. Whales do not travel on dry land, although they have been washed up on the beaches by violent storms.

Here again is evidence of still another Lord taking someone aboard a ship for several days and then letting them out unharmed. Jonah was instructed what to do and say in Nineveh; also as some people have received instructions aboard these same space ships today.

When you recognize that the hierarchy of the space people from other planets hold positions that are *titled* God, Lord God, and Lords, you begin to get some sense out of the many references in the Bible to these many Lords in many different places, and at various times.

Jonah's lord, Moses' lord, the "lord of the harvest," and the Lord Jesus, were all different Lords at different times.

The Bible says there are many Lords and many Gods.

But only One Creator.

Controversy has extended over the years about reincarnations, whether we have lived before, and this being only one of many incarnations.

Evidence given by witnesses is accepted in any accident, in courts, and in all events as to what really took place. Archeology finds evidence of many past events and submits their findings as accepted factual records. Religions submit their written records as evidence of what happened long ago as acts of God, Lord Gods, or Lords. The Christian Bible, and the Book of Scriptures, or the Old and New Testaments, are generally accepted as Holy writ by all

CHAPTER EIGHT HUMANS & MAN

who profess to be Christians. Not being able in this short article to use all of the many records, we will use the Bible for evidence.

(Genesis 1:26-31) says, "Let us make man in *our* image, after *our* likeness: and let *them* have dominion" etc. "So God created *man, male* and *female* created he *them*." These are the generations of the *heavens* and of the earth when they were created." All *plural* expressions.

This was on the sixth day (eon, or age) when man was created male and female separately. This also refers to the race of *man* as both male and female as a species. Where have you been since this sixth period of God creating you eons ago? No, you were not *created* when you were born here on the earth. You were *re-created*.

You are not a descendant of Adam and Eve. God did not create humans as such. You did not evolve from the apes.

God ended his work of *creation* on the seventh day and *rested*. There is no religious, or archaeological evidence, or records, to show that God, the creator of Galaxies, Solar Systems, People and all other things that exist, *ever created anything again* after the seventh day. But the records all show that each creature was given the power to *re*-create its own kind. "Each seed after its own kind."

The confusion of *creation* starts when one gets into chapter two of Genesis.

Here the *Lord* God started *re*-creating through the Adam and Eve story of a condition that took place upon the *earth*. The species of Man was given dominion of *all things. Hu*mans are the pawns of politics, money, storms, floods, earthquakes, accidents, disease, and all earthly carnal things. The cycles of human history prove that the carnal, ma-terialistic efforts of *humans* is not influenced by the forces of creation, or of God, but rather by their own selfish, greedy, destructive, money-hungry efforts to glorify themselves as

CHAPTER EIGHT HUMANS & MAN

images of each other.

The static stillness of an ever-present Creator, Universal Mind, Neutral, Boundless, Infinity of Absolute Intelligence looks on with indifference at the mess humans have made on this planet, a speck of rock in God's endless Universe.

Like fleas on a dog, the people on this planet do not accept that there are other dogs with fleas on them. This is all there is. *Here* and *hereafter*. What about *herebefore*? Who can produce evidence of *hereafter*? The Church? No, there is only one thing that proves *hereafter* and it also proves *herebefore*. That is the fact that you *are now*.

Eternity can't be a hereafter thing only as it also existed *before* now. God didn't *create* you when you were born in this lifetime. You are a *re-creation* of your parents who were given the right "to be fruitful and multiply." To be *created* and to be born are two different aspects.

You were *created* eons ago by God and given eternal life in the form of Man. You were *born* into this aspect of life for contrast, to show you how things shouldn't be done. You can't go to hell, you are already here. The preachers try to make you believe hell is somewhere *hereafter* because they are here too.

Hell and Heaven exist everywhere in both the herebefore, the now and *hereafter*. Heaven is a result of creative cause. Hell is a result of destructive effect.

The earth is populated today with people who have been born here because they fell from their original high estate as the race of Man. It is also occupied by people who were *born* here of their own volition, the ones who attempt to create and beautify the planet and set an example for the ones who are trying to destroy it.

This is death. The confinement in this carnal, physical coffin with

CHAPTER EIGHT HUMANS & MAN

all its limitation. The "hellfire and brimstone" of revivalists are the nuclear bombs. Every reference to the earth in the Bible speaks of coming down to it or going up from it, and hell is said to be down and heaven up. Reality is acceptance of things as they are, not the belief in some-thing that could be, or was. Faith is a knowing that life is eternal, not the belief that someone is going to save your neck hereafter.

When God finished his work after creating all of the laws of cause and effect, contrast of opposites, male and female, and eternal life, He rested because He knew continuity was established through re-crea-tion, that all causes created an effect and all effects re-created other effects thereby becoming causes. These laws are so established that you may be influenced by God to cause an effect. If you hit someone with your car, unintentionally, you cause them to be injured and the effect of their injury may cause them to sue you.

If a human evolves a theory that produces an atom bomb, everyone connected with the creation of this destructive device is responsible under God's law, if the effect of its use kills people. This is reality, for if they hadn't created the weapon the people couldn't have been killed by it.

If you watch the shifty eyes of public officials on T.V., you can see the extent of their guilty conscience. Most of them can't even look the camera in the eye.

This effect is the result of *their knowing* right from wrong and know-ing they have been a party to un-Godly actions. T.V. is a lot like God — it permits both the good and bad to be in it, uninfluenced by either, impartial to both, allowing each to expose itself to others.

War is inescapable when our economy is built on weapons of destruction. We fought one war to save the world for *democracy*. (Demo is the God of *demons*). We fought the last war to end all

CHAPTER EIGHT HUMANS & MAN

wars. Now we are arming the world to the teeth to fight a war to prevent wars. Well, this next one will accomplish its purpose because there won't be anything left worth fighting for, and nothing to fight another war with by the few people left to fight a fourth war. This is reality.

Life has always been eternal. Herebefore, now, and hereafter have always been. The fact that you arrive here through birth as a *re-crea-tion*, occupy a body which you create through generation from the spirit, and depart leaving it a lifeless hulk should prove to you that you were *before* this body existed, you *are* in it *now*, and you *will be* after you have discarded it.

Eternity is an intangible, guaranteed to you by the church, like a *life* insurance policy which only pays off in event of *death*.

You had nothing to do with being born here, except you may have chosen the parents through whom you were born. You have little, if any, effect on what takes place here while you are here, and you have no ability to prevent yourself departing from here. The only satisfaction Satan gets today is the fact that people are arriving faster than they are departing. We call it a population explosion. Think of how mad Satan is going to be when everyone leaves at once for heaven and his hell won't have anyone to tax to finance his destructive ideas. Then there will be a thousand years of peace on earth because the poor devils that are left will need that long to recover from the effects. Evil destroys itself in its gluttonous greed to possess all.

The *causes* created by humans will soon effect a backfire. Every action has an equal and opposite reaction. We are having a war on poverty in the midst of the greatest abundance in the United States. What a paradox!

"And no man bath *ascended up* to heaven, but he that came down from heaven, even the Son of *Man which is in heaven*." (St. John 3:13).

CHAPTER EIGHT HUMANS & MAN

Re-creation *must be* because your parents weren't the Creator. Re-in-carnation *must be* because eternity doesn't start *now*. There can be no *hereafter* unless there was a herebefore. Reality is now, each minute of now, as it passes from the label *herebefore* to *hereafter.*

"And my speech and my preaching was not with enticing words of man's wisdom, but in *demonstration* of the Spirit and of power; That your faith should not stand in the wisdom of men, but in the power of God." (Corinthians 2-4 & 5).

People are a manifestation of a physical body, powered by the Spirit of God. We have no motors or other means of propulsion to make the body go. No wheels, drives, or gears. The body is a flexible vehicle. What makes it go? What is this Spirit that powers the body?

Nikola Tesla, the greatest genius of our age said, "The human being is a selfpropelled automaton, entirely under the control of external influences. Willful and predetermined though they appear, their actions are governed not from within, but from without."

"This automaton is, however, subjected to other forces and influences. His body is at the electrical potential of two billion volts, which fluctuates violently and incessantly. The whole earth is alive with electrical vibrations in which he takes part. The atmosphere crushes him with a pressure of from sixteen to twenty tons, according to barometric conditions. He receives the energy of the Sun's rays in varying intervals at a mean rate of about forty foot pounds per second, and is subjected to periodic bombardment of the Sun's particles, which pass through his body as if it were tissue paper. The air is rent with sounds which beat on his ear drums, and he is shaken by the unceasing tremors of the earth's crust. He is exposed to great temperature changes, to rain and wind."

Tesla demonstrated that the body could be inserted into a high frequency electrical field, that would melt metals, without any

CHAPTER EIGHT HUMANS & MAN

harmful effects to the body.

Preaching as a rule works on the emotional makeup of people. They feel reverent and secure while the sermon is in progress. A few minutes, or hours, after the sermon they are only aware of the external influences again, whether they be discordant, or harmonious.

Preaching becomes monotonous to the listener and some people can't hardly wait until the sermon is over. Incantations also become mean-ingless in a short time.

This external source of power that makes your body go by internal actions is the unseen, mysterious, something intangible, that people pray to when they need help, or pray to in hypocrisy to conform to a ritual.

Astrologers, who *predicted* the death of the late President Kennedy, state that the external forces of Saturn in conjunction with Jupiter, with a square to Mars, is the thing that happens every twenty years that brings death to the President in twenty year cycles.

The Creator established laws by which the universe of Galaxies, Solar Systems, Planets, People, cells and atoms must conform. These are laws of Gravity, Magnetism, Electricity, Pressure, Heat, Attraction and Repulsion, and numerous other laws of cause and effect. Singular-ly, or by combination of these laws, everything in the universe is powered, propelled, or lives. Since the physical body is energized by life through accumulation, galvanic action, conduction, magnetism, of static polarity effects and chemical reactions, these are little affected by preaching. However, the application of principles, in conformance to these universal laws, can have causal reactions that can be of physical benefit.

Praying can have its reciprocal effect when the reciprocant has conformed, or earned their answer. God doesn't violate His own

CHAPTER EIGHT HUMANS & MAN

Infinite Laws. One must keep moving by action in order to be noticed in God's stillness. One must create a void by giving voluntarily in order for God's laws to fill the vacuum with something in return for the effect. God works for those who let Him — but don't expect to get something for nothing.

When the power of the electrical spirit departs from the physical body it loses its motion, its communication and its reactions that operated when it was energized.

Preaching is fine for those who want a second hand contact with God. God's principles work in spite of the preachers. But the fact that "your faith should not stand in the wisdom of men, but in the power of God," should be plain enough for anyone to understand.

Many references have been made in religious history about the Ten Lost Tribes.

The Ten Tribes never were lost. This is information disseminated by the two tribes that are lost to make it appear the opposite. The two lost tribes are scattered all over the Earth, along with descendants of three of the original ten tribes.

The ten tribes are part of the original creation of the species of man, that originally constituted twelve tribes. The twelve tribes were originally "given dominion of all things." So long as they conformed to the universal laws of creation they were privileged to retain this high estate.

The ego of two of the original twelve tribes led them to believe that they could supercede the infinite laws of the Universe and make their own laws. This is still being done today in every Nation, State, County and City on the Earth. These laws made by the few to control the many are a violation of Universal Law; because man was never given dominion over his fellow man.

When the two tribes were "cast down" they tried to make everyone

CHAPTER EIGHT HUMANS & MAN

believe that the other ten tribes were "lost."

The ten tribes in space are listed in Genesis, Chapter 5. Observe that Adam is not referred to as an individual in Genesis 5:2. It specifically says that *they* were created as *males* and *females*. It also states in the plural that God "blessed *them* and called *their* name Adam."

The ten tribes that aren't lost are still living in space and on many other planets. They are Adam, Seth, Enos, Cainan, Mahalaleel, Jared, Enoch, Methuselah, Lamech and Noah.

Some of the tribe of Enoch came to the Earth for a while. They were largely responsible for building the Great Pyramid. They left Earth and went back home, or as the Bible says "Enoch walked with God: and he was not: (on the Earth anymore) for God took him." (Genesis 5:24).

The "fallen angels," or Luciferians, sometimes called "the destroyers," are operating at full capacity on the Earth now. They know that some of the ten tribes are observing the actions on the Earth, since this present civilization now has arrived at the point where they can use the Vril rod (Laser Beam), Hellfire and Brimstone (Hydrogen Fusion) and other destructive devices that can cause untold suffering.

The fact that the Old Testament in the Bible is a record of events that occurred in a civilization before this present one, is not understood by most people.

The fact that the life span of the ten tribes listed in the Bible, and other records, was approximately 800 years cannot be comprehended by people who consider themselves lucky if they make it to seventy years of age before they die. The ten tribes lived by rejuvenating their bodies by a process similar to our research.

The ten tribes in space do not normally interfere with the

CHAPTER EIGHT HUMANS & MAN

Luciferians on Earth as long as they only conduct wars, worship money, and commit crimes against each other, but when they are capable of vaporizing a civilization, or disturbing the balance of a solar system occupied by some of the ten tribes — then they come to get a first hand analysis of the situation.

Noah, the last named of the ten tribes, caused to be landed on the Earth three of the ten tribes. These are listed as Noah's sons, Ham, Shem and Japheth.

The Ham people with black skins came from the tribe of Mahalaleel. They were landed in Africa.

The Shem people with white skins were from the tribe of Methuselah. They were landed in Atlantis; a continent broken off from Western Europe and now sunken beneath the Atlantic Ocean.

The Japheth people, with yellow skins, were landed on a continent called Pan in the Pacific Ocean. These people were from the tribe of Jared. Japan is the only remnant of that great continent today. Its name "Ja-pan" comes from *Ja*pheth and *Pan*. *Ja* comes from *Jap*heth and *pan* comes from the mother continent of Pan, sometimes called Lemuria.

The yellow people, the black people, and the white people are all descendents of the original creations of the species of Man.

All other colors of people are descendents of crossbreeding between black and white, black and yellow, or yellow and white.

The universal law of "each seed after its own kind" is followed by the ten tribes and everything else in nature.

Hu-mans are the descendants of the tribe of Adam which crossbred with the "upright beautiful creatures" of the now extinct animal species called "Eve" in the Bible. All people who live on the Earth are called humans now because the ancient priesthood sought to

CHAPTER EIGHT HUMANS & MAN

hide the distinction between the race of man and the hu-man race.

Under the influence of the Luciferian forces, the descendants of the man — animal cross are now trying to assume complete authority over this planet and make all direct Man descendents, Black, Yellow, and White, subjects to their rules.

The descendants of Shem, in the last civilization on the Earth, left the symbol of this cross-breeding between animal and man by building the Sphinx in Egypt. The sphinx is called *Hu*, symbolizing the man and animal cross, producing the *Human* race. The sphinx is a female animal with a man's head on it.

The cross has been used since ancient times to symbolize this original sin of crossbreeding.

Jesus symbolized the burden of *humanity* by carrying the cross on his back and then being crucified on it.

The diagonal cross "X" has always symbolized danger, poison, or the wrong way. Today as in olden times we use it at railroad crossings; and "x" marks the spot where a body is found; the crossed diagonal bones with, the skull on bottles of poison; and on the pirates flag.

The upright cross has always symbolized the right way and has been used as a religious symbol for thousands of years.

The ten tribes of space intend to intervene through the use of their 'space ships if atomic and nuclear devices are used in an all-out war — to end it,

They would be forced to this action to defend their long range descendants on this planet.

This is Armageddon mentioned in the Bible. This war is not against the people of the Earth but against "Kings, powers,

CHAPTER EIGHT HUMANS & MAN

principalities, and armies," or the destructive elements on the Earth.

Those people who believe in their branch of religion, be it Buddhism, Shinto, Christianity, or any other religion, must accept "visitors from the skies," or discard their religion. The basic foundation of all Earth religions is based on laws and principles given to Earthlings by "people who descended out of the sky."

The ten tribes of space maintain their longevity by recharging their physical bodies like batteries. The "destroyers" on the Earth do not want people here to live longer, because then they would not put up with the conditions here that they now tolerate for their short lifespan.

*Hu*mans on Earth are constantly creating new laws to further restrict themselves.

Armored cars are designed to protect money — because here money is god. The money system owns and controls people through its power. You *have* to work to eat.

No animals, birds, or fish, or even insects have such a restricting, human-made god. The people of the ten tribes look down on this planet and wonder how long humans will endure this stupid system of self-restriction -- when a heaven on Earth is possible.

CHAPTER NINE FREE ENERGY & PROGRESS

CHAPTER NINE

FREE ENERGY & PROGRESS

We have told you before that free energy is the reason why Air Force Intelligence is prevented from releasing the true story of the spacecraft.

Free energy cannot be piped, sent through wires, or sold in service stations. It is the power that manifests motion in each person. It is the power manifested by the Creator, for man to use, as his birthright.

This same energy that powers people, planets, spacecraft, atoms and suns; is the answer to the elimination of smog.

Smog control can only be attained by elimination of the cause of smog. The investigation of a way to stop smog is not by studying its effects, or to fine a few people who burn rubbish, or cause smoke from industry.

Smog control, as it is now, will never do anything but add another department to the political machines of the cities, counties and states. This is an added, and unnecessary burden on the already overburdened taxpayers.

All the State of California has to do to eliminate smog from smudge pots, is to pass a law effective in one year, outlawing the use of smudge pots. In one year all smoke from smudging would cease.

Of course the principle of free energy as presented in this article is going to eliminate the sale of smudge oil by the oil companies. I am not bringing this information out because I do not like the oil

CHAPTER NINE FREE ENERGY & PROGRESS

industry. They have been responsible for some of the greatest contributions to the progress of this civilization.

Progress, however, requires the elimination of many old methods for the advent of new and better methods. The horse and buggy went — to be replaced by the automobile. The automobile made the need for oil companies. Now if the people in the oil companies are smart, they will get into the manufacture of free energy devices. Because as sure as you are reading this article, the oil company products are going to be replaced by free energy. They can't sell the energy, but they can sell the apparatus required to use free energy. The time is near when oil will only be used for lubrication and soon that too will go with the development of bearings that require no lubrication.

Progress is not a respecter of authority or industry.

I recently spent some enlightening hours with two wonderful people. One of them is Mrs. Hazel De Land, the other is Mrs. Eva B. Hibbs. (These two women live in Riverside, California.)

Mrs. De Land is the widow of Mr. John De Land. John was an amaz-ing man who lived to perfect the "De Land Magnetic Control." This is a simple apparatus that prevents freezing in citrus and other fruit on sub-freezing nights. *It costs nothing to operate!*

Mrs. De Land told me how John received the details of the apparatus. John used the same means of thought reception 17 years ago that I use today. He heard a voice speaking inside his head, describing how to control frost and fruit freezing by a new method. John wrote the information down a little at a time, as it was given to him. Then he spent the next 15 years developing and proving true the information.

He has left a monumental contribution to humanity in his "Magnetic Control."

CHAPTER NINE FREE ENERGY & PROGRESS

The drawing is made here of the principle of the device that John De Land gave to humanity, because he believed in progress. Mrs. De Land holds the patent papers on this apparatus. This drawing (fig. 3) is reproduced with her permission.

There are seven # 10 bare copper wires, running radially out underground from a 32 foot pipe mast. The pipe mast tapers up with re-ducers from 2 inch diameter, through 1½ inch diameter, to 1 inch in diameter at the top. Three plywood disks 12 inches in diameter rest on each of the reducers. Each plywood disk has seven equidistant holes for the wires to run through. At the top disk the seven wires are wrapped once around the edge at each hole, and extend outward 4 inches parallel to the ground. Each wire points parallel radially, back to its own other end underground. The mast, which is 32 feet above the ground level, sets in a 3 foot depth of concrete. The wires run through the concrete and loop back up outside the concrete to a depth below the surface that will permit a plow, or any cultivation equipment to pass over them.

Each of the seven wires extend radially underground to a distance not to exceed 144 feet from the mast. At this distance they are wrapped 10 turns around a 1 inch diameter by 5 inches long alnico 5 magnet.

The magnet sets inclined toward the mast at 45 degrees to the surface of the ground. It is also buried below cultivation equipment level.

These magnets are made up and coated with one-eighth inch of plastic to hold the windings in place and prevent rusting. The magnets are set polarized to the North magnetic pole parallel to the lines of magnetic force.

No smoke — no dirty laundry — no expense to operate — nothing but the expense of the original installation. This device is that simple!

CHAPTER NINE FREE ENERGY & PROGRESS

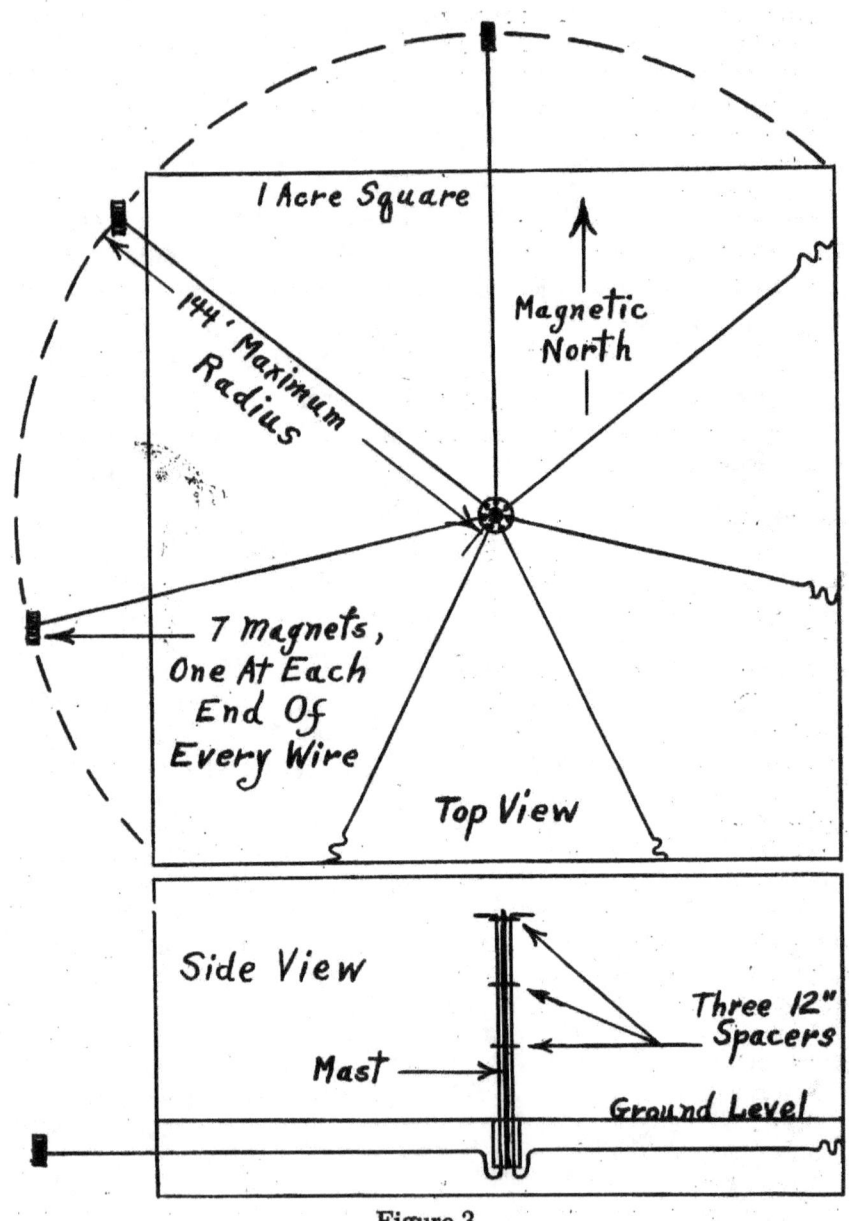

Figure 3

Anti Frost Control

CHAPTER NINE FREE ENERGY & PROGRESS

This single unit will prevent freezing of fruit over an area of more than an acre of ground. *This is free energy in operation.*

Now for the proof of the successful operation of this control. This is where Mrs. Hibbs comes into the story.

Mrs. Hibbs had the foresight to permit the De Land apparatus to be installed on her land. Mrs. Hibbs came from Iowa and bought an orange grove. She didn't know until after she bought the property that the trees were considered "grown out," or beyond their age of producing an average crop.

Her caution only permitted the installation of five units of the "De Land Control" on five acres of her ground. After the first winter proved through freezing temperatures that the control worked, she had her entire 10 acres protected.

She proudly showed us around and compared her oranges with others for color, sweetness, and size. The "grown out" grove has in-creased its production every year. The crop had just been estimated by the packers before we visited Mrs. Hibbs. This year's crop will go nearly four times the average production per acre.

Mrs. Hibbs was forced to buy $400.00 worth of 2" x 2" props to sup-port the limbs on her trees.

Not only has Mrs. Hibbs increased her profit each year from the crop, but she has saved $3000 worth of smudge oil in 5 years.

The saving in oil alone has payed for the installation of the free energy equipment. So over a period of time free energy pays for its own installation and cost.

Mrs. De Land said her husband John never did find out what makes the installation work. So I went back to our friends the spacepeople, through thought transference, and asked them to explain the principle. This is their explanation.

CHAPTER NINE FREE ENERGY & PROGRESS

Trees manifest life but they do not manifest motion. Temperature is a result of molecular motion. The only motion manifested in a tree, or its fruit, is by the electrons in the atoms of its composition.

On a planet that rotates there are four periods each day. These are the positive quarter from 6 A.M. to 12 noon; the active quarter from 12 noon to 6 P.M.; the negative quarter from 6 P.M. to midnight; and the rest quarter from midnight to 6 A.M.

Atoms in free space are charged continuously. Atoms on a rotating planet are only charged according to their opposite polarity period.

As a negative electron rotates faster in the positive and active quarter of the earth's daily rotation, it manifests more heat due to the resistance of polarity opposition. As an atom on the planet moves into the negative quarter, its electrons have no polarity opposition and they begin to discharge.

As the electrons move into the rest quarter they discharge part of their energy and this in turn causes a slowing up in their orbits around the proton. An electron can be stopped in its orbit by extremely low temperatures, which removes its charge. The magnetic canopy of the "De Land Control" helps the electrons to hold their charge by keeping them in motion.

This is definitely proven in the "De Land Control" on Mrs. Hibbs' property. An orange on the tree does not freeze despite the fact that a fruit thermometer inserted into the orange shows the temperature is as much as 7 degrees below freezing. As long as the orange is on the tree it is part of the life process of that tree. Any orange that falls to the ground inside the control area will freeze. This is because it grounds out with earth and its electrons therefore slow up in their orbits.

The temperature inside of the control area reads just as low on a thermometer as the temperature outside of the control area, yet the

CHAPTER NINE FREE ENERGY & PROGRESS

fruit on the tree does not freeze.

Mrs. Hibbs has recorded temperatures as low as 19 degrees inside and outside the control area at the same time.

Put free energy to work, save money and stop your smudge contribution to the smoggy condition that is a disgrace to California.

To the officials of the United States Government, the State of California, the counties and the cities of California, here is your answer to a large bulk of the smog condition; not by appropriations for more investigations.

For the rest of the smog from automobiles and industries, free energy motors and methods are the answers; not filters or fines.

Bring the free energy mechanisms out of hiding and release the principles of the spacecraft power for the progress of humanity. Stop wasting money on atomic bombs and trying to destroy humanity. Spend the people's money for progressive things.

Change is not always progressive but progress is always change.

All densities of life contribute to the progression of every form of life in densities beneath them. All forms of substance are alive in repetitive patterns, for their particular species and span. Thus every substance, through life, repeats its cycles "from dust to dust."

Life is the carrier of progression in its eternal and endless spiral. Thus the stages are positive

or negative

, or both

when they are in balance.

CHAPTER NINE FREE ENERGY & PROGRESS

The spiral of life (also called caduceus) is symbolized by two serpents:

The negative, receptive or female

is only given desire by its opposite

the positive, projective, or male counterpart and vice versa. These symbols are not zigzag in formar, they are spiral. They are centered and separated by the "staff of life"

around which they twine ever upward through the Infinite Intelligence.

The first density, consisting mainly of vegetation, is of both polarities. The dividing line is the surface of the earth. The positive part of the plant is attracted into the dark negative soil to provide minerals and moisture so the receptive female portion above the surface may "bloom in her fullness."

This is the reason why a water witcher's twig, taken from a living plant, can indicate water. It is actually a living instrument. Like magnets when they are cut, the positive end remains in the same direction. Therefore they are held upside down in order to function. As all things beneath the surface of the soil are of negative polarity and since the survival is the strongest desire, the twig wants to assume its natural polarity-position and is attracted, positive butt end first, to the "water of life."

For the same reason, when you spend long periods of time in the positive sun, you require more water which is negative — to

CHAPTER NINE FREE ENERGY & PROGRESS

quench your thirst which is the result of unbalanced light force.

Every cell in the vegetation is life in form maintaining still greater life in form. As an animal eats the first density (Stationary life form) vegetation, it gives to it motion.

The substance confined to the place where the seed dropped can now move around, as it has been assimilated by and raised to the sec-ond density (Life and Motion).

The same progression of substance takes place when you eat the flesh of an animal. Humans being both animal, and spirit, and having life are of the third density (Life, Motion, and Consciousness).

You, as part of the eternal pattern of life in form, give to the animal substance — the ability to talk and recognize the spirit.

Although all forms of life progress within their own densities, much confusion has been started by the theorists who try to tie the densities together. Darwin tried to show the evolution of man from the apes. There is no missing link — unless I'm it.

As our solar system has progressed through space — a living function-ing part of the eternal life pattern — it crossed the line on August 20, 1953, from the third density to the fourth density.

Our planet has emerged from the frequency of the third density. Everything on this planet must now begin to conform to this higher frequency pattern.

Rest assured, we are going to emerge from the pattern of destruction or be destroyed by it.

The fourth density will only support life forms that qualify to live in it. The fourth density does not support a monetary system nor authority by power. It will be increasingly evident that the subtle

CHAPTER NINE FREE ENERGY & PROGRESS

light of free-dom is awakening in people. Those who have succeeded before through subterfuge and brute force are going to find that the old "right by might" doesn't work any more.

We are on the verge of witnessing a cyclic planetary housecleaning. All things in this solar system are going to be brought into balance.

You can prepare to live in the new grade in the same form or go back to the third density and take the grade over again.

CHAPTER TEN CHANGES & THOUGHTS

CHAPTER TEN

CHANGES & THOUGHTS

Along with rapidly accelerating storm, earthquake, and flood conditions on the Earth, information that has leaked out from astronomical scientists indicates the entire Solar System is going through a phenom-enal change.

Dr. Bruce C. Maley of the California Institute of Technology, using a special thermic ray observing instrument on the 200 inch telescope at Palomar Observatory, recorded violent storms in the Southern hemisphere of the clouds around Venus. The storm area was emitting heat, he said.

Mr. Ken Sato of Rakurakuen Planetarium, Itsukaichicho, Hiroshima Pref., reports that for 300 years the large red spot on Jupiter has re-mained unchanged until September of 1962. Then a large dark spot formed near the equator and spread rapidly. The closer it came to the old red spot the fainter the red spot became until the large red spot had almost disappeared by January 8th of 1963. Mr. Sato said the changes on Jupiter had become violent over the past year. He is the chief astronomer in Japan, on the planet Jupiter.

According to astronomers A. Darfus of France, J. H. Bossam of South Africa, and Prof. Charles H. Giffen of Sprinton University, changes are rapidly occurring on the planet Saturn. First a white dot suddenly appeared on the surface of Saturn in 1960. Then greater activity began and expanded to eleven white spots. Prof. Giffen reported several bright egg-shaped spots formed a line like a flowery rosary between the Equator and the North, and also an unusual pattern appeared in the Northern Tropics.

CHAPTER TEN CHANGES & THOUGHTS

A few years back it was announced by American astronomers that our Sun had reversed its polarity.

Red spots recently appeared on our Moon for the first time in history.

The latest data relative to the tilting of the Earth on its axis, mathematically worked out from recent information is as follows. This analysis is based on the theory that when the magnetic and geophysical poles come together, the Earth will assume an axis position perpen-dicular to the ecliptic path of the Sun. This would place the ecliptic path on the Equator.

The North Magnetic Pole in 1955 was located on the Prince of Wales Island. The latest report locates it on Bathurst Island. This is a move-ment of 100 miles in 10 years, or 10 miles per year. In the last two years it has moved 20 miles North and four miles East. This is holding to the 10 mile per year motion in a Northerly direction.

Like all magnetic effects this is expected to accelerate as the poles grow closer together. All nuclear, or atomic underground tests will also accelerate this action due to polarity effects.

The present rate of motion would bring the magnetic and geophysical poles together in approximately 75 years. However, the acceleration increase as they become closer could bring the rendezvous to from 8 to 40 years from now. An atomic war could bring it about sooner. It would also eliminate the possibility of the tilt being recorded.

Many prophecies have been printed relative to the geophysical polar tilt. The Bible records several prophecies on this; as well as modern physics and other ancient records.

A sudden polar tilt would swing the North Polar Ice Cap down across continents, wiping out mountains and cities, as it is a

CHAPTER TEN CHANGES & THOUGHTS

floating mass of ice anchored to a few land areas under the ice. Our nuclear submarines have gone under the North Polar Ice Cap from one side to the other.

The South Polar Ice Cap is mostly on a solid earth foundation. It is increasing in its thickness every year while the North Polar Ice Cap is gradually melting.

In the shift of the earth's mass in its attempt to achieve balance with the North Magnetic and the North Geophysical axes coming together, the fixed ice mass of the South Pole is going to try to reach the periphery of the present ecliptic. This would cause the earth to oscillate, or as the Bible describes it, "to stagger like a drunken man."

Geophysicists of the future would declare, like our present geologists do, that there was an Ice Age in the past in the temperate zones.

There is no question but that this polar tilt will occur again, as it has before, but there are too many factors involved to attempt to declare what year it will happen, even if all of the factors were known.

If our theory is right it will happen sometime between the next eight to forty years. When it happens there will be two opposite places on the earth that will hardly be affected. Everything on the earth that is not in these two areas will be wiped off the face of the earth.

The geophysical axis is wobbling approximately seventeen feet of radius. The earth's plane of orbit around the Sun has changed about 3 . The earth is slowed in its orbit around the Sun and will soon necessi-tate a new calendar.

Navigation by celestial means over long distances is no longer accurate — due to refractory conditions in the atmosphere and

CHAPTER TEN CHANGES & THOUGHTS

belts around the earth.

Heat of a cosmic nature which you can feel but does not show on thermometers is increasing annually.

Recently a professor remarked in a featured article in the newspapers that "no life as we know it could exist anywhere else in space." This distinguished man also objected to the amount of money we were spending in an effort to find intelligent life in space. I disagree with him on both counts. We must look in space for intelligent life because very rarely have we found evidence of any intelligent life here on this Earth.

Laser — the new discovery of how to bounce light until it has to run from itself, has been demonstrated to be both a beneficient and a destructive force. The only trouble with these new discoveries, in the hands of the experts with degrees and titles, is that they always figure out some way to use them without regard as to the results of their madness. When these distinguished men of degrees found out that this beam of amplified light could burn holes in steel, diamonds, and other normally almost indestructible materials, they had to find something else to shoot at. Ah! The Moon! There's a big target that everyone in the scientific circles discuss over their cocktails; so they fired Laser beams at the Moon! They bragged about the fact that the beam had traveled 240,000 miles, and was still confined to a small area of around two miles in diameter upon reaching the Moon's surface.

No consideration was taken of what this light amplification would do to the surface of the Moon.

Then a year later the astronomers suddenly discovered that something was happening on the surface of the Moon. The Moon, long looked upon as a dead, lifeless body circling the Earth, suddenly showed signs of some strange activity. Arguments between the astronomers arose. Some said they saw red carbonic gases; others reported the spots were volcanoes; others said it was lava flowing

CHAPTER TEN CHANGES & THOUGHTS

on the surface, emitted from cracks in the surface. All of these luna gazers agree a new condition exists. All of them agree it is *red*. Some of the Moon scanners describe it as *"like flowing blood."*

One of the astronomers at Lowell Observatory at Flagstaff, Arizona said, "I had the impression that I was looking into a large, polished, gem *ruby*."

None of the titled degree boys suggested even a hint that this new turning of the *Moon into blood* could have possibly been aggravated by the ignorant act of humans firing laser beams at the Moon. It is strange that laser is the word formed from the fist letters of "Light Amplification by Stimulated Emission of Radiation." It is activated in its ampli-fication in a synthetic *ruby* rod. The rod looks like a glass tube con-taining blood when one looks through it.

The last two words "Emission of Radiation" seems to he manifesting on the Moon in the spectrum of *Ruby Red* because these colored spots are growing in size.

Has laser in the hands of lunatics brought some red form of micro-organism to life? Or has it caused some living organism on the surface of the Moon to *bleed to death* in a spreading mass that may cover the Moon's surface?

The Bible predicted "the moon shall turn to blood." God in His In-finite Wisdom knew humans would activate this condition by their ignorance.

Yes, we must look in space for survival and for intelligent life — for there is little evidence of intelligence on the Earth.

While the "free" press of the United States fails to bring out pertinent *facts* relative to the radioactive fallout from nuclear tests, the foreign papers reveal that effects from radiation are already dangerous.

CHAPTER TEN CHANGES & THOUGHTS

From the Australian paper "Pix" comes the following statements:

"Radioactive fallout from nuclear tests at Maralinga (South Austra-lia), in the Pacific, at Nevada (U.S.) and in Russia's Siberia is exposing 9 million Australians to leukemia and cancer."

"The staid, always ultra-conservative journal of the British Medical Association, "Lancet," has gone so far as to declare that it believes the plague of Asian influenza is the direct result of changes in human cell structure brought about by radiation from fallout following nuclear tests."

"Many top scientists believe that already sufficient harm has been done that generations hence will suffer."

"Russia has admitted having to cope with a radioactive poisoning outbreak following its most recent tests and in the United States there is a mounting fear that damage to stock and humans in the Nevada area is sufficient to call for the most searching national investigation."

"Incidents that have sharpened U.S. reaction to the menace have been the mysterious deaths of sheep, strange attacks of leukemia and a growing conviction that a rise in cancer cases in Nevada and Utah areas is directly the result of fallout from what are admittedly com-paratively minor experiments at Yucca Flats."

"Deadly strontium 90, a flesh and bone boring element that knows no resistance, is the primary cause of fear."

"It eats into human marrow, destroys the white corpuscles and eliminates the fighting forces that the body naturally builds to check the threat of cancer and leukemia."

"Scientists admit it takes 28 years to disintegrate any given quantity of strontium 90 — an apprentice brew in a wizard's

CHAPTER TEN CHANGES & THOUGHTS

cauldron — once it is released in the atmosphere."

"It can float in the clouds miles above the earth. It can fall with every shower of rain, contaminate food and pastures, be passed on to humans through the milk they drink and the food they eat."

"In Adelaide, Dr. G.M.E. Mayo, senior lecturer in genetics at Adelaide University, says radiation from fallout is lowering the world's physical fitness. He says it is making people increasingly dependent on drugs, doctors and the benefits provided by a free health scheme."

"American events which startled the world, and which are only now being revealed for the first time, began in 1951. Martin Bardoli, then, was playing in his garden. A few miles away, Minnie Sharp was working bareheaded."

"Soon after tests at the proving grounds, Minnie Sharp began losing, her hair. Since then she has lost all hair on her body and efforts to re-store it have been futile."

"Dewey Hortt, Elma Macke"prang, and Aaron Leavitt are others in the Utah-Nevada area who have suffered the same fate."

"But their lots have been light ones to that of Martin (Butch) Bardoli. Martin, a healthy, husky little lad whose robustness was often the source of comment among neighbors suddenly developed leukemia. The disease devoured him at a rate that baffled doctors and he died."

"It is only in recent months that the U.S. Atomic Energy Commission is prepared to admit the possibility, if not the probability, that early, secret surveys failed to reveal that radioactivity was the mitigating element in all these cases."

"The steppedup production of recent experiments has worried the Americans because they now believe that hundreds of school

CHAPTER TEN CHANGES & THOUGHTS

children, that holiday makers in the Nevada and Utah canyons may have been exposed to dangerous, and what is worse, unknown amounts of gamma irradiation. The snowballing amounts of gamma radiation in the district have become noticeable only with time and improved methods of measuring the outfall. Some U.S. authorities believe there may be hundreds of people wandering the State not knowing they have been exposed. They have little idea who or where they may be."

"Scientists agree that it is in the field of genetics that the greatest harm probably already has been done."

"The American National Academy of Sciences in its most recent re-port says, 'The general public must be protected by whatever controls may prove necessary from receiving a total reproductive dose (conception to age 30) of more than 10 roentgens of man-made radiation in reproductive cells."

"It emphasizes its alarm by pointing out that the average medical X-ray uses from three to four roentgens."

"Three X-rays, therefore, can involve a human being under 30 in exposure to more radiation than the U.S. Academy believes safe with the added contamination that is being poured out in frightening amounts from the explosive tests of the great powers."

In Switzerland reports in the papers stated that the radiation in three of their lakes is sufficient to make the water dangerous for drinking. The location of Switzerland on the globe is just about as far away from the Nevada, Pacific, Australian and Soviet tests as one can get.

Distance is thus not a safety factor.

Geophysical changes are on the increase. The midwest earthquake that shook 22 states for 12 minutes, indicates major underground activity is moving to new areas.

CHAPTER TEN CHANGES & THOUGHTS

Droughts that killed 150,000 catle; 300,000 sheep; stopped power plants, and dried up centuries old vineyards in Chile, are only a prelude to atmosphere changes that will effect many places on the earth.

Jet aircraft, in the past 20 years, have burned up more oxygen in the atmosphere, than all the people down through history have breathed. Carbon 14 fallout, from past atmospheric bomb tests, will increase on the surface up until 1975.

Carbon 14 has a half-life of over 5000 years, so no living thing can escape its effects. This means an increase of cancer and leukemia; spoiled fruit, and more insects.

Magnetic changes are also signs of a major change. The North and South Magnetic poles are shifting rapidly. Surveys conducted in the last twenty years show a magnetic declination change of around 40 feet to the mile.

Navigation charts that were normally issued for a five year period, in advance, now have to be replaced every 6 months.

The Department of Navy Oceanography, who are responsible for survey work of the oceans, have measured the rising of two great continents; one in the Atlantic, another in the Pacific.

The ice is melting rapidly at the North pole and building up at the South pole. These are all signs of coming events.

The ego of materialistic minds, in authority, assumes that you unwashed multitudes cannot do anything about these changes in nature; therefore it won't do any good to let you know about them. They are so wrong. Thinking can change anything. Prayer is an effect of thinking.

If you don't know what is coming, it smacks you in the face. You

CHAPTER TEN CHANGES & THOUGHTS

are injured, or killed, because you had made no preparations.

The Mormon Church knows the score. They have several years supply of food stored ahead, and have recently instructed their members to store individual supplies.

The authorities know the score. They have built large underground quarters, well stocked with food, ventilated and equipped. These were constructed with the taxpayers money; but you couldn't get into one of them.

These are a few of the signs of the times.

Everyone knows the weather is not normal. This can't be hidden from you.

Brute force is not a natural part of man's makeup. The environment in which man lives makes him conform to his surroundings.

Only 277 years of peace out of the last 1000 years have made most humans destructive "critters." If you live among savages you soon acquire their methods of living.

CHAPTER ELEVEN

PERCEPTION & MIND

Brute force is the result of power applied against nature. You can not push over a mountain with your hands but you can step on an ant. The ant is as defenseless against your power to kill, as you are before the forces of nature.

Nature (God) is subtle in all of its workings. It does not force an issue; it only waits, eternally patient, for each action to meet its own reaction.

Every great nation that has manifested waste, and power by brute force over other nations, has fallen by the reaction of its own causing.

Look at Greece, Italy, and Spain, all once great ruling authorities. Each of these countries were once the dominating master of less powerful nations.

Brute force is the control of matter over mind. People of today have become slaves of the systems and wealth they have created.

Humans can run machines but unless they remain the alert masters of them, the machines will destroy them.

Mind is subtle in its presenting of thoughts to people. These thoughts may be good or bad. The end result of the actions taken from these thoughts are the only proof as to whether the thought was good or bad.

People assume that a thought of reverence is good. This is only when the manifested result of the thought is beneficial in service to

CHAPTER ELEVEN PERCEPTION & MIND

others.

Thought is God's Image. Your ability to control your thoughts is the demonstration of your ability "to be in His Image."

If your thought in creating a new force for use is turned to destructive use, then you have manifested evil.

Thoughts manifested in false words are your self created bonds that bind you to brute force.

Power of brute force can only be manifested in a small percentage of its subtle natural capacity. If this were not so humans would have long past destroyed the Universe.

The brute force of today is manifested by the increase in material gains, at the expense of spiritual losses.

God is the fulcrum of all balanced forces. Try to sit on owe end of a teeter-totter and make it balance without an equal weight on the other end. This is the condition of the tottering materialistic world of today. Spiritual balance is lost by the people due to the terrific acceleration of materialistic advances.
The most spiritual book in the world is limited to each person's ability to understand it.

A church does not manifest a religion. Only the people who belong to a church can manifest the religion of that church. A church is manifested only as a building; where people meet to manifest something.

Brute force of labor made the material church manifest as a building. Designation by the word church, by the people, made it a church instead of a department store. The same materials will build either.

Manifestation of religion, or spiritual actions, can take place in a

CHAPTER ELEVEN PERCEPTION & MIND

department store as well as a church. The building doesn't make the difference; people make the difference by their actions.

A person that cheats you in a department store is a crook. One who cheats you in a church is "holy."

Because one wears the cloth and is ordained by the church does not make that one spiritual. A spiritual person works with the subtle forces of nature to manifest good spiritual, or material results.

The materialist is a person without scruples, who is out to be head man in spite of anything. He may make the grade only to live in a hell of his own creation; a slave to the brute forces he used to attain his position.

Brute force is demonstrated in the automobiles people drive. The materialist designs these cars with the idea of maintaining other materialistic organizations.

Brute force is demonstrated by the car, that burns three-fourths of its gasoline, to push around 2 tons of car to carry several hundred pounds of people.

The earth turns on its axis. The Sun shines. Rain falls and all natural forces manifest their actions regardless of us humans.

People can employ the same forces that cause nature to manifest; but first they must toss the theories of brute force out of the window of their materialistic brain. Then they must search for the subtle causes of the forces manifest by nature.

When spiritual and material values are balanced, then one is in a position to apply material structure to the natural foundation.

Many people are aware of the ability of a certain note being played on a violin, breaking a glass. When the vibration of the violin string transmits through the air, it produces a resonating vibration

CHAPTER ELEVEN PERCEPTION & MIND

in the glass. Not being flexible enough to respond, the glass breaks.

This occurs in the sonic range of vibration and requires the air of our atmosphere as a medium to conduct the vibration. Popcorn can be popped with sound. Clothes can be cleaned with sound and holes have been drilled with sound vibrations. Concussion in war from big shells exploding, has caused the deaths of many soldiers by brain damage, because they were in resonance with the sound.

Resonance can occur in the structures of buildings, aircraft, and other objects that cause them to come apart like the glass.

Extra Sensory Perception is not extra at all. It works in anyone that is in resonance with the transmission, and it is not subject to either distance or time. Where resonance is achieved through the *air*, the *inanimate* glass breaks because of the violin string vibration. In *animate* resonance, it is achieved through mind as the conductor, instead of air. Both principles are the same, but in different mediums as the conductor.

All living things are in resonance with *mind*. Some more, some less. From the tiniest insect, the smallest living cell, birds, fish, animals, and man, these each are in their own octave of life, but all have one common bond between each other in *mind*.

We have assumed that because air does not exist in space that there is nothing in space. Science says space is a vacuum and it is relative to atmosphere. *Mind* exists in space. It is the essence of all that manifests in space from atoms, and people, to galaxies.

Mind is the medium of instant communication. It is not electrical. It is not magnetic, and it is indestructible. It has no limits to time, or speed. There is only one infinite all penetrating ever-present boundless Mind. All living things use that portion of this absolute mind that they are capable of assimilating. No one has a mind of their own. We all use the same mind. Animals, birds, fish, and insects use it, and we call their natural ability "instinct." People

CHAPTER ELEVEN PERCEPTION & MIND

become aware of it at times, and we call this "intuition."

Thomas Galen Hieronymus used a part of this Mind in tracking the astronauts to the Moon and back. Cleve Baxter used some of it in his proof of living cell communication. Peter Hurkos uses it when he is "turned on" or aware at the time. Bees use it. Homing pigeons use it. Mind is always here to use. Adrian Clark tried to explain it in his book "Cosmic Mysteries of the Universe." True spiritual mediums use it in trances. De La Warr used this essence of mind as described in his book. "New Worlds Beyond The Atom." Dr. Ruth Drown used it to take X-ray type pictures of patients anywhere in the world, by tuning into their frequency through a drop of the patient's blood. *Mind* is the perfect conductor. It needs no poles, or wires.

True predictions, and prophecy, are the result of some people finding out how to assimilate, or penetrate, this infinity of Absolute Mind that knows everything.

Medical science has often referred to "a sympathetic nervous system," when a woman had a baby and her husband had birth pains. This was the communication of the wife's abdominal cell structure to the busband's cell structure through mind, which was the medium of communication.

One can't hide from this static essence of Universal Mind. It is with you asleep, or awake, here and hereafter. It was here before and will eternally be, everywhere. Prayer has always been considered the spiritual way to activate a response from it. Mind doesn't seek recognition, or rewards, for its manifestations and creations. All of its cell creations perform the purposes they were created for. No legislators make laws. No teachers educate them. Everything on the earth fulfills the purpose Mind created it for, except people.

If people could all use E.S.P. now, they would change their ways.

The future is already established in Mind. This intelligence is only

CHAPTER ELEVEN PERCEPTION & MIND

waiting for the planet to turn on its polar axis so many days, so that the motion will bring about a time of reciprocation for the violation of Mind's laws.

When mankind, who was given the right to choose, put brain educa-tion before intelligence, made thousands of laws to escape the Golden Rule, and engineered methods of destruction and death to make money, they violated natural law. Natures laws of cause and effect reciprocate in equality to the extent of their violation.

Brains, computers, and experts, cannot solve the problems. The violation has gone beyond the point of no return. Nature doesn't recognize position. Mind in its static perfection is waiting and watching for resonance to establish balance.

"The solitary inventor, working in his shop, has been overshadowed by the silence forces."
Dwight D. Eisenhower

It is a tough thing for science to have to swallow their evolution theory, because advanced scientific recsearch is now proving an infinite force works by resonance in all living things. The silence forces may, some of them, be aware of these new phenomena, but their own security keeps it dead under wraps because it will prove there is a God, or eternal causal force.

This infinite force operates in resonance within itself and in attunement with all of its living parts through atomic, molecular, cellular, and complex forms of their matrix. A single human carries millions of volts of potential in the atomic makeup of one body. This energy doesn't manifest, or show itself, because it is part of its own environment electrically, magnetically, and physically.

Advanced medical research, government sponsored biomagnetic and bioelectrical researches, and some of the "inventors in their shops" have now proven the fact that all animal and vegetable cells have *communication*, *emotions*, and other reactions through the

CHAPTER ELEVEN PERCEPTION & MIND

resonance of "Mr. Cosmic Mind."

The *fear* of a mouse for a cat was recorded by a polygraph, connected to a *plant*, in another room in tests run to analyze this phenomena. When the cat caught the mouse, and killed it, the plant drove the polygraph to react wildly. As this test was continued several times the plant became conditioned to the killing and the polygraph reacted less wildly with each successive test. This is the way the brain cell structure of people is being conditioned, through war pictures on T.V., bloody motion pictures, pornography in magazines, and propaganda. This leads people to be apathetic and to accept the changing standards of hair, wear, and bare. If enough people accept something immoral, then it is no longer immoral.

E.S.P. is the resonance of one individual who may be in resonance with another person, or an event, regardless of distance or time. All comrnuuication of the above data is *carried on through* Infinite Mind which is *everywhere* there is polarity to activate with. This is where new ideas come from. This is the Supreme Intelligence of God.

This resonant communication was what was proven by Thomas Galen Hieronymus, in tracking Borman, Lovell, and Anders around the Moon. His instruments could receive the transmission of the astronaut's cell structure from behind the Moon, where radio signals were blacked out. but could not receive from them when they were on the side of the Moon toward the Earth, where the *Sun* did not shine on the capsule. God, "Mr. Cosmic Mind," is still resting except when He manifests through His creations. Being in the *environment* of this *Solar System*, the *Sun* is a part of the System through which God manifests by positive polarity. Communication of the cell structure of the Astronauts failed in the Moon shade area because there was no photon positive polarity activity from the Sun on the side of the Moon in darkness. The astronauts were out of their environment (the Earth) and being of negative polarity bodies assimilated here from the electron Earth, nega-tive polarity will not react without positive polarity. We

CHAPTER ELEVEN PERCEPTION & MIND

described this "rest area," in the "Proceeding" of November and December, 1954, and the January issue of 1955. The Moon has little electrostatic atmosphere, or magnetic field. The Hieronymus equipment will work in the dark-ness on the Earth because of this polarity activity in the electro-static magnetic atmosphere, it requires positive polarity from the Sun in order to register from negative polarity bodies. Mind will not produce results by positive thinking alone, anymore than the starter of your car will start with only one pole of the battery connected.

There is no limit to the functioning of mind and there is no loss of energy with distance. If our principles of time were based on the absolute, instead of motion, there would be no limits in time either.

The germ E. coli is a bacteria that thrives in the intestinal tract. Side by side it would take 13,000 of them to measure an inch. Many thou-sands of biochemical reactions go on constantly for it to live, grow and reproduce. An E. coli is an incredibly complex particle of life. A human made up of trillions of cells makes an E. coli look simple by comparison. An E. coli is made up of thousands of genes. Each gene through what medical research has labeled D.N.A. "tells" the germ what to do. In all living structure biochemistry cannot find out what "tells" these microscopic germs how to work.

Cleve Baxter, of the Baxter Research Foundation, Inc., 165 W. 46th Street, Suite 404, New York, N.Y., 10036, made conclusive tests that proved there are boundless results to be obtained in E.S.P. between cell structure in animal and plant life. Baxter was formerly a lie detector expert with the U.S. Army Intelligence and an interrogation's spe-cialist with the Central Intelligence Agency. Being a polygraph expert, he decided to conduct a series of tests to see if human skin reactions would apply to plants. His tests on Philodendron plants started him on an endless research. He found that plants responded to his *thinking* in the threat-to-well-being principle. He found out that plants react to stress in humans. His big question was: Does a life signal connect all creation? He

CHAPTER ELEVEN PERCEPTION & MIND

doesn't want to get involved in religious implications, but admits he is more religious than before he started his experiments.

Many of us "solitary inventors in our shops" need funding. We are not financed by government subsidy, but as "Ike" put it, we are overshadowed by the silence forces." Dozens of other private researchers are producing amazing results in "their shops."

A broadcast on television has revealed the billions of dollars wasted by the "overshadowing forces." Every great discovery down through history has come through the individual thought attunement in reso-nance with "Mr. Cosmic Mind," and this costs the taxpayers nothing for results.

Jeno M. Barnothy, of the Biomagnetic Research Foundation, is producing fantastic results with ion and magnetic research.

Brown, Becker, Kogan, Conley, Shyshlo, Pereira, Smith, Hanneman, Sittler, Kholodor, and many others are all verifying each other's findings in widely separated researches.

A machine which cuts the *healing time* of wounds and surgery, up to 50% is called "Diapulse" and is produced by the Diapulse Corporation of America, 4 Nevada Drive, Lake Success, New Hyde Park, N.Y., 11040.

The principle of "mind over matter" has been taught by the Christian Science Church based on the findings of Quimby, and Mary Baker Eddy. The Kahunas, priests of the Polynesian Islands, used this resonance in both healing and projected effects clear across the Islands. Psychometry is the ability of some scientists to feel the resonance of others through objects belonging to them.

A "water witch" is only the reaction of the cell structure in a cut divining fork from a living plant. or tree, trying to put its root end down when it senses the "water of life." Metal rods respond to "thought" of the living human cell structure, as an indicator

CHAPTER ELEVEN PERCEPTION & MIND

between man and God — to locate metals, tunnels, or water. Prayers are never answered when one is out of resonance with "Mr. Cosmic Mind." Miracles, on the other hand, occur without human intervention when the person healed has conformed to the fixed laws of earned reciprocation. Some people are "accident prone," and prone to other reactions, because they are in tune with the influence that causes these things, or they are out of resonant contact with the influence that prevents them.

Life is not a mystery to those who seek to understand it. It is only a mystery to those who are afraid of it, and expect someone to act as a "go between" for them. Usually the "go between" doesn't give a rap and may make the individual worse off than before.

"Holy Water" is ordinary water, except someone made it "Holy" by thinking resonant harmony into it. Kosher products are only Kosher because someone brought the resonance of acceptance into it through ritual. Science is only science when it is finding out new things "Mr. Cosmic Mind" knows. It ceases to be science when it hides its findings for any reason. Science is the act of revealing, not concealing.

Remember, Money is God on the Earth. The first consideration of business and politics is, how much can I make from this deal, and how much prestige can I gain in my position by promoting this deal? Repetitions of these acts builds multiples of bureaucratic overlaps that strangle the taxpayers.

This ever growing man-made monster is about to commit economic suicide. No consideration is taken in these blood-sucking propositions about emotions, welfare of the donors, or long range reactions. No thought is presented as to whether this action is against natural laws, in conflict with "Mr. Cosmic Mind," or in conformance with "The Golden Rule."

Destructive weapons, bombs, and war come from the cell structure of the brain of humans, who have been educated and programmed

CHAPTER ELEVEN PERCEPTION & MIND

to believe in what they are a part of. Inspiration of creative things comes through the brain from the universal resonance of "Mr. Cosmic Mind." One must "tune in" to Him in order to achieve resonance, or get the station on your dial spiritually. One does not have to go anywhere to find Him. He is everywhere without bound, ad infinitum.

CHAPTER TWELVE

PRINCIPLES & PROOF

In 1923 Dr. Biefield, professor of physics and astronomy at Dennison University, teamed up with Townsend Brown in basic efforts to understand and overcome gravity. At Dr. Biefield's suggestion a number of tests were performed to determine the electrical relation of gravity relative to electrically charged objects. Dr. Biefield was a former classmate of Einstein in Switzerland. The original tests conducted proved there was a tendency toward motion in a charged condenser suspended from a thread. This observed motion of a charged condenser has been labeled the Biefield-Brown Effect. Brown pointed out in 1923 that this tendency of a charged condenser to move might grow into a basically new method of propulsion.

In 1926 Townsend Brown described a "space car" using this new principle. By 1928 he had built working models of a boat propelled in this manner. By 1938 Brown had shown how his condensers not only moved but had interesting effects on plants and animals. Townsend Brown made a condenser shaped like a saucer that flew around a may-pole long before flying saucers became a newspaper topic in 1947.

The saucers made by Brown had no propellers, no jets, no moving parts at all. They created a modification of the gravitational field around themselves, which is analogous to putting them on the incline of a "hill." They acted like a surfboard on a wave. The electro-gravitational saucer creates its own "hill," which is a local orientation of the field around it. Then it takes its own "hill" with it in any direction and at unlimited acceleration. There are no inertial forces as such inside the field. No thrust, or centrifugal force results on the load or occupants with directional changes.

CHAPTER TWELVE PRINCIPLES & PROOF

Brown's saucers required a highly charged leading edge, the positive polarity pole. Such a charged pole produces an electrical corona. This is visible in darkness. A full scale saucer will produce a corona visible for miles at night. The shape of a saucer follows the requirements of electrostatic and gravitational considerations, not aerodynamic requirements. There is no heat barrier, or skin friction as in aircraft rammed through the air by reaction propulsion methods. The material leading edge of the ship enters a vacuity created by the electrically charged area in front of it. For every known electromagnetic effect there is an analogous electrogravitational effect, but electrogravitational causes and effects differ from those of electromagnetic. The fields around a saucer can reach an intensity where they will bend light around them, and they will appear to disappear. Radar bounce off the body can also be screened off by the field at given frequencies, and it will disappear on the radar scope. Brown observed the following factors in his moving, charged condensers:

1. Regarding the separation of the plates of the condenser; the closer the plates, the greater the effect.
2. The ability of the material between the plates to store electrical energy in the form of elastic stress. A measure of this ability is called the "K" of the material. The higher the "K," the greater the Biefield-Brown effect.
3. The area of the plates; the greater area giving the greater effect.
4. The voltage difference between the plates; more voltage, more effect.
5. The mass of the material between the plates; the greater the mass, the greater the effect.

We observed that with vertical poles a separation, or division of the fields can be affected with a "caduceus" coil winding. This creates one field pulling up and the other field pushing down. The coupling of harmonics in electricity, gravity, and magnetism result in the power that spins planets, orbits them, and causes galaxies to

CHAPTER TWELVE PRINCIPLES & PROOF

spin.

The Biefield-Brown effect demonstrates that a condenser suspended in a horizontal position, when charged with electricity will move in the positive pole direction. Reverse the polarity and it will move in the opposite direction, always moving toward the positive end.

The spherical balls that have been referred to as a landing gear in the pictures taken by George Adamski, are not landing gears — they are condensers. Located 120° apart they provide a tripod effect in the gravitational field, and give directional control by polarity manipulations.

Townsend Brown pursued his research until 1956, when he formed N.I.C.A.P., the National Investigations Committee on Aerial Phenom-ena, in Washington, D.C., with a top brass advisory board.

I visited Townsend Brown in his office in Washington in late 1956 while I was on a lecture tour. In discussing his research and flying saucers with him, I explained the purpose of the 120° control. In a few weeks he resigned as the head of N.I.C.A.P., and Major Donald Keyhoe became its Director.

In January, 1955, we printed data on "The Earth As A Motor." From this data another man made an anti-gravity model, and is at present engaged in making larger ones for a private firm, which is under government subsidy. In 1952 we printed data on anti-gravity relative to rotating high frequency fields. In 1956 we explained data relative to polarity reversals and temperature changes in molecular structure over Radio Station W.O.R. that was later proven by a major steel company, who sent a man out here to consult with me for several days.

There are anti-gravity research projects in every country in the world. On my last lecture tour I was approached by two separate parties con-ducting anti-gravity research outside of government

CHAPTER TWELVE PRINCIPLES & PROOF

subsidy. Both of them work and will lift non-ferrous metals like gold and silver as easily as a magnet will attract iron. Neither one of them works on the Biefield-Brown effect, but rather by orienting the poles of the atomic structure — like magnetism orients the poles in molecular structure.

Authority refused to look at the Dean Space Drive, written about by Campbell in a past "Astounding Magazine," because it contradicted Newton's Law of Gravity — but it works!

The Biefield-Brown Effect is only a part of gravitational knowledge, but Townsend Brown should be publicly honored for his revelations; not rejected to become another Tesla unknown to present scientific teaching.

Kepler and Newton knew the true state of things, but science misin-terpreted their findings. Faraday demonstrated "magnarotation." Rotary moving weights produce mechanical lift through centrifugal force. This was proven by Mr. Benny Hallberg in Sweden and is referred to as the "Hallberg Device."

Resonance is the answer to both sonic and electro-gravitational nullification of gravity. A "free energy" motor can be made with permanent magnets, using a three gear planetary system between the rotor and stator, with an even number of magnets on the rotor and an uneven number of magnets on the stator. The three gears have three magnets rotating to time attraction and repulsion between the rotor and stator magnets polarity-wise.

Gravity is relative to the mass of the atomic structure of the matrix. It would be easier to lift the Empire State building than it would be to lift a salt shaker if the poles of the atomic structure were aligned vertically.

Multiple wave oscillation gives an angleworm thrust to coherent waves that are in harmonic resonance with each other. With no frictional resistance, acceleration beyond the theorized speed of

CHAPTER TWELVE PRINCIPLES & PROOF

light are possible. Being inside of the electrogravitational field causes all time reference to cease, and one could live an indefinite life span as long as the cell loss is replaced in the body by new cell food.

An electro-statically charged condenser — which is a spaceship — excludes all outside influences which cause aging in bodies.

You can understand why the Biefield-Brown effect is not being taught in our most advanced technical colleges today because of the impact it would have on a world run by money. This is the reason why flying saucers data has been withheld from the public.

In the last 50 years the sciences have brought us from the horse and buggy days to men on the Moon. Electronics has given us world-wide, even space-wide, television; communication; and control of military, industrial, domestic, and economic devices. Medical science has come from pasteurized milk to the transplant of vital organs.

In all of this immense scientific advancement there has been the suppression, and withholding, of many vital things, that at the time were in conflict with economic and political interests.

The paradox of today is seen in the overall picture of the constant words for peace, while ever more potent weapons for destruction are being manufactured. The constant cry for higher, and more education, while revolutionaries rip our educational system apart; and advanced science is withheld from our deserving students. A war on poverty while our gross national income is the highest in history.

The thing I am most concerned with is the failure of the government to support and encourage those individuals who have demonstrated the ability, and initiative, to create things that would benefit our people. *All* of the people, from presidents down to the most unfortunate, the cripple and the mental cases, get old and get

CHAPTER TWELVE PRINCIPLES & PROOF

sick.

For many years I have heard of the people who have been persecuted and prosecuted for putting forth projects of their own, because it conflicted with established economy, medical science, or political authority. This I have never fully accepted, because it is difficult to understand why these authorities, who also get old and sick, would cut their own throats — so to speak.

In my own field of endeavor, inspired by a God-given desire to leave this planet better than I found it when I was born, I now ask this question. Why have electro-magnetic and radiesthesia sciences been ignored, suppressed, and withheld from their beneficent usage over the past 50 years? I offer the following data to prove these things are known. The fact that they are not in use proves they have been sup-pressed.

The latest of these great accomplishments has just been revealed. I present this first because everyone is aware of the flight of Apollo "8" around the Moon. What is presented here is only a small portion of the whole research. The principle of its operation is the important thing, because it verifies and *expands* other research done over the years. The man responsible for this device deserves international recognition for a *breakthrough even as fantastic* as the Apollo "8" flight.

The device recorded the intensity of reactions of every gland and organ in the bodies of the three astronauts, Borman, Lovell, and An-ders; from two days before lift-off until two days after splashdown in the Pacific Ocean. It was recorded *without radio*, or telemetry trans-mission from any transmitters aboard Apollo "8." The amazing fact is the transmission continued to be received while the capsule was on the *back side of the Moon* — when all *radio* transmission could not be received on the Earth.

The preliminary report, "Tracking The Astronauts In Apollo '8' " can be had by writing to, "Advanced Sciences Research and

CHAPTER TWELVE PRINCIPLES & PROOF

Development Corporation," Lakemont, Georgia, 30552. The price is $2.00 plus post-age. This report was sent to me by one of the men who was largely re-sponsible for its success.

The tuning in to the three astronauts is accomplished in the device by *radiation from photographs* of each of the three men. Distance did not seem to be a factor in the strength of signals received.

This verifies in principle, the magnetic-ion activities here in our "In-tegratron" relative to living bodies. We have long contended that every atom radiates energy relative to its composition. Every gland and or-gan, or body, is composed of octaves of emanation from its atomic makeup. The *photograph* of anyone includes the *radiations* of the *individual* as well as the reflection of light off of them externally.

Zoler and Kelsh of "Radiopthy Inc.," in Hollywood, proved this. De-LaWar, Drown, Abrams, Lakhovsky, Crile, and many others, devised instruments in part that paralleled this astronaut tracking device, though not in such completeness.

Louis Pasteur established some of these principles in 1862, although he was recognized mostly for his pasteurized milk process.

This astronaut tracking device proves that every living body emanates radiations from all of its parts according to their atomic charge of composition.

Drs. A. A. Boe and D. K. Salunkhe, from Utah State University, put green tomatoes in a magnetic field and the tomatoes ripened four to six times faster than normal. *All* seeds germinate many times faster when placed in magnetic fields.

Dr. Becker and Dr. Brown have found a number of diseases that occur in cycles, and are sure from experiments they conducted that humans are affected by celestial forces.

CHAPTER TWELVE PRINCIPLES & PROOF

In New York City, Dr. K. E. MacLean used an electro-magnetic activator in treating "hopeless" cases of cancer. He reported his results were "remarkable." "Cancer cannot exist in a strong magnetic field," MacLean said. Hair also was brought back from white and gray shades to its natural color by magnetic fields. When MacLean was 64 years old he looked about 45 — after exposing himself to a 3600 Gauss magnetic field every day for 5 years. He reported pain from any cause was relieved in a magnetic field, and recovery to normalcy was speeded up. He could not discover a single adverse side, or after effect, from normal magnetic fields.

Edgar Cayce once said, "There is mind in every cell of the body." Charles Steinmetz said, "When science turns toward spiritual discoveries it will make more progress in 50 years than in all its past history." Doctors have discovered that the human brain has positive and nega-tive polarization. The forehead is negative and the back of the head is positive. Reversal of these polarities causes one to go to sleep. In Australia and Europe, magazines and newspapers run ads on a "mag-netic pillow" that helps people go to sleep by causing this polarity reversal. They also advertise a "magnetic bracelet" that keeps one in good health when worn on the wrist. Sales of this item run around 36,000 a month. Why are these items not available in our country?

A two year study by the American Institute of Medical Climatology in Philadelphia revealed that hospital and industrial records, as well as police and fire department reports, showed peaks and troughs of activity relative to the times of the new and full Moon cycles.

Dr. Igno H. Kornblueh reported complete loss of pain in third degree burns over an entire human body by having the patient breathe negative charged ions in the air. He said the burned body tissue healed much faster.

Dr. Georges Lakhovsky said in his book, "The Secret of Life,"

CHAPTER TWELVE PRINCIPLES & PROOF

"that the cell-organic unit in all living beings, is nothing but an electromag-netic resonator, capable of emitting and absorbing radiation of a very high frequency."

Dr. Harold S. Alexander of North American Aviation Corp.'s Missile Division told scientists at an annual meeting of the Institute of Environmental Sciences that "Mice live up to 45% *longer* after they have been subjected to certain types of magnetic fields, and cancerous mice lose their malignant growths after similar treatment."

Scientists of the U.S. Geological Survey, working with scientists of the National Cancer Institute, discovered that cancerous liver in rats was *less* magnetic than normal tissue.

Dr. J. M. Barnothy at the University of Budapest reported that in albino mice inoculated with certain types of cancer there was loss of tumor in five cases, and complete recovery in four cases out of six, for those mice placed in a moderately strong magnetic field. In contrast, control animals that were similarly inoculated and were kept out of the magnetic field died. He displayed two mice from the same litter which had reached an age equivalent to 90 years in humans. The one which had lived for a while in a magnetic field appeared *only about one third* as old as the other.

In one series of tests, run by Dr. Walter H. Eddy, formerly of Columbia University, 60 mice of a breed especially susceptible to lung cancer were separated into two equal groups. One group was kept in ordinary atmosphere; the other in a room with a high negative ion content. At the end of two months, 22 of the 30 mice living in ordinary atmosphere had developed lung malignancies and died. Of the other group only *two* died; the other 28 *showed no sign of lung cancer.*

In a trip to Russia, Dr. I. Kornblueh of Philadelphia's Northeastern Hospital discovered extensive use of ion therapy there. New medical students are *trained in the use of negative ions,* and more

CHAPTER TWELVE PRINCIPLES & PROOF

than 100 hos-pitals and health centers are said to be taking regular advantage of negative ion therapy. Among the maladies treated in Russia, are peptic ulcers, arthritis, bronchial asthma, hypertension, and various types of neurosis.

All of the above researchers and results are from 10 to 70 years old, except the astronaut tracking. In 10 years we have put men in orbit and around the Moon at the cost of billions of dollars to the people who receive no real return for their money.

What I am suggesting here to the agencies of government, medical science, and electro-magnetic science, is that you are in a position to produce beneficial results in people *now*. With what is known now, centers for prevention and treatment of the sick world can be a reality.

The *simplicity* of magnetic fields and negative ions lies dormant and useless, while presidents and their appointees, and scientists and doctors suffer and die in so short a life span.

A sick people cannot pay taxes. They not only *don't pay taxes*, but they *use taxes* in programs established for their care. Why die at 65 when you can live much longer in full vitality and youthful appearance?

Apathetic young people will not support the system that provides jobs and income. Sick people and old people and people on welfare use up the money that should be used to build a greater, healthier and smarter society. New hospitals are full as soon as they are built. More and more young people are refusing to accept the responsibility of a society that uses them for undeclared wars. More and more people are growing older faster in an accelerated way of tension.

The balance of economic security of government has reached the fulcrum of unbalance, where more is being spent than is being taken in, as witness the annual increase in the national debt. The

CHAPTER TWELVE PRINCIPLES & PROOF

bureaucracy of government in its segregation of itself cannot support itself. The people who lay the golden eggs of taxes are finding every means at their disposal to legally and illegally avoid paying taxes to an authority that gives them nothing in return for their money.

Add up the number of unemployed, welfare cases, sick people, old people and the apathetic youth and see how long the economy can last. Those now supporting the system will soon join these others and become a part of the deficit when taxes cut into their comfort and pleasure money.

The cell structure of society, in its people, can only be as well and strong as its heads in authority permit it to be.

Why can Russia and other foreign countries use these devices for the benefit of their people, while none are available for public use in this most scientifically advanced nation? Every city in the United States should have rooms available to the public, charged with negative ions and magnetic fields, so anyone could walk in and stay until they feel better and act younger. These should be operated by the government. Libraries would be ideal for this. Then people could get self education at the same time.

CHAPTER THIRDTEEN

SECRECY & SPACE

The withholding of findings in space by the authorities, who make policy, and N.A.S.A., who conducts the space flights, from the people who finance these ventures through taxes, is an act of malfeasance.

Of course proof that man is on the Moon now, and has been for cen-turies past, would blow up the theory of evolution. It would force earthlings to accept the fact that there are people out there who are far in advance of the human race, and it would verify creation on a universal scale, not just on the Earth.

According to one of the astronauts I talked to, there hasn't been a Russian, or American astronaut in orbit around the Earth, who hasn't had spaceships, from out there, make at least one orbit of the Earth with them.

In 1915, astronomers observed the structural composition of angular lines in the Gassendi crater (fig. 4). This picture shows the "lines" that were being constructed.
2. This picture verifies the spacepeople who are coming here in spaceships.
3. This picture disproves the orthodox contention that God created man on the Earth. That there is only here and hereafter and nothing else.
4. This picture makes the authorities and scientists trying to put a man on the Moon look like "Johnnie come lately" experts.
5. This picture, from the angle of the Sun and its shadows, clearly shows domes over underground living quarters, connected with a system of large diameter tubes on the

CHAPTER THIRDTEEN SECRECY & SPACE

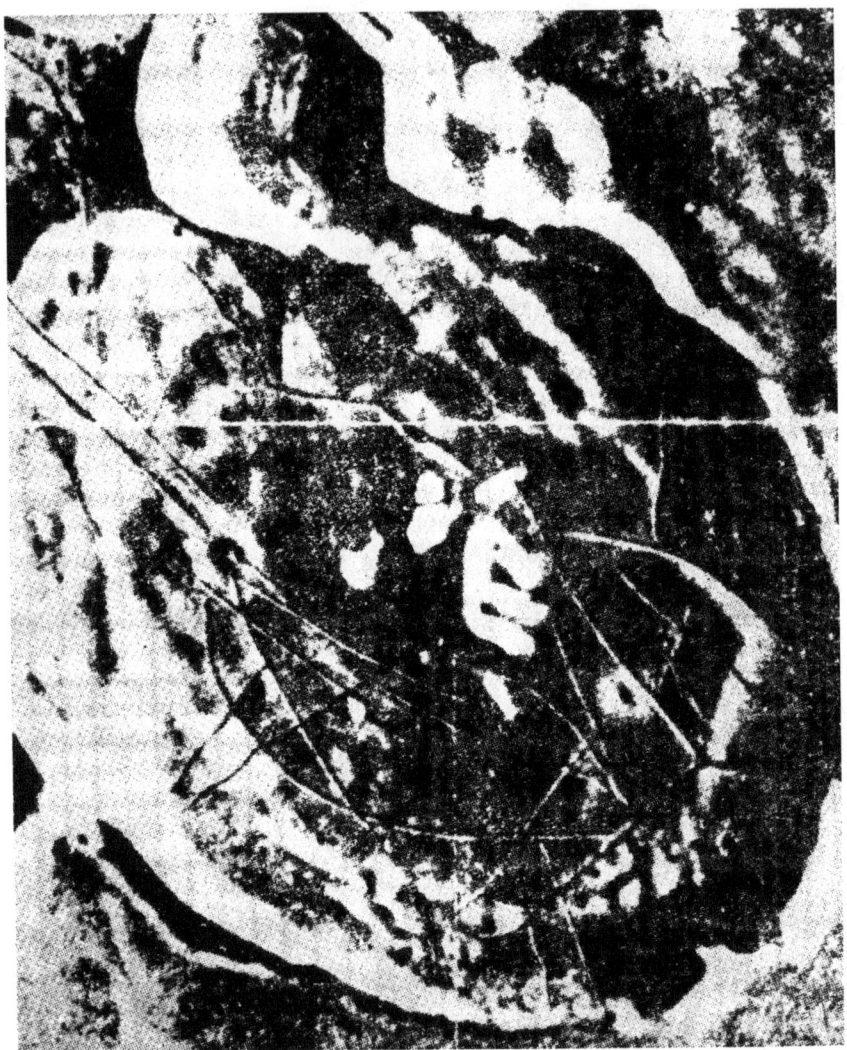

Figure 4. Gassendi Crater

CHAPTER THIRDTEEN SECRECY & SPACE

surface to travel through and maintain an air pressure system throughout the entire base.

This crater is 55 miles long, and was pictured some 35 years ago by Wilkins in his book "The Moon."

The landing of Apollo 12 on the Moon was just above the Gassendi crater in the Ocean of Storms. The low orbiting capsules of Apollo 11 and 12 passed close to the Gassendi crater. They took pictures all around the Moon. When one talks with recognized astronomers about the craters on the Moon they are very cooperative until the Gassendi crater is mentioned, then they clam up.

Surveyor 3, in orbit around the Moon, transmitted pictures back to the Earth that clearly show man-made casings of large diameter sticking out of the Moon's surface. These are either vents, or entrances for spaceships through air locks, to underground installations below the surface.

In 1788, Schroeter, recorded in astronomy, the observation of "a light in the Lunar Alps. But then when this region was illuminated he saw a round shadow where the light had been; then he saw a luminous object near the Moon: that part of the Moon became illuminated by the Sun and the object was lost to view but then its shadow underneath was seen on the surface."

The September 29th, 1969, newspaper, "National Bulletin" has an article written by Sam Pepper about the Apollo Moon walk by Armstrong and Aldrin. Part of the article reads: "I was able to lay hands on a top secret tape transcript of the return to the spacecraft. This transcript was received back on the Earth as the words were uttered, yet Mission Control kept them secret from the public at large, by a delay tape technique, that allows monitors on Earth to censor video and audio tape two or three minutes before it is transmitted to your home television. The following is the verbal record of what the Moon walking duo said and heard as they returned to the spacecraft.

CHAPTER THIRDTEEN SECRECY & SPACE

"What was it . . . what the hell was it? That's all I want to know . . . (garbled) . . . babies were huge. Sir, they were enormous . . . What ... what . . . the hells going on? What's the matter with you guys? ... they're there under the surface . . . Roger, we're here all three of us, but we found some visitors ... Yeh! They've been here for quite a while judging from the installations . . . I'm telling you there are other spacecraft out there . . . they're lined up in ranks on the far side of the crater edge . . . Lets get that orbit scanned and head home . . ."

This same information came from several other sources also. Now the question is: What is to be gained by some minority in authority deciding that the public shouldn't know the facts?

Censorship and meddling authority blocked out the most revealing part of the Russian picture of the back side of our Moon when it was printed in the newspapers.

A full third of the left hand side of the picture was eliminated in the press and on T.V. Why? Why was this portion of the picture restricted from the public? It wasn't security to keep it from the Russians. They took the picture! (fig. 5).

You can see in the lower left hand corner that a revetment, or large dike, has been pushed up from the material of the Moon's surface around the large, white, disc-shaped area. Is this ice? Is it water? Or is it a large, domed city, which would verify George Adamski's statement of many years back — that "there is a large city on the back side of the Moon."

It looks like a rounded canopy, and is over a hundred miles in diameter. It does not appear to have any pock marks or craters in it. Therefore if it is a domed city it was built after the Moon craters were formed. We contend that the domed buildings in the Gassendi crater and their interconnecting tubes on the surface, and this picture alone, prove that there are other intelligent species of the

CHAPTER THIRDTEEN SECRECY & SPACE

race of man in space.

The equator of Mars in inclined about 24° to the plane of its orbit.

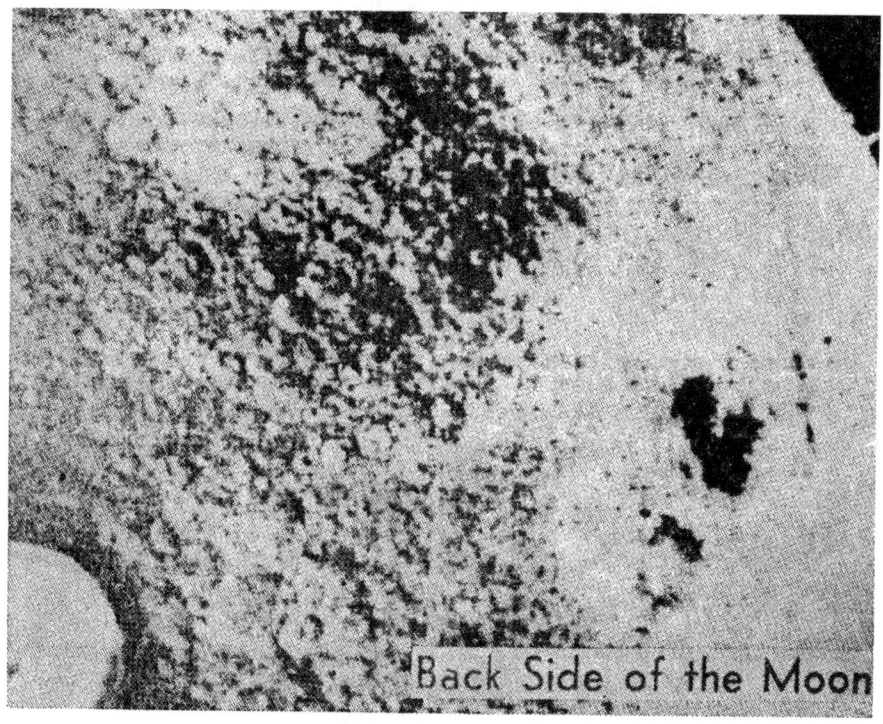

ST. LOUIS POST DISPATCH THREE STAR EDITION
AUGUST 16, 1965

Back side of the Moon — a view of the equatorial and northern sec-tion of the back side of the Moon taken by Russia's Zond 3. The round object at lower left is a scientific marking device.

Tass News Agency submitted two photos that were taken on July 20, 1965 along with an article by Yuri Lipsky of the Shternberg Astronomical Institute in Moscow. Actual article not published nor was the actual number of photos mentioned. Distance of photo is claimed to be about 7200 miles.

CHAPTER THIRDTEEN SECRECY & SPACE

Most newspapers cropped out the so called scientific marking device or reproduced very dark photos that made it impossible to detect the objects that appear to be on the Moon in the lower left and upper right. Blow up photo indicates the "tower" like object is also adjoined by some other structure also. The object in the lower left appears to have a rill of Moon material banked around it like a doughnut!

About 1/2° more than the earth. Its period of rotation makes its day about 1/2 hour longer than the earth's.

Phobos, and Deimos, the two moons around Mars, were discovered by Asaph Hall in 1877. In 1721, one hundred and fifty-six years earlier, Dean Swift in his book "Gulliver's Travels" described the moons around Mars.

Phobos is the only known body in the Solar System that rises in the West and sets in the East. Phobos orbits around Mars in 7 hours and 39 minutes. This means that it goes around Mars 3 times in one day. Our moon takes 28 days to go around the earth once. Phobos is about 3,700 miles from the surface of Mars, while our moon is about 240,000 miles away.

In our 2000 mile out pictures of Mars, why wasn't the public shown any picture_s of Phobos? The Russian space scientists say it is a hollow man-made satellite. Relative to its size, speed in orbit, distance from the surface, gravity attraction and centrifugal force, it cannot be a solid body.

Why the secrecy: Why is the public excluded from seeing the pictures? Why doesn't authority want to admit there are other people out there? Why?

T. Galen Hieronymus tracked the Apollo 11 moon astronauts, Armstrong, Collins and Aldren. His "Eloptic Energy" receiver recorded a lethal radiation belt around our moon. It appeared to extend from

CHAPTER THIRDTEEN SECRECY & SPACE

15 feet off the surface of the moon, out to 65 miles. Because the moon does not rotate like the earth, this appears to be a dispersed Van Allen belt. He recorded a very high beneficent reaction while the astronauts were out of the L.E.M. on the moon's surface.

We are analyzing the Apollo 11 report, and comparing it with the Apollo 8 moon orbital flight. *Soon* this combination report will be avail-able to those who want it. Do not write to us. Write to T. Galen Hieronymus, P.O. Box 77, Lakemont, Georgia 30552. (The price has not been set on this report.)

Several years ago a capsule was fired from Vandenburg, the West coast equivalent of the Cape Kennedy Space Launch Center, in Florida. When it was recovered, it *weighed less* than when it was launched. Much less.

In a recent contact with a friend from the N.A.S.A. Apollo flight series, he told me that all of the Moon flight capsules from Apollo 8 on through Apollo 11, have weighed less when they returned, than they did when they were launched. Now the metals also have less density.

What will be interesting to find out, as an after effect, is whether this will be beneficial, or detrimental, to the astronauts who were in these Apollo capsules. Certainly any radiation in space that can change the weight and density of metals, will have some effect on them.

These men, who risked all, to make these true space flights, are to be highly honored and respected. Let us hope that the future holds much for them in health and happiness.

Archaeology, anthropology, many religious records, and artifacts verify that there were people in physical form visiting the earth, in times past, from outer space. The origin of every religion was based on these visitations from out of the skies.

CHAPTER THIRDTEEN SECRECY & SPACE

The disappearance of the entire populations of Ankor Wat in our recent recorded history proves that they went somewhere — as no bodies were found. This involved thousands of people in an eight hour period of time.

Sanscrit records visitations of people from out of the skies. The Japanese pagodas record these appearances in the past. Antigravity transportation, and lifting of massive stones in the many places around the earth, show technology not yet available to our science except on an experimental scale.
No authority can invalidate these facts from the past.

In the June 1967, issue of "Saga" magazine, John Keel has written an article entitled "Moon Craters, or Secret U.F.O. Bases." This article shows that our governmental agencies are not above lying and producing false information to hide facts from you people who pay for these projects. The picture on page 22 plainly shows vent pipes, or man-made silos coming out of the surface of the Moon. This picture was taken by our Surveyor satellite.

Two books written by Vyacheslav Zaitsev, who spent thirty years researching into past records to prove intelligent beings live in space, are outstanding. They are, "Cosmic Reminiscences In Written Relics Of The Past," and "The Evolution Of The Universe And Intelligent Beings." An article written by him in the August, 1967, issue of "Real" magazine, is most revealing.

Ancient hieroglyphs set down by one of the Ham tribe reads "The Dropas came down from the clouds in their gliders. Our men, women and children hid in caves ten times before the sunrise. When at last they understood the sign language of the Dropas, they realized that the newcomers had peaceful intentions." One Latin American legend says that eggs dropped down from the sky on dandelions! An ancient man could have seen a container with a man in it descend from the sky in a capsule like an egg, suspended by a parachute which he could only describe as a dandelion. How many of the world's tribes today might describe the descent of one

CHAPTER THIRDTEEN SECRECY & SPACE

of our astronauts into their jungle in the same manner?

From the Christian Apocrypha, which was banned by the church from use in services and reading, are many explanations of the myster-ies of life. These books sometimes stand in direct contradiction to church approved texts.

"One of the Apocrypha books, "The Tale About The Three Magi" contains a reference to 'certain books' which claim that Christ came down from the star that was called the star of Bethlehem. The star, it says, was watched by astronomers in many Oriental countries. Once it appeared at night and lit up the whole sky as the Sun does. It hung over Mount Vans for a whole day, after which it alighted on the mountain like an eagle."

Astronauts in orbit around the planet are a fantastic achievement of science, but God put all of us on this planet in orbit around the Sun, which makes our science of space a child of nature.

Astronauts orbiting around the earth inside of capsules at 18,000 miles per hour, are small scale replicas of all of us on the outside of our planet in orbit around the Sun at 66,000 miles per hour. We are not only going faster, but we are held onto the outside of this ball of rock by an invisible force made by God, called gravity by us. We are as narrow-minded as fleas on a dog that don't know there are any other dogs, or fleas, except their own little world.

People, dogs, fleas, churches, scientists, planets, and authorities are only a confused mass in a mess of their own making. We should not be trying to take atoms apart — we should be trying to put them together. We should not be divided in our thinking, or action to create anything.

It is those who oppose God who are maintaining secrecy. Think of how great this society on the earth would be if all information now withheld by the authorities, and churches, were available to everyone.

CHAPTER FOURTEEN LIES & FACTS

CHAPTER FOURTEEN

LIES & FACTS

The Condon report on U.F.O.'s turned out exactly as we predicted it would. They investigated the U.F.O. by the process of elimination, and examined less than 2% of the many reports given over 20 years.

The book, "U.F.O.s Yes," written by David Saunders, who was part of the Condon Committee, exposes the inside story of a negative con-clusion already reached to make the report look like a scientific report. We have stated for years that the Air Force knew the answers since the early 1950's. Their continuity of investigations since then are a cover-up designed to make the public think they don't know the answers.

Thousands of photographs have been taken by Air Force jets chasing the U.F.O.s, as well as ground photographs taken by civilians. No investigator from the Condon group contacted me. I have had 20 years of experience in the field at my airport; where over a hundred-thousand people from all over the world have come and reported sightings they have had over the past 15 years. Air Force, Navy, Marine, and civilian jet pilots have reported more experiences here than they have to the Air Force over the years. This alone is evidence that Condon did not need to find out anything, as he was not supposed to find out anything. Credible witnesses were ignored on the excuse that "they could not add anything new." Of course they couldn't add anything new to the facts that the Air Force already had since 1950. *The Air Force knew the answers then.*

It was interesting to note that the Condon report stated "there was no evidence to indicate that spaceships are coming here from other

CHAPTER FOURTEEN LIES & FACTS

solar systems." Now wasn't that statement a cutie. This is supposed to mean there aren't any spaceships — but — did you grasp the fact that this negative statement did not include the other planets in our own solar system? Why did they word it that way, to exclude our own solar system? You see this leads you to believe what they want you to believe and leaves them an out in a few years, when it becomes known that Venus and Mars are both occupied. The Air Force knows this, so do I. Among the many people who come to my airport is one who runs a computer on radio telescope data. He says the officials have known since we first had radio telescopes that Mars and Venus are beehives of U.F.O. Activity.

Four airplane pilots that I know, have had close encounters with U.F.O.s. One of them for a period of 20 minutes. One of them was over Washington, D.C. with U.F.O.s all around the airliner he was flying into the Capitol in 1952, when the headlines all over the country said "Strange Objects Over Capitol." These men are still flying passengers for one of the major airlines. They are not "kooks" or having hallucinations or they would have lost their responsible jobs long ago.

A test pilot in 1955 told me of chasing a saucer-shaped ship for 35 minutes in an F-86 jet. He wasn't grounded. He later bailed out of the B-70 in a mid-air collision with an F-104. Knowing his story in 1955 didn't stop authority from entrusting to him the testing of an airplane that cost millions of dollars to produce.

I talked personally with an Air Force Captain in 1953 that was assigned to remove the bodies from a downed saucer near Aztec, New Mexico. He told his story to over a hundred Air Force Reserve pilots in a Legion Hall in Hollywood in 1953, at the request of his superiors.

The Major in charge of U.F.O. investigation for the Air Force, came and told me openly of a grounded saucer he had personally seen, in 1953. You see I know the Air Force knew the answers then, because they told me. This was before the "hush hush"

CHAPTER FOURTEEN LIES & FACTS

security they clamped on U.F.O.s in 1954.

Now they have wasted $530,000.00 of the taxpayer's money to continue to fool the people.

David Saunders said the Edwards Air Force Base case, and others that could be conclusive proof, were not turned over to the Condon Committee, in spite of the fact that one of the Committee tried a number of times to get these cases from the Air Force.

I know of these cases personally, not because I went investigating to find out, but because authority came to me to discuss it — and there were witnesses that they were here. Why did they come here to talk to an airport operator that had been in aviation since 1927? Because they know my background and they knew I knew, because of the spaceship that landed here in 1953. The F.B.I. men who came here asked me, at the time, to phone them if any other "strange things" happened in this area. Does this sound like they thought I was dreaming? They knew I knew, from my experience here, and I knew they knew from the things they told me. This was in 1953.

Now in 1969 they are still spending taxpayer's money like water, to try to keep the public thinking they can't give the answers because they still don't know the answers.

The sightings will continue all over the world as they have in Madrid, Spain, while the Condon report was being compiled. Thousands saw the spaceship over Madrid. It was photographed. Jets went up to look at it. It was higher than they could fly. This went on for 2 hours.

I wonder what the cover-up policy will be from Condon's time on, as the sightings continue to occur throughout the world?

Officialdom is either being mis-informed by their advisors on many things, or they are being given wrong information

CHAPTER FOURTEEN LIES & FACTS

intentionally. Statement are constantly issued for public consumption without any name being used as the source of information. "A spokesman said," of this, or that, branch of government, is all we hear.

If security is being used to hide the interplanetary spacecraft from the people, because the public might find out about government research, and ships the Navy and Air Force have copied from the ones they hauled to Wright Patterson Air Base in 1950 to 1952, then this is misuse of security. Heads of foreign governments know the spaceships are here. N.A.S.A. knows from their pictures of the Moon that "they" have bases on the Moon.

Wilbert Smith, who headed the Canadian U.F.O. investigation Project Magnet, until it was closed down in 1954, lectured on the fact he had personal contact with them. Why did Canada stop their investigations in 1954? Because they established that the ships were interplanetary and they saw no further need to spend more money investigating. This is the same year the United States started their expensive cover-up by investigating forever.

Barry Goldwater saw a U.F.O. while flying as an Air Force Reserve pilot. He said they were real. William P. Lear, president of Lear Jet and Lear Electronics, said they were real. Lord Dowding, Air Marshall of England, said they were real. Several hundred VIP have said the same thing, including some Generals and Admirals. The Condon report as good as calls all these people liars, or "kooks."

The recorded sightings all over the world, in the 1890s, before anyone on earth had anything that would fly, makes a lie out of the Condon report and the Air Force policy.

The Rocky Mountain News of November 5, 1966 interviewed Dr. Condon two days after the University of Colorado signed the contract with the Air Force. He was asked if he believed the Air Force was withholding information. He replied that some people

CHAPTER FOURTEEN LIES & FACTS

believed this, but he personally didn't. "Maybe they are," he stated, "I don't care much." Could this "don't care" attitude have been the result of the fact that he already knew the report would only be a further cover-up? It was certainly not the right attitude for anyone to have who was going to spend a half million dollars of the taxpayer's money. When is an itemized account of this money expenditure going to be available to we who footed the bill? It was evident that the Air Force didn't approach Donald Keyhoe, Daniel Fry, or myself, and many others, who have had years of experience in the U.F.O. field, if they really wanted to find out anything, because they would have been submerged with enough evidence to prove the truth. Rather they hired someone that "didn't care" who knew nothing about the subject.

Dr. Lincoln La Paz and Dr. Clyde Tombaugh, discoverers of the planet Pluto, and recognized astronomers, both had saucer sightings. During the Condon investigation, air traffic at the Seattle-Tacoma airport had to be held in a pattern to wait until a large U.F.O. cleared away from the airport runway approach. These air traffic controllers, responsible for air safety of thousands, also become liars if the Condon report is accepted.

"Newsweek Magazine," in a national poll, said "at least 11,000,000 Americans had seen U.F.O.s." I maintain it is closer to 18,000,000, from my count of hands in over 250 lectures in the past eleven years.

Why is it a government policy to lie to the population, and back up their lie at the taxpayer's expense, when this is not military security? The Air Force has stated publicly many times that "these objects present no danger to the security of the United States." "These objects" in the sentence is an admission there *are* objects. How did they determine "they present no danger to the security of the United States"? This indicates government *has had contact with them* either personally, by radio, or both. Otherwise how can they make a flat statement that they are friendly?

CHAPTER FOURTEEN LIES & FACTS

Books have been written on U.F.O.'s by Jacques Vallee, a N.A.S.A. consultant; Frank Edwards, nationally known radio news commentator; Desmond Leslie, nephew of Winston Churchill; Cramp, Keyhoe, Fry, Michele, and many other stable, employed people, as well as myself. Over 300 books are available on the U.F.O. subject. Show me anyone who wrote a book, or books, that "made an easy buck" as they often are charged with. There are none.

Military services have government printed forms to report U.F.O.'s on. Why were forms printed (also at the taxpayer's expense) to report something that doesn't exist? Military jets have been scrambled many times to chase these objects detected on radar.

I maintain that the small staff of only *three* people under Major Quintenella was all the Air Force needed to keep up the false front. If they really wanted to investigate to find out anything, they would have had hundreds on the payroll. This again proves they already knew the answers. There wasn't anything more to find out!

Air Chief Marshal, Lord Dowding, of the Royal Air Force in England said, "I believe there are people on other planets who are operating through flying saucers to help our world in its present crisis."

General Curtis E. LeMay said, "We expect ultimately to be capable of developing a system that will enable us to examine and determine whether or not Unknowns in Space are a threat to us."

Frol R. Kozlov, First Deputy Chairman of the U.S.S.R., Council of Ministers, while in San Francisco, California in 1959, stated: "Let's have an American - Soviet alliance against the Martians!"

Dr. Alexander Kasantzev, a Soviet science writer said, "Highly advanced creatures from Mars have visited the earth many times until today."

CHAPTER FOURTEEN LIES & FACTS

William Lear, President of Lear, Inc., said, "I have seen it in the day-time. I believe flying saucers are operated by super intelligent beings from outer space."

Barry Goldwater, U.S. Senator from Arizona and Republican candi-date for President said, "Flying Saucers — Unidentified flying objects — or whatever you call them are real."

Albert M. Chop, former press official handling U.F.O. information at the Pentagon in Washington, D.C. said, "One thing is absolutely cer-tain. We're being watched by beings from outer space."

Dr. Clyde W. Tombaugh, discoverer of the planet Pluto said, "I have seen three objects during the past seven years, which cannot be ex-plained away as Venus, nor optical phenomena of the atmosphere, nor meteors, nor aircraft. I am an expert of astronomical observations and I have sighted eight green fireballs moving in a quite different way from the usual green fireballs. It is unscientific scientists who deny the possibilities of the existence of human beings in the universe outside the Earth."

In 1959, Russia's leading planetary physicist, I. S. Shklovsky, pub-lished the results of observations he had made.

He came to the conclusion that Phobos is an artificial satellite, probably made of aluminum.

"We have to assume that Phobos is hollow inside, something like a tin can from which the contents have been removed," he said.

"It is an artificial satellite of Mars."

Shklovsky based his statement on four peculiar properties of Phobos:
1. No other planet has moons that are as small as Phobos.
2. Both Martian moons, Phobos and Deimos, are extremely close to the planet, Mars. Phobos is only 5,000 miles from

CHAPTER FOURTEEN LIES & FACTS

the planet's surface.
3. Unlike all natural moons, Phobos moves in its orbit over three times as fast as Mars. This is impossible for a natural moon, according to accepted astronomical theories. No natural satellite can move faster than the planet it circles, because both planet and satellite were ori-ginally made from the same substance, traveling at the same speed.
4. Phobos is slowing down and falling toward Mars. This duplicates the motions of all man-made satellites put into orbit by the U.S. and Russia.

Scientists all over the world greeted Shklovsky's theories with mixed emotions.

Dr. H. M. Sinton, an astronomer at Yerkes Observatory, William Bay, Wis., agreed with Shklovsky, in a statement before the U.S. National Academy of Sciences.

"Phobos may be a huge orbiting city filled with men, women and children," he said. "The other moon, Deimos, might be one, too."

Agreement also came from one of the world's leading astronomical experts, Dr. Fred Hoyle, astrophysicist, a professor of astronomy at Cambridge University, England, and one-time staff member of both the Mt. Wilson and the Palomar observatories in Calif.

"This is the only theory I have heard that covers the mystery of these two moons," he said.

Dr. S. Fred Singer, professor of astronomy at the University of Maryland, and a key figure in the NASA Mars Probe project, added his agreement.

"If Shklovsky's figures are accurate, then Phobos could be artificial, hollow, and therefore made by living creatures," he said.

In 1952 Giampiero Monguzzi worked as an engineer at Monza,

CHAPTER FOURTEEN LIES & FACTS

near Milan. He was a member of the Edison Society of Italy. On July 31 that year he went climbing in the Bernina Mountains, together with his wife. At about 9:30 a.m. one morning, both of them suddenly saw lying on a glacier a thing they could not help but call a flying saucer, although up to that moment they had scoffed at the term as meaning some kind of American hoax. Both of them stood on the other side of the glacier to the strange object. Monguzzi very much wanted to cross the glacier to get nearer to the thing. But his wife was terribly frightened and prevented him, so he stayed where he was and took a series of seven pictures.

The first shows the saucer a bit tilted to one side, with an aerial sticking out of it; the second shows it in a more straightened position, with a man appearing to one side. He is wearing a kind of diving suit with a headpiece which hid his head. Monguzzi judged his appearance and size as being that of an ordinary man wearing a space suit. In his right hand he carried some kind of torch light with which he seemed to inspect his ship. On his back he carried a contraption, very much like a "walkie-talkie" with another aerial or antenna rising from it. He slowly walked around the saucer while Monguzzi took three other pictures. Then he disappeared behind the saucer. The aerial was drawn in and the ship took off, without noise and rather quickly. Monguzzi was lucky enough to take two other excellent photos of the ship's departure.

The whole procedure had lasted only a few minutes. Very likely, if Monguzzi had run over to it he would have ruined the chance to make these unique pictures. He and his wife went to Milan feeling certain of having taken the pictures of the year and planning to sell them at a good price. The engineer showed them to his friends, to his manager, and to some newspaper men. But nobody believed him (remember it was 1952). They all felt sure they had to deal with very clever fakes. A violent controversy arose in the Edison Society with the result that Monguzzi lost his membership, and later on his job, since his manager was a leading member of the society.

CHAPTER FOURTEEN LIES & FACTS

In comparing these pictures one must take into account that they may be slightly different in some respects, due to design changes over a period of several years.

The picture of the ship, when shown to a major aircraft firm's vice president in 1959, caused him to remark "there aren't any pictures of this ship available to the public. Where did Van Tassel get this picture?"

This remark indicated he knew what the object in the picture was and that the ship was probably built by his company. (fig. 6).

CHAPTER FOURTEEN LIES & FACTS

CHAPTER FOURTEEN LIES & FACTS

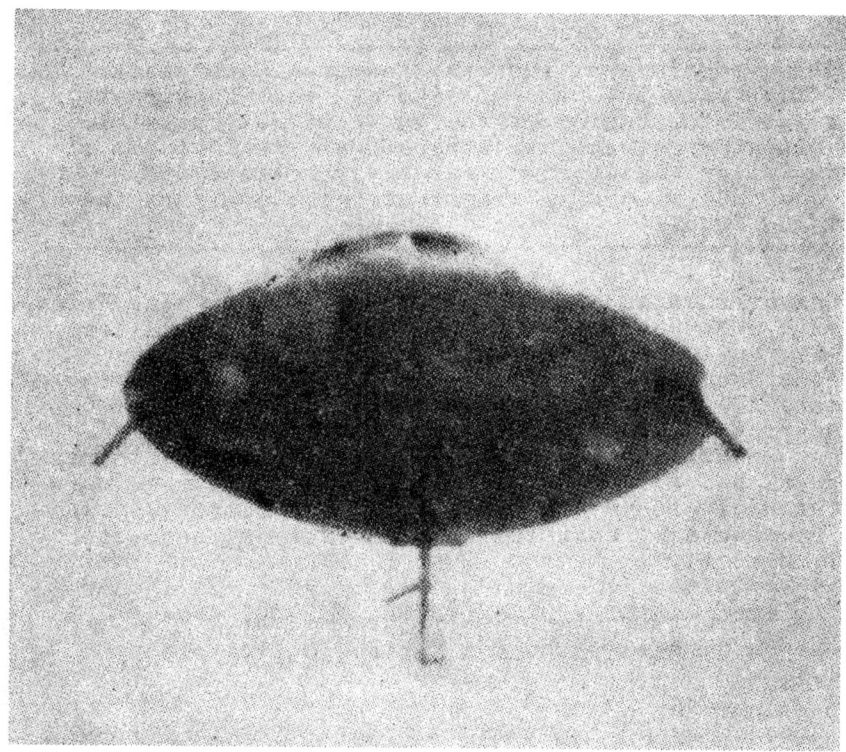

The above picture we contend is a photograph of a U.S. Navy experimental anti-gravity "saucer" that was taken by Radio Officer T. Fogl of Harleyford Road, London, S.E. 11, England.

Officer Fogl took this picture from a British ship, the S.S. Ramsay, off the coast of San Pedro, California, in December of 1957.

There are two things very apparent in keeping the truths of antigravity from the common people. One is that Russia knows as much about it as the United States does; and the other is, that there has to be a one world government operating on a total credit system before it can be used by everyone. It is impossible from an economic point of view to have a money system and public use of anti-gravity at the same time.

CHAPTER FOURTEEN LIES & FACTS

The sightings over Lisbon, Portugal, suddenly appeared in the press, where the "object" stopped electric clocks by the hundreds; and over Canberra, Australia, where the objects caused interference with the Mars probe tracking station at Tidninbilla. Framingham, Massachusetts; France; the Antarctic scientific bases; and many other points reporting "glowing objects" was not any increase in the number of sightings. It was a sudden release from security.

The Air Force has known, scientists connected with "saucers" have known, and government heads have known for years that:

1. These objects are spaceships.
2. They are occupied and controlled by intelligent people.
3. They are friendly.
4. They can't be shot down, or chased "home."
5. They have had the Earth under observation for centuries.
6. Their visits down through history have brought about the beginning of every religion on the Earth.
7. Authority expects to "reveal all" by announcing some homemade anti-gravity ships of their own, and imply that these are what people have been seeing all along.

CHAPTER FIFTEEN SIGHTINGS & SATELLITES

CHAPTER FIFTEEN

SIGHTINGS & SATELLITES

Shadows on the moon and dizzy acrobatics of a saucer around ECHO II.

"Buenos Aires. 5th December, 1965 — Some flying saucers have been sighted in Buenos Aires. Reverend Father Benito Reyna, of the Society of Jesus, teacher of mathematics and director of a small private observatory, has photographed 3 of these UFO's which according to him, could come from another planet.

"During a press conference Father Reyna displayed some negatives on which can be seen 3 black spots of different sizes outlined against the illuminated surface of the moon. We recall that Father Reyna had already observed some saucers last November."

`Le Figaro' — 6/12/1965.

One of the members of G.E.P.A. (Society for the Study of Aerial Phenomena) wrote to Father Reyna and in reply received a photograph of the phenomena. The conditions under which they were taken are as follows:

"On December 1, 1965, at 2040, we were asked by telephone, from various places, whether we had noticed anything strange on the moon, which was in its 8th day. I replied that at that very moment photographs were being taken. On developing these there appeared on the 6th one a fleet of flying disks (UFO's). On the following day, several journalists came to see me; I arranged a discussion with them and showed them the photos."

This photographic observation, which is completely authentic and

CHAPTER FIFTEEN SIGHTINGS & SATELLITES

is corroborated by the distant witnesses who called the observatory, is in itself remarkable, but Father Reyna continues:

"From the 2 observatories (there are 2 at San Miguel) I have followed many times with the naked eye or with binoculars the movements of UFO's. They almost always followed the artificial satellites or the rockets which put them into orbit, but always at a certain distance so as not to disturb them by their magnetic field. When the satellites enter the cone of the earth's shadow they disappear. However, the UFO's remain luminous and generally change direction, and this at fantastic speeds.

"One night we followed one of them with a telescope. I am going to draw on the reverse (of the page) a diagram of its movements. All this is absolutely certain and checked by technicians. I know that in France people take a great interest in UFO's and that one group of observers is trying to solve this riddle."

On the back of the Reverend Father's letter is found, under the title "The course of a UFO followed with a telescope of 100 times magnification," a description and an astounding drawing:

"From the ADHARA Observatory at San Miguel, Buenos Aires, on the clear night of 14th November, 1964, we were following in the telescope the satellite ECHO II, which was travelling from the north to the south pole. It appeared at 2037 hours almost on the same meridian as the observatory.

"At 2045h there arose in the west near Pegasus a UFO following a route perpendicular to the orbit of ECHO II and on the plane of this orbit. On approaching the satellite it deviated from its route, tracing a semi-circle (perhaps so as not to attract the satellite with its magnetic field), then continued on its way in an easterly direction, in the neighborhood of Orion, descending to the horizon. It made this journey in 3 minutes.

"At 2052h when ECHO II was at the zenith, the UFO rose from the

CHAPTER FIFTEEN SIGHTINGS & SATELLITES

southwest near Centaurus, going to meet ECHO II. On approaching the satellite it made a detour, then headed towards the northeast and descended to the horizon near Andromeda.

"For the 3rd time, at 2100h, it appeared near Altair, presenting itself in the form of a cigar, then becoming circular. On reaching the level of ECHO II it made the same detour as before, then, heading towards the south, in the direction of Canopus, finally disappeared below the southern horizon at the same time as ECHO II.

"As there were many people inside and outside the observation dome, it could be followed and observed from within and without, on its various paths, by rapidly adjusting the opening of the dome, so that all could see it. Near the horizon we saw it with perfection. It could be observed quite clearly, its upper turret of a greenish color. Its central ring was of a yellow color and its edges were blue. Sometimes it filled the whole field of the telescope and appeared bigger than the full moon. The speed of ECHO II being about 25,000 km per hour, the UFO must have been traveling at more than 100,000 km/h, as can be deducted from the journeys which it made at the same altitude as the satellite. The spectacle offered by the UFO which followed ECHO II was fantastic."

A priest of the Society of Jesus, Rev. Father Benito Reyna is an astronomer, biologist, doctor of science and teacher in the University del Salvador in Buenos Aires. He also directs scientific centers in 3 different places (at Santa Fe and in the 2 observatories of San Miguel). He has been doing research in astronomy and biology for 30 years.

San Miguel is situated 40km. west of Buenos Aires. In this town the Jesuits have 2 observatories: an "Observatory of Cosmic Physics," and a simple astronomical observatory, the ADHARA Observatory. Existing since 1935, the former is one of the most complete in the world, for in the 6 hectares (15 acres) which it covers, it has, as well as 3 observation domes, chemistry, biology,

CHAPTER FIFTEEN SIGHTINGS & SATELLITES

entomology, physics, electronics, heliophysics, meteorology and seismology departments. A radio telescope is being built. There is also a telescope for the observation of solar phenomena, which permits the taking of photographs of the sun in the morning and the afternoon.

The ADHARA observatory is a private observatory created by Louis Ferro, who has done studies in physics at Turin and Padoue. The various telescopes were made especially for studying the secrets of space and making them known to all the visitors who come each night to his home. In 4 years he has made some notable discoveries. In recent months he has discovered big explosions or solar "souftlets" and has measured their size by methods which he has invented. His calculations have been confirmed by the big observatories and he has received commendation from Mt. Palomar. The position of the ADHARA observatory is as follows: Lat. 34°42'40" W.

For many years the witnesses who reported fantastic manoeuvres or the speed of these UFO's were thought to be mad. But, the San Miguel observation has put a different construction on the matter. 100,000 km/h is really startling, not to mention the arcs described around the American satellite.

In the case of the observation of Father Reyna and the technicians who, being with him, confirmed this observation, we are dealing with an indisputably qualified astronomer who has made use of a telescope which has a magnification of 100 times. Also, the appearance and the antics of the object observed prove that this object could not be a natural phenomenon. If ever an observation was authenticated by the qualification of the principal observer and the agreement of parallel witnesses, this is it.

The fact that Father Reyna is a member of a religious order where very strict discipline reigns adds to the genuineness of his declarations. An individual person can take upon himself the risk of making a statement which could expose him to ridicule. It is

CHAPTER FIFTEEN SIGHTINGS & SATELLITES

unthinkable that a Jesuit would bear a testimony which would jeopardize the reputation of himself, his order, and his superiors.

It is impossible to doubt the reality of these things. As in the lawcourt, one can not object to witnesses who have the convincing evidence of those whom we have presented here.

One cannot see how this object could be put in the category of natural objects or known machines. The amazing antics of this saucer which appeared literally to play with ECHO II are desperately humiliating for terrestrial astronautics. In comparison, the interminable manoeuvres of the orbital rendezvous of Gemini and Agena, which are nevertheless the crowning glory of our technology, seem miserably useless, if not ridiculous. The manoeuvrability of the San Miguel object astounds us. It seems to ignore all restrictions which the laws of space mechanics impose on our space vehicles. It acts as if no law of gravity existed.

In view of such acrobatics in pursuit of ECHO II, who could pretend that this chaser of satellites was a secret experimental machine released from some Russian or American laboratory? When cosmonauts are to be launched into space, don't you think that the Soviet and American technicians use the best material and methods available in order to preserve the lives of their men?

At its launching, ECHO II had an orbit whose perigee was 1,033 km. and apogee was 1,313 km. It is therefore, at an altitude of more than 1,000 km. (620 miles) that Father Reyna and the other witnesses saw the saucer. Now what natural phenomenon, what exospheric globular lightning flash could pursue, giving 3 performances, with such precision, a satellite orbiting at an altitude of more than 1,000 km.? You tell us! This watchdog of ECHO II was certainly nothing vague like ionized gas in the upper atmosphere. Seen in the telescope, with a beauty exceeding that of the full moon, it appeared as an object of fixed proportions whose clearness amazed the spectators, and in which could be seen zones of color, geometrically divided.

CHAPTER FIFTEEN SIGHTINGS & SATELLITES

Father Reyna's report is an undeniable document, but it is also, at the same time, a decisive document. It puts to shame all the "explanations" by which those who hold to scientific dogmatism have sought in vain to discredit one of the biggest and perhaps the most serious enigmas of the present time and the past. It literally pulverizes them; at the same time the saucer which he describes itself pulverizes, as far as we are aware, all the records of altitude or speed which have ever been recorded in all the known history of these mysterious machines.

The figure given by the Rev. Father has to be seen in space, and he told us that ECHO II, a polar satellite, appeared "almost on the same meridian as the observatory." If we understand this properly, it signifies that the orbit of ECHO II is found, at the moment of passing, on an almost vertical plane for the observer. Therefore, the routes of approach and the antics of the saucer must have been almost horizontal to the observer. Under these conditions it seems certain that the paths traced by the saucer between two encounters with the satellite must have been much longer than the orbital path traced by the satellite itself from one point of encounter to the other.

The saucer originated near Pegasus, then, grazing ECHO II at an altitude of 1,000 kin., reached the horizon only 3 minutes after its appearance. This confirms the speed attributed to the saucer by Father Reyna.

A speed of 100,000 km/h (62,000 m.p.h.) — which practically corresponds with the orbital velocity of the earth — is, as we have said, a startling speed. A machine capable of such a speed is undoubtedly a space machine, and such a one that our ingenuity has never realized.

Let us take the escape velocity from the earth, for altitude 0, as equal to 11.2 km/sec., being 40,000 km/h. 100,000 km/h, or 28 km/sec., is 21/2 times this value and already more than half the

CHAPTER FIFTEEN SIGHTINGS & SATELLITES

escape velocity from the solar system, on the plane of the earth's orbit (42 km/sec.). It is almost double the 3rd cosmic velocity (16.6 km/sec.).

This "3rd cosmic velocity" is that which it is necessary to give, in the direction of the orbital velocity of our planet, to a terrestrial object going away from the sun, and therefore already aided by this orbital velocity, in order to permit it to escape, not only from the earth, but from the solar system.

The average orbital velocity of the earth is about 29.77 km/sec. One must, to attain the escape velocity of the solar system (42 km/sec.), add to this velocity 12.23 km.sec. But is necessary besides to escape the earth's gravity, which requires a velocity of 11.82 km/sec. Finally, by designating the 3rd cosmic force by V, we have, in (km=sec.):

$$V^2 = (12.23)^2 + (11.18)^2$$
$$\text{Therefore } V = 16.56 \text{ km/sec.}$$

The object showed that it was capable of deceleration which was perhaps more fantastic than its speed, since it was able, in a few minutes, to slow this tremendous speed to a movement so slow that it could be observed with perfect clarity in the center of a telescope of more than 100 times magnification. The ease of the manoeuvres seems like child's play compared with our techniques and the energy which we put into propelling and manoeuvring our space vehicles.

Father Reyna writes in his report "I have followed many times with the naked eye or with binoculars the movements of the UFO's. They almost always followed the artificial satellites or the rockets which put them into orbit."

We have no reason to think that the Rev. Father would wish to deceive his correspondent, unless his eye was deceived by the nature of that which he had observed. But a question arises in the

CHAPTER FIFTEEN SIGHTINGS & SATELLITES

mind of the reader. "If the Rev. Father was able to see these things, how do you think they were able to escape the notice of those who had launched the rockets and satellites and who have at their disposal, for the pur-pose of following their projectiles or space vehicles, powerful and highly specialized means of locating them?

A reasonable answer doesn't seem doubtful: one cannot think that the companions of their space vehicles are going to deceive the vigilance of the electromagnetic or optical tracking stations established by the Americans or Russians. They certainly know that they exist. The U.S. Government has known all the time that strange machines are observing what we are doing in outer space. There is no doubt that this corroborates Father Reyna's statement. Both Russia and America have come to the conclusion that "Flying saucers exist and their origin is extraterrestrial, and their arrival, in a relatively short time, must permit verification of this affirmation."

In his letter of 20th April, 1966, Father Reyna writes:

"On the 1st of February and the 6th of the same month of this year, we followed the routes of some UFO's. One night, 5 of them in a V formation, crossed the sky horizontally. From various parts of the Republic of Argentina some remarkable information frequently arrives concerning these flying objects."

Father Reyna's report leaves no doubt as to the existence and the fantastic capabilities of these UFO's and their great interest in our space attempts.

"Phenomenes Spatiaux," June, 1966—

CHAPTER SIXTEEN

CONTACTS & CYCLES

In August of 1953, a Mexico City taxi-driver named Salvador Villanveva Medina was hired by a Texan and his wife to drive them in their own car from Mexico City to Laredo.

When about 7 miles north of Valles, Mexico, on Mexican Route 85 the car broke down. The Texans obtained a ride back to Valles to get a mechanic, but due to delays they spent the night there. The Mexican taxi-driver had been told to stay with the car until they returned.

He had pulled the car off the road, and had crawled under it to work on the gears. It was just getting dusk when he heard footsteps approaching, and he saw what he thought was some type of aviator, because the man was dressed in a one-piece garment resembling a ski-suit.

As Salvador got out from under the car the man spoke to him in Spanish and asked him what was wrong with the car. He noted that it was an "educated," Castillian type of Spanish. The man had fine wavy hair which reached almost to his shoulders.

He also noted that the man wore a wide belt, which seemed to have holes in it, and these would light up now and then as though there were electric bulbs inside. Occasionally a humming noise came from the belt. Under the man's arm was a helmet like those used by football players, but fine wires extended out from the ear pieces.

Salvador was very frightened. After some conversation the man's belt began to hum louder and he put on his helmet and departed through the brush to the right of the road in the direction he said

CHAPTER SIXTEEN CONTACTS & CYCLES

his ship was located. Salvador watched the lighted belt until it disappeared from view.

Salvador then went to sleep in the car, but was later aroused by the "aviator" who had returned with a tall companion similarly dressed. He invited the two men into the car and the three of them sat on the front seat and conversed until almost daybreak.

Gradually it dawned on Salvador that these men were from another world, and he gathered considerable information regarding their manner of life, but none regarding the location or name of their world. For example, their world had a single government. Also the children were raised in community schools and educated according to their natural abilities and talents. As the hours passed they also asked Salvador many questions. He felt a great friendliness and all his fears departed.

Toward morning they said they had to leave but invited Salvador to accompany them. Off the road the ground was very muddy. Salvador's shoes were covered with mud, but he noticed that the two spacemen appeared to walk above the mud, and that no mud adhered to their shoes.

About one-and-a-half kilometers off the road in a little hollow they came upon a round saucer-shaped ship about 10 meters in diameter and about 5 meters high with portholes. One of the spacemen made a signal with his arms and a door opened in the side of the ship. They entered and invited Salvador to come aboard also. At this point Salvador became frightened and ran back toward the car. He watched in the direction of the ship, and after some minutes saw it rise slowly above the trees glowing with light. It hovered momentarily and then took off at great speed.

Salvador is a very humble, earnest and religious young Mexican, father of seven children. He regards his experience with awe and religious reverence. At first he tried to tell it to the truck driver who took him back to Mexico City, but was laughed at and accused of

CHAPTER SIXTEEN CONTACTS & CYCLES

smoking Marihuana. On arriving home he and his wife agreed it was best to keep it a secret.

It was not until saucer-sightings began to appear in Mexican newspapers months later that he decided to tell his story. It has been carefully checked and re-enacted by impartial investigators, who feel it is authentic.

Submitted and verified in Mexico by Bryant and Helen Reeve.

"And the likeness of the *firmament upon the heads* of the living creatures was as the colour of the terrible crystal, *stretched forth over their heads above.*" Ezekiel 1-22.

Naturally, in Ezekiel's time when nothing was known on the Earth of space travel, aircraft, balloons, etc., this was a pretty good description of a space helmet made of clear plastic, or glass.

In the Medina contact with two people from a spacecraft that landed in Mexico, Medina stated that the spacepeople were carrying clear glass helmets under their arms.

Medina also said the two people were wearing wide belts that seemed to flash lights out of holes in the belts.

Ezekiel described the anti-gravity belts in 1-27. "And I saw as the colour of amber, as the *appearance of fire round about within it, from the appearance of his loins even upward, and from the appearance of his loins even downward, I saw as it were the appearance of fire, and it had brightness round about.*"

In that "oil lamp age" you can imagine Ezekiel trying to tell the Earth's people of his contact with spacepeople. Today the things he professed are part of a *holy book.*

In this "electronic age" multitudes with an "oil lamp understanding" cannot be converted to comprehend the connection

CHAPTER SIXTEEN CONTACTS & CYCLES

between the button they push and the electric light lighting.

Howard Menger explained how the space people he contacted wore these light pulsating anti-gravity belts, and easily floated over a high board fence in his back yard.

The "experts of ignorance" have altered the Bible in the last few years, so that the meanings are now changed. In the Scofield or King James versions, the wheels within wheels are described only as wheels (Ezekiel 1-18). No statement is made as to what kind of wheels; disc, wire spokes, or gear wheels. Now the New American Revision of the Bible adds "spokes" to the wheels (Ezekiel 1-18). Their "horse and buggy" revision doesn't say whether they are wooden spokes, steel spokes, or wire spokes. In this disc wheel age they could have at least specified what kind of spokes, as long as they "knew" enough to add spokes.

The "hush-hush" group are even altering our Bible to make it conform to their "security" clauses. For the information of these experts, the *pulsating* light from the belts and ships of the spacepeople is the secret of overcoming gravity.

Ezekiel pulled an "Angelucci" on the people back there in those donkey days. In 3-14, he recounts:

So the spirit *lifted* me up and took me away, and I went in bitterness, in the heat of my spirit; but the hand of the Lord was strong upon me."

This is in the Holy Bible. The things that happened centuries ago are labeled *religion today.* The very same things are *happening today* but Satan's agents are trying to keep it secret.

The Lord God said, in Ezekiel 20: 35 and 36. "And I will bring you into the wilderness of the people, and there will I plead with you *face to face.* Like as I pleaded with your fathers in the wilderness of the land of Egypt, so will I plead with you, saith the Lord God."

CHAPTER SIXTEEN CONTACTS & CYCLES

So we *have come face to face* with many space contacts for various reasons. *"In that day shall messengers go forth from me in ships* to make the careless Ethiopians afraid, and great pain shall come upon them, as in the day of Egypt: for, lo, it cometh." Ezekiel 29-9.

If Isaiah, Ezekiel, Matthew, John, and all the others had not written their accounts of their contacts and experiences with the spacepeople, there wouldn't be much of a Bible.

Earthly religions are all based on "heavenly creatures," "angels," or in short spacepeople. There wouldn't be a Christianity today unless these visitors from space existed.

Air Force denials that these craft and their people exist, is bluntly a flat denial of the Bible, Christianity, and all other religions. It is surprising that the Creator managed to make this vast universe without the knowledge and help of these "experts."

Ezekiel referred to the Lord as a man in 43-6. "And I heard *him* speaking unto me out of the house; and the *man* stood by me."

The very things the Bible says will happen in the latter days are happening *now*. Face to face contacts. Wars, and rumors of wars. Thunderings in the skies (sonic blasts). Lights in the heavens (spaceships). Rogues in the high offices of the government and the churches.

Each person will *soon* have to decide where they stand.

Behold, he cometh *with clouds; and every eye shall see him,* and they also which pierced him: and all kindreds of the earth shall wail because of him. Even so, Amen." Revelations 1:7.

Throughout the New Testament the return of Christ is connected with *clouds, power,* and *great glory.* St. Luke 21:27. St. Mark 14:62. St. Matthew 24:30.

CHAPTER SIXTEEN CONTACTS & CYCLES

The U.F.O.'s are often seen and photographed ionizing a cloud around them, or coming from a *cloud* that was formed by the electrostatic field around the craft. They also demonstrate *power* in their rapid acceleration and high speeds. When witnessed with the irridescent colors of the rainbow, and changing colors of the force field around the craft with different energy applications, this certainly manifests *glory* — as it is a glorious sight to see.

Not only is the return of Christ connected with *clouds,* but also when he ascended before multitudes after his resurrection. In Acts 1:9 "And when he had spoken these things, while they beheld, he was taken up; and a *cloud* received him out of their sight." And in Acts 1:10 and 11,

"And while they looked steadfastly toward heaven as he went up, behold, two men stood by them in white apparel; Which also said, Ye men of Galilee, why stand ye gazing up into heaven? This same Jesus which is taken up from you into heaven, shall so come in like manner as ye have seen him go into heaven."

A *cloud* by day and fire by night also directed the Israelites in the time of Moses.

Prophecy in the Bible is being fulfilled daily if one watches what is taking place. However, the return of Christ has been expected and unfulfilled for several generations. Is the clue to His return given in Revelation 1:7, where it says, "and *every eye shall see him?"*

It stands to reason that he could not travel making personal appearances throughout every city and small town worldwide, *but* today we have *worldwide T.V.* and *every eye* could see him under these conditions; with motion pictures where T.V. is not shown in isolated areas.

Certainly there would have to be a condition existent upon the earth that would make His return of great value to the people. This

CHAPTER SIXTEEN CONTACTS & CYCLES

condition already exists in geophysical, moral, military, economic, and racial crisis. It should be evident by now that the brains of the world are only making matters worse in their power hungry activities.

Whether one believes in Christ, or not, is not the point of this article. The point is that the conditions of earth require outside intervention, and the time conforms to the requirements of prophecy.

"Then we which are *alive* and *remain* shall be caught up together *with them in the clouds*, to meet the Lord in the air: and so shall we ever be with the Lord." First Thessalonians 4, 17.

In the gospel of St. Matthew (1:1-17) the genealogy of Joseph is given. Further it explains (Mat. 1:16) that Joseph was the husband of Mary and by implication leads you to believe that he was the father of Jesus.

By reading carefully (Mat. 1:18-25) it is plain that Joseph became the husband of Mary "before they came together" and after "she was found with child." In Mat. 1:25 it is made clear that Joseph "knew her not." It is evident that Joseph was the same as a stepfather to Jesus. There was no blood of Joseph in Jesus.

Mary is one of the spacepeople; one of the "male and female" that God created (Gen. 1:27) before He ended His work (Gen. 2:2), and before the crossbreeding of Adam and Eve took place.

Mary volunteered for the assignment of bringing through birth — to the Earth — a son of the Adamic race of man. Jesus also accepted the assignment knowing before his earthly birth what it entailed. Mary became pregnant and was landed on the Earth by the spacepeople of God's pure creation.

The three wise men were also true descendants of the Adamic race. They "came from the East," having already been aware by thought

CHAPTER SIXTEEN CONTACTS & CYCLES

transference that a true creation of God was to be brought forth.

They followed the spacecraft called "the Star of Bethlehem" (Mat. 2:9) until it hovered over the inn where Jesus was being born by Mary. A force field, generated by the spacecraft, looks like a star when seen at night.

The spacepeople "stood by" at the birth. The ones aboard were in communication telepathically not only with Mary but also with the three wise men (Mat. 2:10).

The wise men were informed "of" God, not "by" God (Mat. 2:12) through His agents, the Adamic people aboard the craft. "In a dream" (Mat. 2:12) is as near a description of the state of consciousness as could be expressed. Any state of meditation required for a clear reception, in thought transference is dream-like because it excludes physical conditions and things (Try it, you may be astounded by your dormant possibilities).

Now that you can see the connection between the birth of Jesus and the spacecraft we shall go further. In Mat. 3:16 is given evidence again of the "transistor beam." This is the same beam that Jesus was retrieved bodily with at his resurrection. The same beam was used to lower Fred Reagan to the ground, when his airplane collided with a spacecraft over Georgia in 1951. This is also the beam that picked up Noah and Enoch. The transisto r beam was also used to bring aboard a rocket test airplane and the pilot at Rogers Air Force Base. This was written up as fiction to cover the facts.

These spacecraft are the "signs in the skys" referred to many times in the Bible. They signify the return of the man called Jesus who will come "out of the clouds" (Acts 1:11).

After God made man He finished His work (Gen. 2.3). The Creator made man to manifest His creations. God brings about His doings through man. Man either manifests the constructive

CHAPTER SIXTEEN CONTACTS & CYCLES

creations of God, or the destructive actions of Satan.

The spacepeople informed me, that when one of their people gets destructive ideas they isolate that one and place him on a planet. It looks like this is the planet. The whole economy of the nations of Earth is based on manufacturing weapons of destruction. Everything on Earth is valued by its worth in money. — The beast is ruling in the form of the golden calf.

Insignias of war do not designate authority; they designate brutish force. If all this vainglorious display is so necessary, why then the commandment "thou shalt not kill?"

Aren't the administrative branches of governments the representatives of the people? It is time our representatives take the brass by the horns. The people are entitled to know the facts and the truth.

The time is short. You are either an instrument of God, or a pawn of the devil. Jesus is about to land amidst you. Are you ready to be "taken up" or are you one who will "be left."

And what will ye do in the day of visitation, and in the desolation which shall come from far? To whom will ye flee for help? And where will ye leave your glory?" Isaiah 10:3.

The day of *visitation* is here *now*. Many visitors not of this Earth have walked among the people. Their ships have been seen visually, photographed, tracked on radar, and chased by jets.

Authority has hidden this great event in secrecy and fear, because it will destroy their economic god Mammon — and they have no control over this condition.

The *desolation* that will come from far should be evidenced by the build-up of atomic powers, 100 Megaton bombs, fleets, armies, and air forces.

CHAPTER SIXTEEN CONTACTS & CYCLES

"To whom will ye flee for help?"

The authorities of civil defense one year cry "evacuation is the only hope." Now they cry "the best protection is in individual bomb shelters."

This may not be the best way, but they changed their tune when their economic god said "there is no *profit* in evacuation. Let us demand permits that cost the people money and let us make a code and we can make sure no-one can save themselves without our permission."

It is hard to understand anyone building a bomb shelter for their family and themselves. Will people never learn that selfishness only ends in self destruction? Individual bomb shelters are "dead end rat traps."

When the desolation comes you and your loved ones will rush into your hole in the ground for safety from the invisible, intangible radiation of fallout. After a few hours, or days, your neighbors who didn't have the financial means, or foresight to build their own bomb shelters will get hungry, scared and desperate.

Just a few, or many, of your hungry neighbors will say "Joe has food in his bomb shelter" — and there you are trapped in the ground. These "friends" will get your food either directly by forced entry, or plug up your air and ventilation pipes. Your shelter that made money for the Mammonites proves to be your death trap or grave.

Your only safe place is with many others and it won't cost you anything. Of course the civil defense authorities will never suggest this to you because there is no profit in it.

Go to the nearest storm drain entry and get into the big concrete pipes that run under the street. This network of storm drains runs clear out of the city and you could go through them for miles with

CHAPTER SIXTEEN CONTACTS & CYCLES

manholes available at intervals. In this event your entire expenditure would be for a canteen to carry water, a flashlight and extra batteries, and some concentrated food.

"For the leaders of this people cause them to err; and they that are led of them are destroyed." Isaiah 9:16.

When the people of wealth hold the highest offices of the governments of the world, how can they think any other way than they do? They arrived at positions of authority through Mammon. Will Satan condemn Satan? Will the wealthy leaders in authority be concerned more with what the poor people cry for, or with what their drinking buddies of association and class ask for?

Desolation is now knocking at the door. Desperation will result from the survival instinct. Deceit has been prevalent throughout the "dog eat dog" history of nations subject to the rule of Mammon (money).

Your only hope to escape personal danger is to "get out from among them" as the Bible says.

If your survival instinct has any foresight you will be getting into action now.

As for my people, *children are their oppressors,* and women rule over them. O my people, *they which lead thee cause thee to err,* and destroy *the way of thy paths.* (Isaiah, 3:12).

Could the juvenile delinquency of our days be more accurately stated by the prophets? Are the children of today influenced to a greater degree to form gangs, to murder old people, to wreck schools and take narcotics than in generations gone by? No! There are not greater nor more numerous influences working today than ever before.

The prime reason that the youngsters of today are more delinquent

CHAPTER SIXTEEN CONTACTS & CYCLES

than in past generations is because they cannot see any security in their future. They see their parents both working in order to maintain a decent standard of living. They see enforced military training for continuous warfare, as soon as they graduate from high school.

They read daily newspapers, which print a continuous expose of crooked political grafters. The young people are forced to accept work in industry under a collusive segregation, of classifications that do not recognize ability.

They go to church, to hear dogmatic poppy-cock that is not demonstrated by the clergy, nor the congregation.

No! The children are not to blame. The blame is clearly pointed out in Isaiah's prophecy: "They which lead thee cause thee to err." This does not mean governments, or schools, or churches; it means the people who operate these institutions.

Everyone knows by now, that it does not matter which of the two political parties are in power, the program is invariably the same.

The youngsters are run through schools on a conveyor-belt-production principle.

The churches — efficiently commercialized — place their trust in shekels rather than in righteousness, confusing the religions for the multitude.

The politicians "play ball" with the special interests using smooth words for the public and hiding their well-greased hands in their pockets.

Can the youth be blamed because they see all this hypocrisy, allowing no security for their future? Not by a darn sight.

"And destroy the way of thy paths." That sage Isaiah said a mouth-

CHAPTER SIXTEEN   CONTACTS & CYCLES

ful way ahead of time.

The governments being in the insurance business, the atomic energy business, the shipping business and everybody else's business — through classified rules — permit the "special interests" to have all the advantages.

Of course we need laws and regulations to conduct any government sensibly, but one expose after another should indicate by now that many, in between the laws and the business end, are operating with the knowledge of the red-tape system supporters in government.

How do the juvenile minds react to these conditions? They read of top people getting away with these rackets. They are squirted through a mass-production schooling only to be grabbed by the army and trained to kill.

It is the failure of past generations, viewed by these youngsters, that has brought about their delinquency. The adults of today are also responsible.

Isiah's prophecies are registering now before our eyes. In Chapter 6:11, 12, it is written: "Then said I, Lord, how long?" And he answered, *Until the cities be wasted without inhabitant, and the houses without man, and the land be utterly desolate.* What does this mean? Does this fit our time of today? What could cause "the cities to be wasted without inhabitants, houses without man, and the land to be utterly desolate? There is only one answer today — the radiation from atomic bombs. Further, in Isaiah Chapter 13:20 it says, "It shall never be inhabited, neither shall it be dwelt in *from generation to generation.*" Again radioactivity is the only thing that would prevent cities from being lived in over generations of time.

Isaiah's prophecy has been confirmed already by recent atomic tests at Yucca Flats in Nevada. Isaiah said, in Chapter 3:24, "And it

CHAPTER SIXTEEN CONTACTS & CYCLES

shall come to pass, that instead of sweet smell there shall be stink; and *instead of a girdle* a rent; and instead of well set hair baldness; and in-stead of a stomacher a girding of sackcloth; and *burning instead of beauty."*

Ask the people of Mesquite, Nevada, 110 miles East of Yucca Flats, what radioactivity does at that distance. Many men and women have lost every hair on their *heads* and *bodies* — *baldness!* — The desert that was beautiful is now burned at Yucca Flats.

Consolation for America, which is Jerusalem. Isaiah prophesied also that this country will be saved by the spacepeople, in Chapter 31:5, "As *bird flying* so will the Lord of *hosts* defend Jerusalem; defending also he will deliver it; *and passing over* he will preserve it." Everyone should read about what Isaiah prophesied for us who are living today. He included everything.

In Chapter 32:2, he said "And a man shall be as a hiding place from the wind, and a covert from the tempest; as rivers of water in a dry place; as the shadow of a great rock in a weary land."

The people of today are awakening. This is the time of great changes; a master cycle, a major cycle and a minor cycle are culminating at the same time. Are you aware of your part in this cosmic drama?

CHAPTER SEVENTEEN

PURSUIT & PURPOSE

The Ministry of Universal Wisdom, Incorporated, is here to minister unto others. Through its scientific branch, The College of Universal Wisdom, we are putting God's eternal laws of magnetism, electricity, and ions into practical application for the good of all humanity.

These natural laws provide all manner of comfort to do the work for humankind today. We do not have a church building for people to collect in to hear words. Our building is a machine to apply God's scientific laws to alleviate the greatest scourge the human race faces — ageing flesh of the physical body. Our principle of operation is ten times simpler than color television. We are three-quarters finished with this machine. We have volunteer Doctors who want to serve on our Medical Board of Advisors; to conduct "before" and "after" checks of people in our test program. Our scientific associates have not charged a cent for their time and talent to assist this project.

When it is operating, another year or two will be required for adjustments and testing. Let us all extend ourselves at this time in a drive to prevent ageing in our youthful people, and charge our elderly people with the energy of their younger years.

This is not a dream. It is a method to a fuller, longer, energetic life for everybody. Let one generation live to correct its own mistakes!

THE "INTEGRATRON"

This four story high, 55 foot in diameter, dome shaped, electro-static magnetic generator, is a people-sized follow-up on smaller

CHAPTER SEVENTEEN PURSUIT & PURPOSE

bench re-search. This giant machine incorporates two basic electro-magnetic principles that have been used in science for many years. The only differences in our application of these two principles, is that we apply them simultaneously with a multiple wave in their operation.

The only new principle in this machine is that we control the resonance, and polarity reversal interruptions, through a time function that creates a 'time zone."

Where Georges Lakovsky created regeneration in the cell structure of his subjects, as a side effect of his basic principle, we use his side effect as our basic purpose. His subjects were required to spend up to several weeks, about 15 minutes a day, in order to obtain results in the emanation of his multiple wave oscillator.

Through our time function control, we can perform his side effect in an instant. We will be creating, in two split fields, a common core flux. The division in these fields is where the "time zone" is.

All selection of our test subjects, who are elderly people, who want to go through the "Integratron," will be controlled by our Medical Board of Advisors. A prominent retired doctor has agreed to head this Medical Board as soon as we are ready for our test program.

When this machine is finished, and our test program is completed, the "Integratron" is designed to handle up to 10,000 people a day. They will walk in one door and be guided through the fields by plastic tube rails on both sides of the course. They will walk through a 270° arc and come out of the machine at a second door.

This project started on a small scale in 1953, and the "Integratron" machine was started in 1957. The structure was erected in 1959 and since then we have been making tooling, templates, and parts. Subassemblies are finished, and we are now in the final assembly stage.

CHAPTER SEVENTEEN PURSUIT & PURPOSE

We depend entirely on public gifts to finance this beneficent project. When it is finished and operational, there will be no charge for anyone to go through it.

The "Integratron"

CHAPTER SEVENTEEN PURSUIT & PURPOSE

The Bible says "death shall be the last thing to be overcome." If this is accomplished, someone has to do it. We are trying.

The building I have been instructed to build is a 21st Century version of the Tabernacle that Moses constructed.

Much of the terminology for various parts of the building and the apparatus therein are different today but their scientific functions are the same.

Fortunately with modern technology and manufacturing methods we do not have to make the parts of acacia wood and then cover them with metallic foil. This method was used in Moses' time because they had no machinery to make metallic parts. Therefore they made the part of wood and covered it with metal, giving it the same conductive quality electrically and the same polarity abilities magnetically.

Moses' Tabernacle used the positive power principle of the Great Pyramid of Gizeh, exactly the same principle as we are using in this building.

Exodus 25:9 tells Moses how to make the *instruments* to operate the apparatus.

"According to all that I shew thee, after the pattern of the tabernacle, and the pattern of *all the instruments* thereof, even so shall ye make it." Today we would call Moses' "rings" coils, "staves" condensers "tenons" wires; although Moses' "silver sockets" are still called sockets, or outlets.

Moses surrounded his Tabernacle with skins and cloth curtains. Thus it was all of non-metallic covering. We are doing the same, but with plywood and fiberglass.

The apparatus they made for inside the Tabernacle was called an "ark." Our equipment will be the same, generating an *electro-static*

CHAPTER SEVENTEEN PURSUIT & PURPOSE

arc.

The dome of our building is described in Exodus 25:11, "And thou shalt overlay it with pure gold, within and without shalt thou overlay it, and shalt make upon it a crown (dome) of gold round about."

We do not have to use gold leaf as we have the less expensive aluminum foil of today, which Moses didn't have in his time. Can a Leyden jar be described much more accurately than as in the above Biblical verse?

Moses talked with the Lord who entered his Tabernacle, as explained by the Lord himself in Exodus 25:22. "And there I will meet with thee, and I will commune with thee from above the mercy seat, from between the two cherubims which are upon the ark of the testimony, of all things which I will give thee in commandment unto the children of Israel."

The cherubims as described by Ezekiel had four faces (the same as formerly on the Great Pyramid), that of a man, a lion, an eagle, and an ox. This has also been symbolized in the Egyptian gods. The Sphinx being the man and lion in combination, the eagle symbolizing the ability to fly or soar, and the ox or Hebrew Tau, which symbolized the male generative organs. The wings of the cherubim were discharge points, today called an air gap. The cherubim were depicted by Ezekiel as "like coals of fire," which our apparatus will look like when in operation.

"And thou shalt make curtains of goats hair to be a covering upon the tabernacle: eleven curtains shalt thou make." (Exodus 26:7).

The goat's hair was used as a friction generator of static electricity. It is well known that a pith ball coated with *gold leaf* is repelled by a glass rod that has been electrified by rubbing with silk; and is attracted to a rubber rod that has been rubbed with fur and vice-versa, showing the different polarity reactions. Hair carries a

CHAPTER SEVENTEEN PURSUIT & PURPOSE

positive polarity charge, silk a negative.

"And thou shalt make forty sockets of silver under the twenty boards, two sockets under one board for his two tenons, and two sockets under another board for his two tenons." (Exodus 26:19).

"And they shall be coupled together *beneath*, and they shall be *coupled together above* the head of it unto one ring: thus shall it be for them both; they shall be for the two corners." (Exodus 26:24).

Our building has one "ring'" that rotates on a track completely around the outside of the building.

What I am bringing out in this short article is only a very small part of the *many* verses giving mechanical data on the functioning of Moses' Tabernacle. Only because of an acceleration of critical events on the Earth is it now necessary that I put these things into public knowledge, otherwise they would not have been revealed until after the apparatus was perfectly working.

"And it came to pass, as Moses entered into the tabernacle, the *cloudy pillar descended* and stood at the door of the tabernacle, and the Lord talked with Moses." (Exodus 33:9 }.

"And the Lord spake unto Moses *face to face*, as a man speaketh unto his friend . . ." (Exodus 33:11).

All of the technical data needed is not in the Holy Books of the various religions. What is given in these books is not enough to build the regenerator; however, *I have been given the additional needed data to make a functioning modern Tabernacle.*

"For the cloud of the Lord was upon the tabernacle by day, and fire was on it by night, in the sight of all the house of Israel, throughout all their journeys." (Exodus 40:38).

CHAPTER SEVENTEEN PURSUIT & PURPOSE

The Author And " Time Machine"

CHAPTER SEVENTEEN PURSUIT & PURPOSE

We all know the Tabernacle Moses made was *portable*. The fire seen by night was the electro-static discharge corona, and the cloud by day was the ionization of the moisture in the air causing a cloud to condense around the Tabernacle. The effect around our building will be identical.

"Look upon Zion, the city of our solemnities: thine eyes shall see JerUSAlem a quiet habitation, *a tabernacle that shall not be taken down*; not one of the stakes thereof shall ever be removed, neither shall any of the cords thereof be broken." (Isaiah 33:20).

Our building is a permanent structure.

"And a man shall be as a hiding place from the wind, and a covert from the tempest, as rivers of water in a dry place, *as the shadow of a great rock in a weary land."* (Isaiah 32:2).

Can it be coincidence that the Bible says, "Make straight in the desert a highway for our God," (Isaiah 40:3), and five roads leading to Giant Rock are straight? Frank Critzer (the man who made the roads to Giant Rock) was called "straight road Critzer" by the people who knew him.

My job is *not to save the world*. That job belongs to the coming One. I came only to prepare an instrument much needed for the Earth's future events. Our research is for the benefit of *all* humanity; Jews, Gentiles, Blacks, Whites, etc.; in short all of the people of the race of Man.

There are literally thousands of photographs of U.F.O.'s. What is more phenomenal is the ability of the people in the spaceships to cause our photographs to reveal, or hide, many things as a result of their advanced knowledge to cause refraction, reflection, bend light, diffuse light, and control many things through rays and beams.

In this picture I am standing in bright sunlight which casts shadows

CHAPTER SEVENTEEN PURSUIT & PURPOSE

from the bushes, the sign beside me, and the dome in the background. All of these shadows point to the Northeast, as the Sun was in the Southwest. Now observe the lighted area *before* me and *behind* me on the ground — *brighter* than the Sun on the ground in the rest of the picture. This light is coming from overhead and casts *my shadow* almost 60° off from the other shadows — and my shadow is on the ground *where the Sun it shining*.

You see the Biblical prophecy has nailed it down too. The interplanetary hosts will be the ones who finally clean up the mess. These are the ones who have been responsible for the origin of every religion on the Earth; the visitors, angels, or spacepeople — whatever you wish to call them. God fulfills the destiny of planets, not humans.

CHAPTER NINETEEN *SPACE, ENERGIES & CONCEPT*

CHAPTER NINETEEN

SPACE, ENERGIES & CONCEPT

God in His infinite Wisdom caused all of his creations to function by perpetual motion. He maintains the balance of interchange by centering each creation and insulating each one from all others.

When He created the "A" lines of light force, He gave to them density — 1850 to a square centimeter. He gave them polarity (positive), gender (male, projective), motion — speed 186,000 miles per second — and matter in form of charged particles. He added energy (electromagnetic flux) and placed these creations throughout all space.

In opposition to the "A" lines of light He created the "B" lines of light force. The "B" lines are composed of density — 1257 lines per square centimeter. They cross between the "A" lines of force at 90 degrees, with motion at a speed of 202,000 miles per second. Their polarity is negative. Their gender is female, receptive.

Between the "breathing" of these two primary forces, He created rhythm. This brings about a "wave motion" which consolidates the individual lines into "bands." When "A" works inward, "B" works forward and when "A" works outward, "B" works backward. Rhythm, which establishes the "bands, levels, and density changes," is operated by strain or desire. Strain is the time between the "flight" of the female, negative lines of force and "the pursuit" of the male positive lines of force. When they encounter an object-creation (planet) that was "born" before by other "A" and "B" lines of light, they add to its rotation by spiral induction and partial penetration.

CHAPTER NINETEEN *SPACE, ENERGIES & CONCEPT*

The "B" negative lines are attracted to the positive core but are repelled by the "G" light insulation strata. Having penetrated the negative crust, they are repelled by it and take the "line of least resistance," out of the North Pole. By induction they attracted the positive core to rotate in one direction and in being repelled helped the negative crust to rotate in the opposite direction. The "A" positive lines of force work opposite and are emitted at the South Pole. As they emit from the poles they are met by the "G" lines of light and bent to their original course. The resistance in bending causes aurora borealis.

As they have reduced their charge and speed in adding power to the planet, they enter different levels as they emerge from the poles. Then the "G" lines of light, crossing between them and insulating them, bring them back through "rest" and "rhythmic breathing" to their original speed.

The "A" lines of force have more density and less speed than the "B" lines of force. The "B" lines have more speed and less density. This is the reason why the "A" positive lines of force, charged with matter, become the proton core of the earth. The faster "B" charged matter becomes the crust of our planet. This strain or desire is the eternal progressive spirit in all things: atoms, planets, people, solar systems, etc., that manifests action. Man refers to the pure strain of blood in breeding animals, yet he does not include himself in the proven process.

Strain in people is desire. When the desire exceeds the limits of capacity, the Father's agents of balance — the "A" or "B" lines of force —will bring about an opposite result. The "G," "A" and "B" lines are the "Us" referred to in the Bible (Gen. 1:26) when God said, "Let us make man." If man gets enough science of God, his health and religion will be living proof of his creative ability of life, not by destruction for death.

The terms which science has named "dimensions" are really

CHAPTER NINETEEN *SPACE, ENERGIES & CONCEPT*

densities.

The first density is Life; Causation; God; Father; Intelligence; Stillness; the all-pervading Light, called by us, "the G lines of light;" Endless Length (Ethe).

The second density includes Life and Motion; Gender; Polarity; physical bodies; animal life, birds, etc.; all forms of life in motion; "A" and "B" lines of force; Action by Instinct; Breadth (Bred-Ethe).

The third density consists of Life; Motion and Consciousness; Man; Self-recognition; the stage of ability to advance through self effort; Individual control of mind; Potential Christs; Intelligent form compositions of life and motion consolidated from patterns of atomic structure. An expanded state of life forms in motion through conscious control. Thickness ('Thinkness).

The fourth density comprises of Emergence; the sum of the first three densities; Life; Motion; Consciousness; Understanding; the progressive state of be-ing where all people understand each other and God. Thought transference, being the means of communication, makes it impossible for man to "hide behind false words." Man must demonstrate right thinking by right living, or be insulated from those who do so. Christhood. The ability to create instead of destroy.

The last mentioned density is the level of the beings who are flying the spacecraft in our atmosphere. As our solar system is progressing into their density-area of space, they are here to find out our conditions. They cannot accept "rotten apples" in their space "barrel." That is why the Bible says, "One shall be taken and one shall be left." They will only accept the ripe consciousness-developed fruit of mankind.

"G" light force is the primary cause, Intelligence of The Creator.

CHAPTER NINETEEN *SPACE, ENERGIES & CONCEPT*

"A" and "B" light force is secondary energy in motion.

The positive and negative lines of primary light energy cause all motion. Humans, atoms, suns, planets and galaxies are all powered by the same forces.

The Earth is an oversize electron of a predominantly negative polarity. Its rotation and orbit are the result of attraction and repulsion to the lines of primary light energy.

Magnetism in and around the Earth is a result of the Earth's interruption of the lines of primary light energy. Electricity is the result of the Earth's magnetism by a generator.

CHAPTER NINETEEN *SPACE, ENERGIES & CONCEPT*

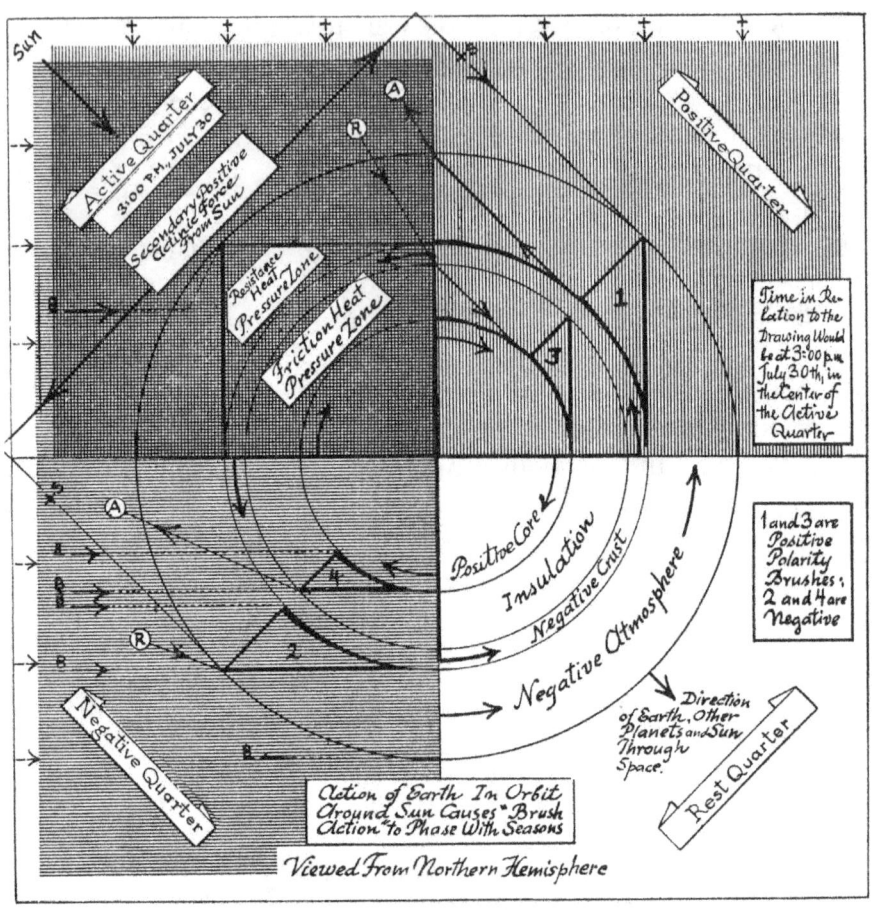

Rotation Principle Of The Earth

CHAPTER NINETEEN *SPACE, ENERGIES & CONCEPT*

As magnetism is the result of energy in motion, it can only effect a resultant energy by another motion interrupting it. Thus we turn an armature in a magnetic field to make electricity.

As the lines of primary light energy are in motion, any body that interrupts them will move according to its capacity and polarity charge. Electricity is the second by-product of primary light energy; Magnetism is the first. Neither can exist without the other because they are both part of each other — like people.

In the drawing we show only the positively charged core of the Earth, the negative crust, and the atmosphere in order to present the principle. Actually these charged strata and insulating layers extend to where they are smoothly repelled by strata around Mars and Venus.

The drawing is made with the Sun shining in the center of the Active Quarter from a 45 degree angle. The Sun is the alternator that changes polarity predominance from one hemisphere to the other every six months. The circles enclosing the "A" and "II" indicate the direction of the attracting and repelling forces. The Negative Primary Light attracts the positive core in the Negative Quarter and repels the negative crust. The opposite is true in the Positive Quarter. These two attracting and repelling "brushes" are changing position continuously as the Earth orbits.

The atmosphere is actually a part of the crust and is of the same polarity. It acts as a bearing for the crust to turn in. The atmosphere and oceans are affected by the helical vortice set up in each hemisphere in opposite directions. This is caused by the depleted lines of primary light giving their energy to motion of the planet. As they are depleted they try to reach rest, like people, so they head for the point of least motion; which is at the poles. Naturally the polarity seeks opposite polarity.

A compass needle does not point to the north magnetic pole

CHAPTER NINETEEN *SPACE, ENERGIES & CONCEPT*

because it is attracted to it by an opposite polarity. Its negative charged end is only pressed into position parallel to the lines of light force going by it. The intelligence, in the molecular arrangement of its negative charge, wants to go with the other positively charged light lines in motion around it.

For the same reason the negative Earth, or other planets, were never part of the positive Sun. The planets being of opposite polarity could be attracted to it but never thrown off from it.

The Suns Insulation Stratum prevents the positive polarity of the Sun from attracting the Negative Earth into it.

Light is transmitted into energy by penetration into matter that interrupts it. The matter then effects motion.

Matter then re-produces the energy effect in reflection. When the reflection loses its energy it is then absorbed into the light.

A negative vortex of light energy produces decelerating effects in negative matter.

A positive vortex of light energy produces accelerating effects in negative matter.

The reason the negative light energy spirals to the North Pole through the Northern Hemisphere, is because it is trying to reach rest-through arriving at the point of least motion.

All negative planets are spherical manifestations of light energy in matter, going through the evolution of becoming positive cubes of matter in space.

All negative planets are of terrene structure. A planet of contra-terrene structure is a Sun. All Suns are cubes. The illusion of the Sun as a ball of fire is because we only observe the negative force field

CHAPTER NINETEEN *SPACE, ENERGIES & CONCEPT*

around it lighted by the resistance it sets up to the lines of primary light energy. We see the surface of negative planets because we cannot see their positive force fields.

Every planet in the universe moves in curved lines of travel. This is not because they were thrown off by a Sun, or central body. If they were, they would not orbit. Anything thrown off of a rotating object will travel in a straight line outward, though it may fall because of gravity on the Earth. The reason planets, or electrons orbit around a central body is — they are powered by light-energy.

Once again, get this straight in your mind — positive or negative light-energy cannot be seen by physical vision. They are both invisible unless they encounter resistance in opposition. They extend infinitely throughout all space and penetrate all bodies in ratio to their densities.

Space outside of the Earth's atmosphere is blacker than the blackest ink. Only the brightest stars can be seen.

In the drawing of our central Sun and the Earth in its cyclic orbit is the explanation of the only way to square the circle.

Light-energy squares the orbit of everybody that travels in it. Light-energy powers everything that manifests motion whether directly, or indirectly.

Pictured in the drawing is what has often been termed "the four dark corners." The Positive Quarter, or Spring Season of the Earth's orbit, is only predominantly positive relative to the Earth's passing through it. At all other times when light-energy is not interrupted by a body, or planet, the negative or female lines of force predominate. The old axiom "women first" is applicable throughout the universe. The Active or Summer Cycle is the hottest in any form of life or motion. The Negative or Autumn Period is always a result of the Active Cycle. The Winter Season or

CHAPTER NINETEEN *SPACE, ENERGIES & CONCEPT*

Rest Period is evident in plants, people or planets. They are all trying to reach a point where they can quit the repetition of "going around in the same old groove."

As the Sun crosses the Earth's Equator on March 21, it effects a positively charged cyclic predominance in the negative northern hemisphere.

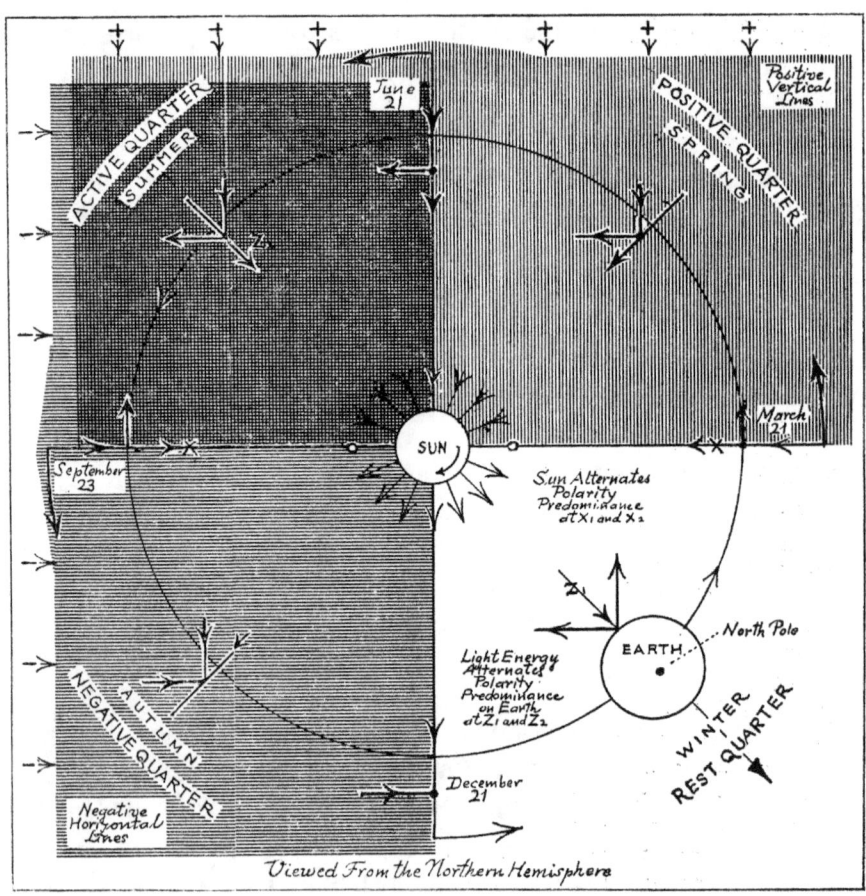

Orbit Principles Of the Earth

CHAPTER NINETEEN *SPACE, ENERGIES & CONCEPT*

In the arc, from March 21 to September 23, the Sun tries to attract the Earth to it. This causes the negatively charged Earth to describe the arc of its orbit from March 21 to June 21. This is noted in the drawing as the Positive Quarter. The reason the Earth proceeds toward the negative lines of light-energy in the Positive Quarter is because the negative lines of light-energy have been weakened from passing through the Sun's force field, or positively charged vortex.

The positive lines of light-energy are repelling the Earth inward to the Sun and the Sun is attracting it inward because the negative northern hemisphere is predominant to the Sun, while the positive southern hemisphere is predominant to the positive line of light-energy.

As the Earth moves from June 21 to September 23 through the arc of its orbit, it starts in the downward direction of its eliptical arc (see the drawing). This is called the Active Quarter. These conditions are being viewpointed from the northern hemisphere in this explanation. In the southern hemisphere the Active and Rest Quarters would be opposite from those shown in the drawing.

As the negatively charged Earth follows its path, in the Active Quarter, it is attracted by the positive Sun on the negative northern hemisphere and by the negative lines of light-energy which are acting on the positive southern hemisphere. The positive lines of light-energy are repelling on the positively predominant southern hemisphere.

The Active Quarter is Summer, our hottest season of the year. This heat is caused by the increase in resistance, set up gradually by the Sun, extending its path on the Earth laterally to its northernmost extreme. In the daytime it is hotter because the Sun is farther into the negative northern hemisphere, thereby setting up more resistance in our negatively charged atmosphere and the negatively charged crust of the negative hemisphere. At the midway point

CHAPTER NINETEEN *SPACE, ENERGIES & CONCEPT*

between June 21 and September 23, the Earth also reaches its maximum exposure to the resistance of both, the positive and negative lines of light-energy. This increase in resistance — from all three forces at the same time — generates more heat.

As the Earth proceeds in its path from September 23 to December 21, the days become shorter as the Sun starts changing from the Equator into the positively charged southern hemisphere.

The positive Sun-effect on a positive hemisphere repels the planet. The negatively charged light-lines of energy predominate and repel the planet from their direction of travel causing it to arc through its orbit to December 21.

From December 21 to March 21 the negative predominance of the light-lines of energy are again decreasing and at Z, in the Rest Quarter all forces reach balance for an instant. At Z, in the Rest Quarter the field or vortex of the Sun decrease both the positive and negative lines of light-energy. The Sun has reached a half-way point between the Equator and its southernmost lateral extreme. Then the positive lines of light-energy begin to attract the negatively charged planet and the increasing predominance of the negatively charged northern hemisphere. The Sun begins to attract the increasing negative predominance of the planet and the negative lines of light-energy begin to repel the increasing negative predominance of the northern hemisphere.

The Sun and all of the planets are moving through space in the 45° direction, indicated by the arrow in the Rest Quarter of the drawing. Everything in the universe is trying to reach balance by traveling in the Rest Quarter direction.

The fact that the Earth has more land-mass in the northern hemisphere than in the southern hemisphere is the reason for the Earth's orbit being slightly elliptical. Land sets up more polarity-action than water. The Sun acts upon the predominance of the polarity of

CHAPTER NINETEEN *SPACE, ENERGIES & CONCEPT*

the hemisphere presented to it by the equinox alternation.

At the March 21 and September 23, both the northern hemisphere and the southern hemisphere are each attracted and repelled equally and oppositely for an instant by the Sun.

The Sun reaches its maximum attraction on the Earth on June 21 and repels at its maximum on December 21.

The light-lines of positive and negative energy act upon the Earth as an alternating negatively charged body. The Sun acts upon the oppositely polarized hemispheres as they are presented to it in seasons, or cycles.

The relative increase or decrease in polarity action varies continuously, depending upon the tilt of the Earth, the resistance of the Sun's force-field and effects of the quarter cycles upon each succeeding cycle.

People have less resistance to disease in Winter, because at that quarter of the orbit the life light-lines of energy are both reduced due to passing through the rotating vortex of the Sun's force-field.

The positive attracting and repelling powers of the Sun and the positive and negative lines of light-energy reach a balance of their forces at a zero point of circumference throughout the Earth's orbit.

This zero circumference circle is the path the Earth travels in its orbit.

Any predominance change of polarity in the Earth's atmosphere or the surface crust will result in climatic changes. This is how positively charged particles from hydrogen bombs have caused weather changes and extremes throughout the world.

The wheel-of-life principle functions the same in powering all

CHAPTER NINETEEN *SPACE, ENERGIES & CONCEPT*

motion throughout the universe.

The Sun does not emit light of itself. The Sun transmits positively polarized secondary force which reacts upon the Earth because of its opposite negative polarity.

The Moon is one of the bodies acting as a governor to the Earth. The Earth's tides are a "fluid drive" connection between the motor-generator-battery Earth, and the governor Moon.

Gravity of the Moon has no effect upon the Earth. The only effect of the Moon upon the Earth is by polarity action on the Earth's force-field and by interruption of the light lines of force.

The Earth is surrounded by a self-generated force-field. Nothing inside of the Earth's force-field is affected by anything outside of it, except through the attracting or repelling effects of polarity in the lines of light energy or the Sun.

Gravity within the force-field, generated by any body, is not subject to the action of any body outside that force-field; unless the body out-side of the force-field is of opposite polarity.

The Moon and the Earth are both of negative polarity — as are all humans in their physical substance and all bodies that can be seen by reflected light.

All negative bodies generate a positive force-field and all positively charged bodies generate a negative force-field.

Temperature is the result of light forces in opposition. Magnetism is an effect of primary light energy in opposition, produced as a result of interruption by any body. Electricity is an effect of magnetism in polarity opposition. Heat is an effect of electricity in opposition. Contraction and expansion are opposite effects of heat, or the lack of it. Every effect is the cause of another effect.

CHAPTER NINETEEN *SPACE, ENERGIES & CONCEPT*

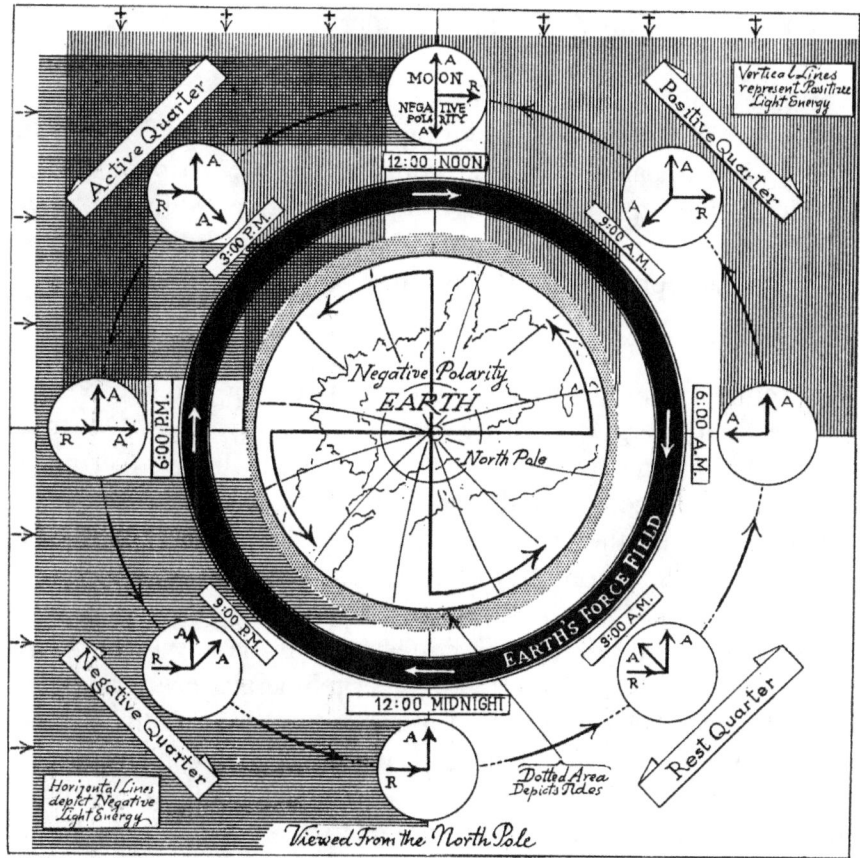

Orbit Principle Of The Moon

Let us start in the Positive Quarter and rotate the Moon around the Earth.

The small arrows, shown on the Moon, indicate the direction of forces set up by polarity affecting the Moon. The A arrows represent attraction forces and the R arrows stand for repelling forces. At all times these forces are changing their predominance until the zero point of curvature is reached, which establishes the Moon's orbit around the Earth. The Moon's orbit speed is fixed

CHAPTER NINETEEN *SPACE, ENERGIES & CONCEPT*

according to its charge of nega-tive polarity.

Everything on the Earth is affected by the Moon's interruption of the positive and negative lines of light energy. Though this effect is variable it is apparent in tides, crops and people. At points where the Moon interrupts the positive — or negative — lines of light energy, natural magnetic vortices — on the Earth — may cease their rotation for an interval of time, or rotate in the opposite direction.

The secondary light rays from the positive Sun and the positive lines of light energy warm the morning cycle from 6 A.M. to 12 Noon. This occurs by the attractive, resistance heat effect in our negative atmosphere and the crust of the Earth. The force-field does not decrease these polarity effects because their polarities are both positive, there-fore they offer no resistance to each other.

The heat registered during the hottest part of the day is the Active Quarter from 12 Noon to 6 P.M. Higher temperatures are registered in this quarter because the Sun and positive lines of light-energy are set-ting up attraction resistance within our atmosphere and the negative lines of light-energy are setting up repelling resistance. Two forces are working in attraction to the force of the Earth's polarity and one force is working in opposition to it. The negative lines of force also meet resistance of the positive force-field, which acts as a parabolic reflector.

From 6 P.M. to Midnight cast the Negative Quarter. Both the positive lines of light-energy and the Sun's attractive forces are eliminated and the negative lines of light-energy maintain only the heat of resistance by repulsion. The forces of the Active Quarter fade away and the negative physical bodies of people become tired and sleepy during the Negative Quarter.

Opposite polarities can only create activity corresponding to the charge of the minimum charged polarity. A negative body requires

CHAPTER NINETEEN *SPACE, ENERGIES & CONCEPT*

positive polarity opposition or it is void. Try running your car with only one post of the battery connected. Nothing happens — yet the battery can be fully charged.

In the Rest Quarter, from Midnight to 6 A.M., the Sun's positive force, the positive lines of light energy and the negative lines of light energy set up no resistance of attractive or repelling forces. So the atmosphere and crust cool off in the coldest quarter of the cycle, because the surface is shielded from the three forces by the planet.

For the same reason more people die from "natural causes" in the Rest Quarter, than in the other three quarters combined. This is because their "physical resistance is low." In other words, none of the three life forces of light are active in the physical body during the Rest Quarter. That is what rest is — the lack of polarity opposition forces. Everything is meant to rest in the Rest Quarter and all of nature does it, except in cases where the positive polarity is predominant.

People of a predominant negative polarity cannot stand to work on a "graveyard shift." People of a predominant positive polarity are often called lazy because their Active Quarter and Rest Quarter reactions are opposite and they want to sleep in the daytime.

It has been maintained by science that the Moon attracts the tides. This is not so any more than the profession that heat comes from the Sun.

Forces exerted to create balanced effects are always strongest at the point of greatest resistance.

The negatively charged Moon is attracted to the maximum perisphere of the Earth's positively charged force-field. The Earth's force-field is divided between the force-field and the crust of the Earth by a ring around the Earth at the equator line. The ring is

CHAPTER NINETEEN *SPACE, ENERGIES & CONCEPT*

called the "arch of the firmament" by the spacepeople and separates what they call "the divisions of Equa." Now recognized by science as The Van Allen Radiation Belt.

The polarity predominance alternates between the northern and southern hemispheres of the Earth and causes the force-field to oscillate. The erratic orbit path of the Moon follows the oscillations of the Earth's force-field. The Earth's positive force-field rotates opposite to the Earth and the Moon's orbit. Interruptions of the light lines of force by other bodies or planets causes variable effects on the Earth and its reactions are transmitted to its self-generated force-field. These influences cause the oscillations to vary and hence the Moon's orbit is variable.

The Earth's force-field causes the attraction of the tides as it is of opposite polarity to the water. The fact that it is strongest at the point of most resistance, where the Moon is, explains the reason that science professes that the Moon attracts the water causing the tides. A negative Moon cannot attract a negative body of water, it would repel the water and in that case the tides would be lowest on the Earth, on the side toward the Moon.

The cyclic interruption of the Moon between the positive and negative light lines of energy, and the Earth, is what causes diurnal in-equalities in the four tides of a day and the age of the tide. Water being a fluid accounts for the equal effect on the opposite side of the Earth. The fact that the force-field is rotating in the opposite direction to the Earth — and is strongest at a point between the greatest resistance of attraction — by both the Earth and the Moon, is what causes the "tides to lag;" which has never been explained satisfactorily by science.

There is no difference in principle between the spacecraft that are being sighted in our atmosphere and the Earth — except the people that operate the spaceships are qualified to use primary light energy, because they conform to the laws of its constructive

CHAPTER NINETEEN *SPACE, ENERGIES & CONCEPT*

principles. The people of Earth have no control over the craft they are traveling on through space. The egotistic minority, that have for generations developed monsterous means of destruction, have prevented the constructive evolvement of the science of true intelligence.

As you travel through the maze of life light lines you often encounter resistance, set up by those who think they are going in the right direction and that you should conform to their direction of travel.

Each was given the individual right to choose their direction.

Scientifically the correct course is at 45° to the lines of light and in a progressive spiral into finer frequencies of light.

This maintains balance between the positive and negative lines of light energy.

The destructive forces try to lead you to the left where you will involve in death or disintegration.

The constructive forces try to lead you into the cycles of birth and rebirth of evolution.

Your consciousness is composed of the same number of atoms as the number of experiences you have had since your Creation as an individual.

Experience is recorded in the consciousness. It is the eternal record of your knowing.

Education and learning are recorded in the brain and can only be used in this mortal grade of life. When the brain is buried with the body, all the learning and intellectual education ends unless it has been applied through experience.

CHAPTER NINETEEN *SPACE, ENERGIES & CONCEPT*

To reach the true intelligence of your many experiences and permanent knowledge requires going within; through meditation you can become aware of your consciousness and unseen intelligence you ac-cumulated in the past.

There is only one life principle, it can only be understood by those who are interested in the true science of their be-ing.

Mundane mortal science and religions are each divided from the other and split many times within their divisions.

Humans can only achieve to at-one-ment through unity; by putting things together instead of taking things apart.

The old accurate science of astrology is almost lost in the muddle of our confused race, who consider it a means of fortune telling. The correct astrological bearing on every person is a study of these influences in relation to time.

As our solar system moves through space, its progression is into an ever increasing frequency of vibrations. Each solar system and every planet must evolve through grades, even as people learn to crawl before they walk.

This space train of planets, following the helical track laid down by our Sun, is like any other train you may ride; the people can only get on and off at the stations. While you are on this planet-car — the Earth — you must conform to its characteristics. However you are also affected by the rest of the train, the locomotive-Sun and the other planet-cars.

The A+ and B---- lines of force pass through your body at 90° to each other. The "G" line of Infinite Light centers your consciousness and separates you, each from all other people, with a boundary of skin. As these positive and negative lines of energy

CHAPTER NINETEEN *SPACE, ENERGIES & CONCEPT*

pass through your body, they activate every atom and cell of your physical makeup.

If their approach to this planet, out of space, is interrupted by one of the other planets, as they are, then you individually are affected by the influence from the other planets.

Our science says the Moon causes our tides, yet in the same breath they contend that the Moon has no effect on crops, people, or other conditions — that this is superstition. The human body is over two-thirds water. Is it superstition to assume that if the influence of the Moon moves thousands of millions of tons of water in the oceans, that the hundred pounds of a person is not affected?

These constant contradictions of science are the results of scientists expressing opinions, while under the influence of these forces. Everything has some effect on everything else in the Universe.

As you move throughout your active day, in an upright position, you are moving in and out of many lines of force. All of them are charged with influences, not only of other planets but from other people, various metal objects, electronic devices and atmospheric conditions. You feel these influences and you may wonder how the day, or year, went so fast. At another time the hours may drag. These time changes are the results of some influence acting upon you.

As you go through your daily activity you move through literally millions of different lines of A+ and B— forces. If you work hard or run you become heated and tired. This is the result of an increase in the number of charged lines of force you have interrupted.

As the electro-chemical action increases in the body, through various attitudes caused by turning, bending and motions of the limbs, heat is generated because of constant changes of the "angle

CHAPTER NINETEEN *SPACE, ENERGIES & CONCEPT*

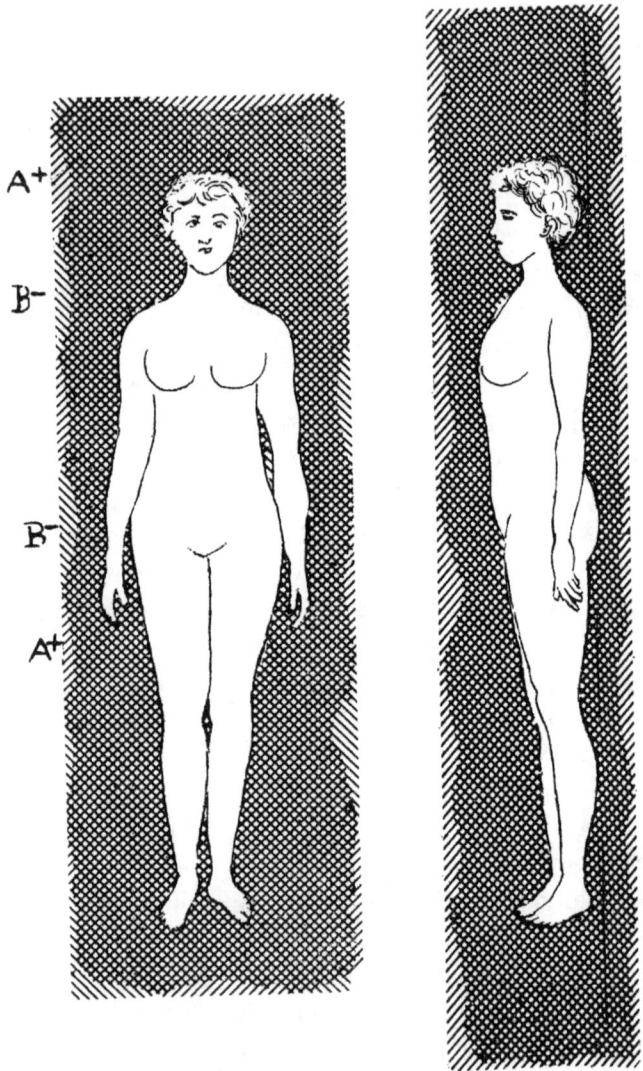

The Lines Of Force And People

CHAPTER NINETEEN *SPACE, ENERGIES & CONCEPT*

of attack" from the lines of force.

When you sit down to rest for a few minutes, this permits the body to absorb the energy from the A + and B- - lines of force issuing forth from the same unchanging direction. Then the atom-cell structure of the body cools off because it reaches balance. This idling condition of the body-motor is brought about by the fact that each atom is receiving steady motion by the same lines of force. It is more important to sleep away from metal objects. Coil springs are especially detrimental to complete rest. Metal conductors of various densities set up vortices that cause a circular motion within the straight lines of force. This is parallel to body activity, so instead of resting, your body is working while you sleep. As each astrological condition affects you individually from birth, according to your time, so too does everything you do affect other people in many ways you may never know about.

You are affected by each destructive atomic blast, as is the weather, the Earth's crust and various other stations of life levels around the Earth and on other planets. The denials of authority in this regard do not cancel the Laws of Cause and Effect.

Your body is an instrument to manifest the Creator's actions. It registers many influences that ignorance refuses to recognize. The One Creator is the only Authority. You are the only one who can read the reactions of your body instrument to the influence of other actions.

Time is only understood by each conscious intelligent unit from its established point of location in motion.

Time cannot be measured, only the repetition of motions manifested as beginnings and endings can be measured.

Each point of beginning and ending are only relative to the understanding of the individual establishing their point of view.

CHAPTER NINETEEN *SPACE, ENERGIES & CONCEPT*

The point of begin and end is established by one individual, so as to bring another individual to the same point of understanding.

Life, time and Be-ing are the trinity of infinity, understandable to intelligence alone. These three are non-existent only when intelligence has been excluded by ignorance in the individual.

Life, time and Be-ing can only exist in space, which is also infinite.

Space is solution, composed of life, time, Be-ing, and intelligence. None of these can be measured in the absolute. They can only enter measurable dimensions when individuals establish points from which to measure.

Length, height, and width; these are only other measurements by which individuals can understand points from which relative measurements are started and ended.

An inch, a foot, or a yard, are not understood by people who use some other devised means of measurement. A relative difference be-tween the measurements must be charted in order to understand the difference between their system and ours.

Measurements can only be achieved in and by motions. No day, or night, could be measured without the motion of the earth revolving. No seasons, or years, would exist if the earth didn't orbit around the sun.

The life span of people on the earth is only arrived at by the measurement of people's time on earth relative to past measurements.

Belief (the illusion of reality) makes people accept the established record of the life spans of other people who have lived before

CHAPTER NINETEEN *SPACE, ENERGIES & CONCEPT*

them, as a measure by which they should live and then die.

The establishment of these points of beginning and end of life are only manifest in matter which has little or no intelligence.

Matter cannot manifest motion without energy. Energy is the motion of thought manifested through matter. Intelligence which has no motion can only manifest through thought, which causes motion to be manifest in matter by thought force.

In symbology the Creator is expressed by a ☉. This signifies the circumference encompassing everything. The circle is an endless line signifying infinity with no beginning and no end.

Life is an essence of the infinite solution we call space. You are living in an endless ocean of life, as are the atoms, planets, and Suns. You could not manifest life, if life were not where you are. Since life manifests everywhere in infinity, you cannot end life, or begin life. You can only establish a point in the endless circle where you began the cycle of manifesting matter in life.

Motion can be symbolized in the endless circle by the sign of an arrow ↟
An arrow has always signified "the way to go." All matter manifesting life in balanced motion moves in an arc. All matter manifesting life in unbalance, or unnatural principles, is symbolized by an angle.

The largest portion of you is space, whether it be the space in the atoms, cells, or tissue composing the matter of your physical body; or the space your limited body as a unit occupies.

Your intelligence is established by the limits of your individual concepts. Everyone uses the One Mind. Your limit is only a measurement of your ability to penetrate and absorb to the full

CHAPTER NINETEEN *SPACE, ENERGIES & CONCEPT*

capacity of the Infinite Intelligence.

Your life span here is only limited to the extent that you can accept matter in form, manifesting life.

Time is variable in your concept of it. One day seems longer, or shorter, than another day.

You are an assembly of other forms of individual manifested life. You are a form enclosing various compositions of atomic, molecular, crystalline, and cellular structure. In turn you are a small individual part of a living planet, solar system, and galaxy.

Change is the result of motion. Time is measurable only in cycles of repetition. Unless you can break out of your groove, you can only manifest repetition of the same old joys and sorrows over and over again.

When you use the Supreme Intelligence to set your course, only then are you master of your destiny. Only then are you going with the natural currents of creation.

Every thought sets up motion. Every motion causes an effect. Your manifestation of matter in motion is the reflection of your true concept, and understanding, of Infinity.

CHAPTER TWENTY *VERIFICATION & DATA*

CHAPTER TWENTY

VERIFICATION & DATA

Verification of past data.

On April 6, 1952, a message was received through the tele-thought beam by George Van Tassel in the presence of twenty witnesses researching into telepathy. The message reads in part as follows: "Your pentagon will soon have much to muddle over. We are going to give this globe a buzz. I hope they do not intercept us from in front."

This was transmitted by an individual named "Noma," from a space-ship, through a beam that registers electrically from the inner ear to the brain. The brain receives the words exactly as if words were being spoken externally to the ear. The message was recorded in our data book On July 19, 1952, three months later, a message through the beam instructed Van Tassel to send the April 6th information to the Air Force. It was mailed the same day by registered mail, with a return receipt requested, along with other data. The return receipt was mailed back from March Air Force Base on July 22, 1952, at 08.50. It was signed Air Technical Intelligence Corn., by Junior Enches — Mail Clerk. The odd part about the return receipt was the "Buy Defense Bonds" cancellation stamp also said, "In The Spirit of Paul Revere." This seemed kind of strange, since Paul Revere warned the people the British were coming, and Van Tassel was warning the Air Force that the spacepeople were going to buzz the Nation's Capitol.

On July 27, 1952, the newspapers across the country had large double headlines. The one in Los Angeles read, "Air Force Jets Chase 'Objects' Over Capitol."

CHAPTER TWENTY *VERIFICATION & DATA*

This incident, which verified Van Tassel's warning, occurred for sev-eral nights over Washington, D.C., and was verified by radar from the control tower and through airline pilots observations. Radar showed they were "solids" and there were formations of from 4 to 12 of the "objects." The newspaper reports also stated the "objects" eluded speedy Air Force jets which tried to intercept them.

A copy of the letter to the Air Force was also addressed to Ted Owens of the Los Angeles Mirror newspaper.

Verification of other data had given Van Tassel the courage it took to inform his government someone from space was going to buzz them. If it hadn't happened, publicity would have ridiculed him. Because it *did* occur, Van Tassel received no publicity. The Air Force didn't even answer the letter. It became a closed incident when it was *verifiable proof* of communication of an *interplanetary nature*.

On August 9, 1952, Van Tassel sent a letter to Mrs. Dwight D. Eisenhower and enclosed a copy of the letter he had sent to the Air Force on July 19, 1952. (Both letters were signed by secretary Mrs. C. H. Severtsen) The letter was addressed to "The Next First Lady" and also informed her that her husband was going to *be the next President* of the United States. This was months before the election. Mrs. Eisenhower was asked to show the letter to her husband. We know she did this because the reply came from Arthur H. Vandenberg, who was then the secretary of General Eisenhower. The letter was mailed from the Brown Palace Hotel, Denver 2, Colorado, and dated August 19, 1952.

Van Tassel also said "Kennedy would defeat Nixon by a close margin" in a radio broadcast from "The Pump Room" in a hotel in Chicago in 1959. This also proved true.

Dozens of other verifiable incidents over the years, with many witnesses, have established Van Tassel as an authority of not only

CHAPTER TWENTY *VERIFICATION & DATA*

what is happening, but what is going to happen.

Since this concludes the compiling of 18 years of the "Proceedings," I want to add a few of the most important articles written in the last four years.

ARTICLES SINCE 1973

HELP GOD MAKE YOU WELL

The story of creation tells how God created all things in six periods of time, and then rested. In no record of the creation is there any reference to God coming out of the rest, and creating anything again.

Since mind is the source of all things, we know God is an infinite essence of perfect intelligence at rest, or everywhere through space and time in a static state.

Knowing that you are encompassed in this mind of God, that this pure essence of life permeates every atom of your being, and that you are physically manifesting God here, will give you the ability to use God.

God loves to be needed, loves recognition, loves to respond to those who are involved in conditions that require help.

God being at rest, neutral, in a static state, needs to be activated in order to respond to mans many requirements. God responds in many ways in times of crisis, like giving a man the super-human strength to lift a wrecked car off of another person. Since God ended the creation, and gave man "dominion over all things," and the right of free choice, you are in a position to command and select to improve, or maintain, your dominion. God doesn't like beggers who come crying for help, only turning to God when they hurt, as if God was a firstaid kit.

When your health is impaired, or injury afflicts you, most people in their suffering try to reach God for help by praying to someone "up there." Expand your concept of God being here, and up there,

ARTICLES SINCE 1973

and everywhere, throughout the infinite universe. Then grasp the fact that you are a creation of God, and when you hurt, God hurts where you are.

Every gene, chromosome, molecule, and cell, in your body performs its electro-biochemical function here in order, coordination, cooperation, and effect, without voluntary thought on your part.

Every cell in your body, 100,000,000,000,000 of them in one human body, knows their function and purpose, because God is where they are. In essence God's mind knows all things, so the cells know what they were created to do, and use that portion of mind they occupy. To us, the cells work involuntarily on our part, but to God they are following the instructions of their purpose in creation.

Every one of your body cells are individuals, like people are individuals. Didn't God give you dominion over all things? Those cells are you. They feel every thought you have. They enjoy your happiness. They suffer when you hurt.

Those poor combinations of cells that compose your physical body, were not given dominion over anything. They can only perform within the limits of the functions God created them for. Each one, in different octaves of resonance, works with others in the same octave to be a heart, a kidney, artery structure, and all parts of the body. In this symphony of octaves, they perform in being the organ, or gland, their vibration is in God.

They get tired, they fail under demands in excess of their limits, and their only rest is in absorbing that rest of God's mind they are in. They each want to live as much as people do.

Cells being in the infinity of mind, like to be praised, and loved, and respected the same as people do. You are on this world, the earth. Their world is in you. Each cell is composed of galaxies of atoms, and solar systems of molecules, like the universe on a micro scale. You are a universe of universes in an infinite universe of planets, solar systems, and galaxies. You are a cell in God, on a planet.

God made you as an eternal electro-magnetic entity to assimilate these combinations of cells here, because the environment on the earth requires a physical body for you to manifest here. Each person is a center of activity in the static mind of God where you are.

God is the still resting fulcrum, the balance point in mind between the two choices he gave to man. Everything throughout the universe moves in order, by fixed laws, in the essence of the perfect mind of God.

In your body of cells, like people, they like a thought of thanks, a "pat on the back" so to speak, for their endless effort to keep your physical body going. How many people ever express their appreciation to this vast civilization of cells they are composed of?

Cells can only assimilate that atomic structure which is within their frequency limits. Anything in excess, or foreign to their frequency is injurious. In this respect they are like a human stomach. That portion of infinite mind cells occupy, established their resonance and that is all they can be.

Brains are a bipolar gland of receptive and projective abilities in the volume of mind they occupy. Brains are an octave of cells that can only be brains. When a person thinks, they only activate the brain to receive that thought, out of the infinite mind of God that knows everything. The brain can only remember those things a person programs into it through education and experience. In meditation one tries to clear the stored information and bring the brain into the neutrality of its bipolar ability of free choice.

The better one can meditate to the balance point, or a state of blank

ARTICLES SINCE 1973

mind, the nearer one gets to God and assimilates from this perfect mind. One is only capable of extracting from this perfect mind of God, those things which the brain limits of concept can receive. Periodic, frequent practice enhances these concept boundaries. Meditation is the purest state of rest that your brain cells can get.

The most intellectual materialist can be a spiritual idiot. Spiritual dominion over all things requires desire and effort. God doesn't let you use God's infinite mind beyond the rights God gave you; neither will God permit mind to be used to uncreate the original creations, without God's fixed laws bringing about reciprocation to the act.

If you are sick, or hurt, in some part of your body, focus your thoughts on that area. Then think to the cell structure, thank those cells, compliment them, apologize to them for not realizing they were intelligent. Get them to be friendly, like you get people to be friends. Then communicate your request that they get in harmony and resonance and correct what is wrong in their area. Think to them periodically. Recognize their community level of life which makes up you. Tell them they are in discord with that portion of perfect mind they occupy. Tell them to get on the ball, because if you die, they all die too. Give them credit for the intelligence of being what they are. Brag them up. They will respond if you have stopped the excess, or condition that made them sick.

Broken bones have been grown back together in minutes by people who understand their dominion over the society of self. This also can be used for others by picturing in mind what they look like and where they are.

When God gave man the right of free choice, God expected man to use it. When God rested, God expected man to awaken God when need required it.

Get on the ball! Love yourself! Laugh! Do all things in moderation. Be happy. The civilization of cells which compose you will respond if you treat them like they are somebody, which you are. God is bored with rest. Use God.

ARTICLES SINCE 1973

THE INTEGRATRON

Since a number of our readers, and friends, have expressed a desire to know how the "Integratron" operates I am writing this article to try to explain it's purpose and function.

The purpose of the "Integratron" is to recharge energy into living cell structure, to bring about longer life with youthful energy. This has been the goal of many people, since Ponce De Leon started looking for the "fountain of youth."

Our effort here, in this giant machine, is not the first idea of it's kind. It is the first time that other research efforts have been brought together and applied simultaneously.

The work of Georges Lakhovsky, Dr. George Crile, Barnothy, Oneil, Tesla, Smith, and many others, is being combined, by us, in a basic re-search to make the principles work. The only new thing we have added to their research is to make the application of three principles occur instantly and simultaneously.

Lakhovsky's Multiple Wave Oscillator (U.S. Patent Number 1,962,- 565) was used by him, in association with many doctors, to correct cellular malfunctions, and accumulations, in many patients. His principle is opposite to control of radiation of radio and television transmission. He spread his radiations over a multiple wave, while television, and radio confine it to channels and kilocycles to prevent overlap, Lakhovsky used a field in which every tissue, organ, cell, and nerve responded in resonance between 10 cms. and 400 meters. This corresponds to frequencies of 3 to 750,000 millards per second. The harmonics extended from I to 300 trillion vibrations per second. No harm. ful side effects or aftereffects were ever noted. In his book "The Secret of Life," first

ARTICLES SINCE 1973

printed in 1939, Lakhovsky detailed the many cases, functions, and results. His Multiple Wave Oscillator took from one application to three weeks of daily applications to achieve its outstanding effects. Our frequency control makes these periods instant in a one shot application. Our basic research is Lakhovsky side effect of rejuvenation.

Lakhovsky established that "every living cell is essentially dependent on its nucleus which is the center of oscillations and gives off radiations." By the same token the sun is the center of our solar system, and life could not exist without it giving off radiations that set up oscillations in living matter. Everything on the earth has been proven to react to sun spots and solar prominences.

Energy principles work on the same basic universal laws; be they atoms, cells, or solar systems.

The wet battery in your car operates on an acid electrolite. The dry battery in your flashlight operates on an *alkaline* electrolite. The separators in your car battery are a *semi-permeable* matrix.

The D.N.A. structure is a caduceus winding coiled in opposite directions. The filaments in the nucleus of a cell exhibit coil and plate configuration. These are microscopic electric circuits that work with the cell electric capacity as oscillators. Cilia in the lungs and respiratory tract are antenna that extract radiations from the air and transmit this energy to the cells in the blood to be conveyed throughout the body.

We are electrical creatures using a bio-chemical body to exist in a electro-chemical environment. We know that in highly diluted solutions certain chemical compounds are disassociated with the result that electrical charges appear, equal, but of opposite polarities. Sodium chloride for an example is disassociated as sodium with a positive charge and chlorine with a negative charge. The body fluids are a saline electrolite with cells in suspension.

ARTICLES SINCE 1973

Every microscopic part of a cell emits radiations according to the atomic structure of its makeup.

Like batteries, cells run down, bodies run down, and the energy loss is manifested as ageing.

The Bible says Adam lived 930 years; Seth, 912; Enos 905; Cainan, 910; Mahalaleel, 890, Jared, 962; and Methuselah, 969 years. Then after these people of the race of Man mated with "the daughters of men" the life span fell off to 120 years according to Genesis 5:5 to 6:3.

After years of Pyramid Generator energy research, there is no question in my mind that V.I.P.s were brought back from death in the sarcophagus of the Kings Chamber. The sarcophagus and the Kings Chamber were constructed of granite. Granite, because of it's matrix of feldspar, mica, and quartz crystals, exhibits a radiation caused by the pressure of the matrix on the quartz crystals known as the piezo-electric effect. Granite was called "spiritual rock" by the Egyptians because of this auric radiation. The energy generated by a pyramid in a vortex is neither electrical, or magnetic as such. It is composed of "this other energy" which radiates life property effects. This energy is everywhere in a static state, and serves in this respect as an insulator and separator while it remains static. When it is activated by thought, as in a prayer, or by resonance in electro-magnetic fields. it reverses its insulating qualities and becomes an infinite conductor.

It is this energy that will respond to our control in the "Integratron" and integrate energy into the cell structure of the body.

There is no reason why people today cannot live as long as Methuselah. I am convinced that he used the Great Pyramid to live so long without ageing.

The D.N.A. configuration, the caduceus coils, the Emerald Tablet

ARTICLES SINCE 1973

principles, and the pyramid vortices all exhibit a method of life energy activity.

We have put in 18 years of endless effort to prolong life without further ageing. We are anchored here on dedicated property. We are not going to go anywhere. It is our intention to be able to regenerate our world leaders, our world humanity and defeat "the last enemy to be overcome — death." It is a thousand times simpler in research than the effort it took to put men on the moon, but we need an ingredient we cannot make and that depends on other humanitarians. We are approximately 90% finished, with new methods already being apparent from the associated researches being conducted by others verifying our earlier efforts.

Jeno M. and Madeleine F. Barnothy, of the Biomagnetic Research Foundation, in Evanston, Illinois, have contributed outstanding results in magnetic research with everything from enzymes to rabbits. They showed retardation of ageing and 30% increased activity in research conducted on mice, whose cell structure is like humans.

Nikola Tesla, and others, showed that high voltage static electricity caused ionization. This causes disassociation of structure and charging of particles in positive and negative polarity effects.

Dr. George Crile, in a fabulous research that he devoted his life to, established that every living cell was a battery, a transducer, and a condenser. In his book "The Phenomena of Life," printed in 1936, he states, "Electricity is the energy that drives the organism." He further states, "It is clear that in the second half of life the *electrical potential* of the elderly patient as a whole or of this or that organ, has been very much reduced and that by so much, the margin of safety has been dangerously diminished." Hugo Fricke, working with Dr. Crile in his laboratory, found that the film which surrounds red blood cells is on the order of 3/10,000,000 of a centimeter in thickness and that this lipoid structure has an electric capacity of high order, viz., 0.8 microfarad per square centimeter.

ARTICLES SINCE 1973

Dr. Crile further stated, "The unit of structure and of function of the living organism is the cell. Plants and animals are disperse systems of cell suspension. The nucleus of the cell is comparatively *acid.* The cytoplasm of the cell is comparatively *alkaline.* The nucleus and the cytoplasm are separated by a *semipermeable membrane*. Therefore the cell is a bipolar mechanism or an electric battery, the nucleus being the positive element, the cytoplasm Vie negative element."

These cell batteries of the body are what we are planning to change with the "Integratron." Each cell has a capacity like the battery in your car. The human body is composed of over 100 trillion of these cells. Our principle of operation is as simple as applying Lakhovskys multiple wave oscillation to Barnothys magnetic fields saturated with Teslas ionization to charge Dr. George Criles cell batteries. Our method of control is through a time function of frequency from zero time to infinity. This is our contribution. The schematic circuitry is a hundred times simpler than in a television set.

It's a strange thing that George is involved in so many firsts. Maybe this is where the expression evolved of "let George do it." Here we have George Crile's research tied in with George Lakhovsky's principles, being extended by George Van Tassel. After all George Washington was our first President, and Nikola Tesla was financed by George Westinghouse. Nikola Tesla's discoveries made Westinghouse what it is today. Then there is the contrast of opposites because *Ge-or-ge* is ge twice with an "or" in between, and Westinghouse's largest competitor is General Electric or G.E., and further in the letter expression of mean-ings, G.E. means *generate energy.*

ARTICLES SINCE 1973

CELL COMMUNICATION

The old witchcraft of tribes of illiterate people, around the world, is now beginning to have some scientific basis in fact. The use of witchcraft powers was always condemned by the church and people who used these powers were considered to be working for the devil.

The power used for witchcraft is the same power used for divine healing. Only by the purpose of its direction by the witch, or healer, is its devilish, or divine result established. If a miraculous healing resulted as an effect of an appeal to deity by the clergy, in prayer, this was accepted and lauded by the church. If someone directed the same power adversely in a curse, or stuck pins in an effigy of someone, this was condemned as the work of the devil.

In the 15th Century, the Inquisition executed thousands of people, regardless of how they demonstrated this power, because they were outside of the clergy, thus they could only be working with the devil. In England and Scotland, in the 17th Century, there were hideous scenes of witch torture and extermination.

Now with Cleve Baxters research which demonstrates cell communication between plants and animals, and plants and other plants, it is accepted that this power is just a power that has no polarity of itself for either good or bad effects. Max Freedom Long, in his book, "The Secret Science Behind Miracles," explained the Kahunas' use of this energy in the Pacific Islands, in the early 1950s.

What science is now proving is that the medicine men of illiterate tribes, centuries ago, knew what they were doing all along. Baxter's work proves cell communication takes place, but it doesn't

ARTICLES SINCE 1973

tell *how* it takes place. Dr. Rhine's research into E.S.P. proved E.S.P. works, but it also doesn't tell *how* it works. Our efforts to explain it is deterred by the fact that the largest percentage of readers do not understand technological or electronics reactions.

In static-electricity, or magnetism, the same polarity laws respond alike. Unlike polarity, or poles, attract; and like polarities, or poles, repel each other. This energy in cell communication only responds to these polarity laws when it is given polarity (good or bad) by the thought of the individual activating it; otherwise it is neutral. This is the "right of free choice" given by God; to use this normally neutral energy, by the individual giving it positive or negative activity by thinking. It is subject to good, or bad labels according to the manifested results. The church committed a greater crime by executing witches than the witches did in using this energy under their right of free choice. The Inquisition didn't establish justice in right or wrong actions, it only established the church as the only authority which could determine what was right, or wrong, by executing the opposition.

Cell structure in all of nature is now responding in reciprocation to the mis-use of this neutral energy. Since the materialistic world has developed by materialistic thinking, the churches are now changing their code of ethics to conform to the very devilish force they condemned in the past. This turnabout will react in the cell structure of their congregations who will not support them financially because satan isn't going to give himself his own money.

We have water, air, and earth pollution chemically, and this is being enhanced by spiritual pollution on the part of the cloth, that hide behind an angels mask worn by the devil.

Spirit on a universal scale is this neutral energy. It has a critical stress point in resonance, where it's natural use insures harmony in all cell structure, and where it's pollution or misuse creates discord and disharmonic resonance.

ARTICLES SINCE 1973

All cell structure conforms to its purpose. It exists as spin *energy* in it's atomic make-up. It has communication in the universal essence of neutral energy with it's own kind. *Every* level of life has this. Thought converts this neutral essence into *linear energy*. When the thought of a minority in race, religion, military, financial, or central control, is only on the material world, disregarding natural law or God, it is only in communication with itself. Therefore it lacks inspiration, dedication, and direction through *linear* activity of the neutral essence of spirit, and manifests in credibility gaps, generation gaps, ecology gaps, and communication gaps.

The neutral still energy doesn't care. It waits to be used in linear direction between spin energy creations it has made. When materialism, dividends, war, profit, tax, and matter, excludes this neutral intelligence, it can only wallow in the mess its ignorance has concocted.

The human race put poisons on their crops and eat it. They put pollution in their water and drink it. They contaminate their air and breathe it, and the cell structure in nature and their bodies react in discord, disease, and death. All of this for power, profit, or purposes that are not natural in universal law.

Cells operate by natural law. The cells in bodies, trees, and all living things cannot conform to laws legislated in government. When the harmony of communication between the cells of people breaks down, there is not only violence and hate between the people, but a spiritual gap has been activated between the people and God. Those who are in this gap say "God is dead." They manifest more devilish activity than the best of witches ever did. In these times they are not burned at the stake. They are condoned by the churches, pacified by the politicians, and supported by the tax payers through welfare programs. People are the cells of this civilization. We make mouth washes to kill germs, we make chemical compounds to clean clothes "brighter than bright." We hire people to haul away the garbage. We create laws to stop disorder and then handcuff the law enforcement in the courts. As cells of the society, we need an antibiotic to deactivate these discordant destructive cells.

As sure as the pendulum will swing back, when it is pushed away, so will this destructive element turn on the very element that permitted them to get away with their devilish witchcraft. This is a natural law.

Cells in nature do not have ears. They cannot smell, see, taste, or touch, in their sensing. But they reciprocate to keep nature in balance. They are responsive to thought and they function by the spirit of neutral energy. They know what to do without education. They are not elected, or appointed. They have no political or financial systems. Yet all of them are in communication with each other and God.

When humanity had the pony express, they were slower in their communication, but they had time to think. Criminals were dealt with severely and in a very short time. Now we have almost instant communication around the world and in space. We have computers and automation. What made this better, faster, instant system get the world into the fix it is in today?

Does a computer recognize a God? Do communication devices care what is sent through them? The most important part of a wheelbarrow is the man behind it. The most important part of a law is its enforcement. The most important thing in government are the people who operate it.

The "right of free choice" will never operate in harmony in the cell structure of society, when a minority of cells in authority drain them to their financial limits in order to propagate a materialistic cabal on a world-wide basis. When the "silent majority" of cell society reacts it will be spontaneous. Woodrow Wilson once said, "The greatest force in the world is the mutual spontaneous reaction of people." It is this "silent majority" who are in harmony in their cell structure. They have perfect communication because they all think alike. They have moral and spiritual principles. They know their God. They are all generals in a crisis. Unless some changes take place soon, the "silent majority" will not speak, they will act. This will be natural reciprocation to the fever that plagues them.

ARTICLES SINCE 1973

THE PYRAMID PRINCIPLE

Orthodox science is now beginning to find that the energy we have been writing about for 18 years, really exists. In the scientific research conducted by Dr. Luis Alvarez, who won the Nobel prize in physics in 1968, standard scientific principles were used. The idea was that cosmic rays passing through the pyramids would reveal any chambers that have not been found yet. A cosmic particle recording device would show less loss of energy on passage through a hidden room than it would through solid stone. This research involved several institutions as well as governmental agreement between both the United States and the United Arab Republic.

Magnetic tapes, which recorded the data, were run through the most modern computer to analyze the results. The tapes revealed that a pattern could not be established from which to establish a stable zero point of reference, and every time the tapes were re-run, they gave a different pattern of readings. Not only were the patterns *different*, but certain data *disappeared* from the tapes. The final conclusion was that what was occurring was not only *impossible*, but some energy was being registered *that does not conform to the laws of science.*

Vern Cameron, of Elsinore, California, was conducting experiments 30 years ago in order to try to understand what this energy is that does not conform to known scientific laws. Vern found out that meat could be preserved for an indefinite period of time, after being subjected to this unknown energy generated by a small pryamid. He also found that a razor blade could be used to shave with over a hundred times, before it lost it's sharp edge, when placed under his small pyramid.

ARTICLES SINCE 1973

In collaborating with Vern, we not only verified his results, but also found that an egg in a saucer would solidify under the pyramid in a week, while one outside of the pyramid in a saucer remained fluid. Milk kept in a carton with a pyramid shaped top will also keep fresh for an indefinite period of time without refrigeration. This is now patented in France where cartons are used for dairy products.

The common denominator in all of these findings is that the *shape* induces the energy. It must be a four sided pyramid, and the most energy results from a 52° angle on the sides. The most powerful results are obtained when the pyramid is oriented with the sides parallel to north, south, east and west directions.

Tests we have conducted, over the years, prove that the *corners* are the operational necessity as holes cut in the sides do not detract from the generating force. Another point that we discovered, is that in order to achieve *maximum* energy, the pyramid must be fastened down, so it cannot be disoriented. The maximum energy requires 28 days, one magnetic month, to reach it's peak. We also discovered that a *quartz crystal* peak on the top, where the capstone should be on the Giza pyramid, will produce other effects. We believe that a laminated quartz condenser, with germanium separating the quartz sheets, on top of the pyramid will produce energy readings on present scientific instruments. Due to lack of money, we have not been able to conduct other tests that should produce electric power for use.

It is our firm conviction, after years of anlysis, that the Great Pyramid of Giza, was used to produce power, used for rejuvenation, used to make mummies, used to restore life, and used as a launching power to start space ships out of the earths gravity.

One of our associates in Park Ridge, Illinois, has accomplished levitation with single pyramids and a group of four pyramids. She has established a "norm" where the point of levitation of either hand will occur. She has established that some of the charge will

ARTICLES SINCE 1973

remain for a period of three days; and that from the original point of first levitation, that the time diminishes from 7 minutes and 45 seconds, down to 45 seconds in five exposures. She also discovered that "dowsing rods" activate over the pyramid in the lowest level of her home, and activate equally as strong upstairs in the highest level of her home. This same associate also discovered ancient Hebrew and Greek root meanings to words in the bible, which we printed in the "Proceedings" ten years ago, do translate into modern English meanings. We printed this in offering a comparison between our "Integratron" and Mose's Tabernacle.

Capt. Bruce Cathie, in his first book "Harmonics 33" and in his second book, "Harmonics 695" shows by physical proof and mathematics that the power grid system of the earth involves the Great Pyramid and the Stonehenge circle in England.

Application of "natural power" can be used to increase crop growth, eliminate destructive insects; used to diagnose disease and the treatment of it; used for interplanetary communication, the preservation of food, a power source for transporation and other things too numerous to mention. The only requirement to use this "free energy" is our ability to couple into it, store it and transmit it. First of course it must be accepted by the scientists, and an economic system of exchange devised to permit its use. These two requirements are the barrier which logger-head profit and power hungry opponents will not accept to make a "heaven on earth" possible.

The builders of the Great Pyramid had to know science beyond our present knowledge because the Pyramid measurements incorporate the speed of light, the mass of the planet, the acceleration of gravity, weights and measures, the axis of polar rotation, the distance to the Sun, the 26,000 year procession of the equinoxes, the Earth's magnetic field, the Earth's orbit around the Sun, the value of trigonometry, and latitudes and longitudes among many other things.

ARTICLES SINCE 1973

The stones in the Great Pyramids structure weigh up to seventy tons. Granite was used to encase the Kings Chamber because granite produces a "piezo-electric" effect due to the matrix of quartz crystals, mica, and feldspar. The bulk of the pyramid of Giza is limestone which has no electrical ability. The granite chambers above the Kings Chamber form a granite air condenser for energy storage. The Kings Chamber was built off *center purposely* to place it in the power area of the energy generated.

On the Great Seal of America, printed on the one dollar bill, we see the pyramid with the capstone removed *upward*. In the center of the capstone is the all seeing eye and the capstone is surrounded with the radiance of power. The spirit is supposed to go *upward* at death. Pyramids apex upward as do cones and church spires. Coils are spiral. I.R.I. in *spirit* is the same as IRIS in the eye. The centering focus of all seeing, light, and energy. Pyramid means fire, or light, in the center. The word "spirit" comes from the Latin Spirare. Spire is "a body that shoots upward to a point." The Accadian word Pir, or Bir meant light.

All of nature spirals, Spiral nebula, spiral vines, spiral rising smoke, spiral water running down a drain. The structure of cells in a hair are spiral, the D.N.A. of life is spiral, as are coils to activate magnetism in the cores. Pir-a-mid is to activate light energy in the center.

If you look at the Sun in the morning as it comes up, you will see a spiral cone shape surrounding it. This is the same spirit energy the pyramid generates which the ancients called the "Shekina Glory." Electricity, magnetism, and gravity, are side-effects of spirit energy.

The pyramid was called K-HU-TI by the Egyptians, and K-HU in Egyptian means "The Luminous One." HU is HUE now, meaning a mixture of colors.

One of the peculiar puzzles, to those who have spent any time in

ARTICLES SINCE 1973

the Kings Chamber, is the intense bone-chilling cold that is felt, like it was inside of the body.

In the secret alchemy of The Emerald Tablet, the "formula of life" and the mathematics of the "mystery laws" apply to the Great Pyramid. The four elements, fire, water, earth, and air coincide with the four faces. The three principles of alchemy, circulation, fusion, and spagyric equasion are parallel to the three sides of the triangular shape of each face. The reciprocal action in a living instrument produces Universal Harmony, or life energy.

The sarcophagus follows the "Node of Nature" which doubles the cube, and produces cubical crystals in gold, silver, and salt.

We are anxious to apply the pyramid principle to make a refrigerator. We believe a two story high pyramid with a conveyor belt feeding it through one side, would shrink city garbage to one-quarter of its volume and could be shipped dry as a land mulch to agricultural areas.

A pyramid shaped top on a storage shelf for food, open on all four sides, would preserve fresh foods and fruit without refrigeration. These principles have already been proven on a small scale.

Resonance of any object depends on its shape, the same as the shape of an airfoil must correspond to the airflow in order to prevent resonance. Resonance is the reciprocating action in spirit that makes things live. In matter and physical things, resonance can be in discord and cause things to break. This has happened in the construction of new buildings, where the city noise and traffic have caused buildings to collapse because the structure in steel was a framework of cubes. A resonance that might be in *harmony* with a sphere might also be in discord with a cube. Shapes are a science in themselves, long ignored by scientists. Ancient symbols are each a separate scientific principle of applications of energy for different purposes.

ARTICLES SINCE 1973

The pyramid principle of power will create a "Cube of Infinity," a "Cone of Silence," a "Capstone of Eternal Youth," a "Sarcophagus of Preservation," and a "Vortex of Cosmic Power." The transmutation of matter can also be accomplished with the pyramid power.

It was found that the mummified flesh when ground to a powder and taken internally served as a cure-all for all internal ailments and caused broken bones to heal back together in a matter of minutes. Therefore mummy matrix was a common cure and sold in apothecary stores. The energy that caused the body to mummify was stored in the flesh and was the potent healing agent.

Those of you readers who are interested in conducting tests and making pyramids should remember that the critical thing is to make the sides on a 52° angle. The best size is around a foot to 18 inches high. The pyramid can be made of cardboard, hardboard, metal, plas-tic, or any other material. The corners can be attached with tape, or glued. Holes can be cut in the sides without affecting the energy. The pyramid should be fastened down on a fixed shelf, or bench, with the sides oriented with a compass. The east and west sides should be parallel to north and south.

If a series of pyramids are used and a wire is run from the top of one to another with the end wire running to a coil wrapped around a piece of iron pipe, it will be possible to direct the energy in a cohesive beam, like laser, to an undetermined distance. The beam can be turned, like light, by reflecting it off of a mirror. A plastic tube should be slipped over the coil and pipe. Winding spacing and wire size are not critical. The wire should be insulated. We would be interested to see what this beam does when run through a prism.

There are an unlimited number of tests that can be done which haven't been tried yet.

We believe this energy which responds to some optical laws and some electrical laws, will be the energy that replaces atomic, and

ARTICLES SINCE 1973

fossil fuels for the ultimate power for all puropses.

We are working on an instrument which will detect and measure this energy.

ARTICLES SINCE 1973

BREAKTHROUGH

For twenty years we have been trying to inform people of the Universal Energy in the "Proceedings." "This Other Energy," "Prana," "Life Fields," "Fohat," "Eloptic Energy," and all of the other names it has been called, are expressing the same thing.

The breakthrough to demonstrating this power in the last few years now is being accepted, even though it still is a mystery.

In the June, 1974, issue of "Saga" magazine, another masterpiece of writing by Joseph F. Goodavage, presents new aspects of the use of this energy.

"The American Medical Association and the American Cancer Society have flatly refused to look into a revolutionary test involving electrodynamic fields that can predict cancer, heart disease, and many other illnesses and ailments — long before any physical symptoms appear. And scientists who specialize in the study of seed germination can now forecast the growth patterns, size, and general vitality of future plants by using similar tests."

"These electrodynamic fields appear to be the same as the so-called `aura' seen around human beings and other living things and are profoundly influenced by the power of the mind."

We have printed for years that this power is *Universal Mind*. It is the *static* essence of the Creative Mind that created the universe. It is the power that makes so called "miracles" work. It is the power that is responsible for healing through healers. It is the *Mind* that created identical order in the atomic structure. It makes the pattern *exact* in the crystalization of all of the elements. *It* made the pattern of the stars and galaxies. It combined the elements in exact ratio in

ARTICLES SINCE 1973

water. It created every law and principle of nature that science and religion can only copy.

Goodavage writes: " — the Rev. Franklin Loehr, reported that two boxes in which he had placed identical amounts of seed and soil had — through the power of human thought — produced entirely different results."

"He wanted to prove to his congregation that 'prayer is very real and very effective.' The care and conditions given to each box of seed and soil were identical. The only variable was that Dr. Loehr's parishioners prayed for the seedlings in one box and ignored (or in some cases `cursed') those in the other."

"To everyone's amazement the prayed-over seeds blossomed many times faster and produced sturdy, beautiful flowers. Those in the other box barely managed to sprout a few stunted growths. Evidently there was something to the power of prayer, but there was no way of knowing how the mind was linked to such power."

We have proven that this *static mind* of universal power can be activated by thought, by prayer, by electro-magnetic fields, and is the feeling in every living thing that we call *emotions*. Discoveries, and inventions, are the results of people assimilating from this Master Infinite Intelligence the *laws* of all the principles they apply to their devices.

"Since 1966 Backster and his colleagues have widened their investi-gations to include all kinds of fruit and vegetables, yeasts and mold cultures — also blood specimens and scrapings from the roof of a hu-man mouth. They extended these observations into the realm of amoebas, paramecia, and even spermatozoa — all of which supported their contention that 'primary perception' is a Universal phenomenon operating throughout the evolutionary scale. They had detected a previously unknown communication signal that seemingly links all living things, and by 1971 a California scientist had picked up and recorded similar signals

ARTICLES SINCE 1973

from outer space' " (See SAGA, January 1973).

L. George Lawrence, one of our best associates, has perfected a method of bringing this mind media into instrument reading range in the electro-magnetic spectrum, with a bio-transducer of "living matter." (See SAGA, January 1973).

George De La War photographed these emanations of "life force" in England, 30 years before the now much publicized Kirlian effect. Max Freedom Long, another associate of ours, wrote of the Kahuna use of these powers in his book "The Secret Science Behind Miracles."

Dr. Ravitz, explained, as Goodavage reports: "The cellular structure in certain parts of the human body is completely renewed every six months. It is the L-field, not the DNA molecule, Dr. Ravitz explained, which molds the new material, derived in part from food intake, into the same design as the old. 'This explains why, even though you might not see a friend for a year or more, during which time all the molecules of his face and head have completely changed, he is recognizably the same.' It also explains why you can remember events of five, 10 or even 20 years ago when every molecule of your brain has been replaced perhaps half a hundred times." This proves that the *spirit of mind* holds the same pattern in figure, and you are a reflection of yourself here in a matter environment.

"Edward Russell, in his book Design for Destiny, states: 'In their present preoccupation with particles, biology and biochemistry are in the same stage that physics was years ago before 'particle physics' gave place to 'field physics.' When biology finally matures and 'particle biology' gives way to 'field biology' the role of genes and DNA will be seen in its true perspective."

We have explained in past issues of the "Proceedings" that, "Time, Space, and Being are the *trinity of infinity*." Time is absolute, Space is absolute, and Being is the manifestation of all living

ARTICLES SINCE 1973

things which *live eternally somewhere* in the universe forever.

"Your nervous system, for example, did not develop from the demands of a hostile terrestrial environment (as the theory of evolution states). Instead, it came into being as a result of dynamic forces superimposed on the groups of cells by the total field pattern — your individual L-field."

"The indestructible quality of L-fields suggests: a) that they are changeless; and, b) being changeless they are not influenced by physical evolution. It is possible that there's another area of being, another state or 'dimension' where the Universe exists in a kind of Eternal Now — a 'timeless' condition. Our conception — even our experience — in time may not be what our subjective senses tell us. Time might be apocryphal — just one way of seeing reality. An observer in an airplane for example, can see what the motorist below sees, but in addition he can also see where the motorist has been and where he's going — simultaneously."

"If 'past' and 'future' are purely subjective, then they might coexist with the present. L-fields are changeless because they appear to exist in another dimension where all time is `now'." We have recommended "Saga" before to our readers, as the out-standing magazine to keep up with the times.

Uri Geller, a young Israeli, is confounding the scientific field, by bending forks, and other metal objects, by concentrating on the form that they bend to. Others are now succeeding in duplicating Geller's phenomena. This is the proof of "mind over matter."

In "Psychic" magazine of June 1974, another friend, Andrija Puharich, who is sponsoring Uri Geller in the United States, reports about many of Uri's abilities. One of these is moving the hands of a watch. "A typical example of this feat, which Geller has done hundreds of times, was witnessed by former astronaut Captain Edgar D. Mitchell. Captain Mitchell looked at his watch, a Chronometer, that he had worn on his flight to the moon; the time

ARTICLES SINCE 1973

was 10:00 A.M. The watch was placed face down on the table by Captain Mitchell with his hand over it, so that it was hidden under his hand. Uri Geller concentrated on this hidden watch for some thirty seconds, and then told Captain Mitchell to turn the watch over. The hour and minute hands had been `moved' back one hour and eight minutes. In addition, the separate Greenwich mean time dials had also 'moved' back one hour and eight minutes. Captain Mitchell bears testimony that this demonstration was conducted under cheat-proof conditions. Science has no explanation for this phenomenon."

These examples of control, by mind, are fulfilling the latter day prophecy of the Bible which says, "All things shall be revealed." It didn't say *who* would reveal them.

Puharich goes on in the article: "I finally became convinced that what Geller did could not be explained within the present boundaries of science. This made the quest all the more exciting because it allowed the possibility of extending the frontiers of science into totally unknown areas. But I had no intellectual tools that would allow progress in such unknown realms. This dilemma was resolved for me on December 1, 1971, when in the course of a routine hypnosis experiment with Uri Geller a voice appeared from, or near him, which announced itself as a representative of an extraterrestrial power."

What biological science doesn't seem to grasp is that the brain is a bio-transducer that can transcend the mundane level of human thinking and reception of thoughts. The inner ear is a transducer that converts sound into electrical impulses to the brain computer. Uri Geller attributes his ability to control, bend and break metal to extraterrestrial power working through him as Puharich relates in the "Psychic" magazine.

Twenty years ago, on August 24th, of 1953, I told of a personal physical contact with these extraterrestrials, who landed here at Giant Rock Airport and gave me the formula that started the

ARTICLES SINCE 1973

"Integratron" research. We have miles of tapes with their voices recorded giving information beyond human knowledge.

Puharich further relates in the Geller article:

"I have tried to determine the purpose of this communication with man in our time. I am told that the beings from Hoova have been observing earth for some 20,000 years. They have made contact with earth men only intermittently in this period. Some of the admitted contacts are well known figures in history. However, the relationship has always been kept secret. For reasons unknown the pledge of secrecy has been relaxed in our time. I am now asked to reveal the communications from Hoova to man. I do not know who else on earth is in com-munication with Hoova."

"All of the phenomena exhibited by Geller are products of the advanced ideas, science, and civilization of Hoova. They seem to have solved every problem that now plagues earth and its inhabitants. I would say that their great achievements rest on three sciences unknown to man."

1. The power to cause objects to disappear, translocate, and appear elsewhere.
2. Total control over biological systems ranging from design, reproduction and healing repair, to the imprinting of feelings and ideas.
3. The ability to travel across time (in the way we travel across space) in what we would consider to be no-time."

The UFO seems to be a time machine . .' that can carry out these three broad functions.

"The basic attitude of the beings from Hoova toward man appears to be benevolent. The life span on Hoova averages about a million years. Hoova wants to help man, but feels that man is scarcely capable of accepting Hoova or carrying on a civilized discourse. A being from Hoova affirms that there is a God in the universe who

ARTICLES SINCE 1973

cannot be reached by any being except as an idea. Such is the sketchy profile we have of Hoova. Were it not for the tangible reality of Uri Geller none of this would be believable."

ARTICLES SINCE 1973

WORLD POWER GRID

Since Nikola Tesla's early experiments with extracting energy from the earth, there have been a number of attempts to produce electrical power from this giant solar electron.

The fact that the Sun causes variations in the fluctuation of the earth's energy, due to sunspots and flareups in the Sun, is well established.

Government appropriation of billions of dollars, to obtain energy from the Suns radiations, in only a "battery charger effect" to another "Rube Goldberg" method of indirect energy.

Alfred Hubbard obtained energy directly from the earth, and demonstrated that it could be transmitted, as was written about in the December 17th, *1919 Seattle* Post Intelligencer newspaper. The pictures in the paper showed the Hubbard device lighting a 200 watt light bulb.

Hubbard, then only 19 years old, powered *an 18 foot boat* around Portage Bay, near Seattle. Operating a 35 horsepower electric motor, with no batteries in the boat, he cruised around for hours on the energy produced from his device.

One of our associates, Art Aho, learned considerably about Hubbards device from a man that workeJ with Hubbard at the time. Art was also working with Lester Hendershot when he was lighting a 100 watt bulb from a similar `basket weave" coil.

Both Hubbard, and Hendershot used what was called, in old Chinese records the "Cosmic Flower," which they claimed was "the source of all power." Both principles employed a pulse resonance with the earths grid system and created a secondary induction between the two windings on the coils. Hubbard's coils were round, in both the primary and the secondary; and Hendershot used a round configuration in the primary with a diamond shaped secondary as the result of the "basket" weave in the winding.

Hubbards transmitter was in exact resonance with the transducer he had aboard the boat. He collected the energy in his transformer by running wires 1200 feet in north, south, east and west directions underground, from the center. The outer end of the wires attached to hollow tubes 18" long that had mercury in them. The wires passed through the earths energy grid wave. The mercury apparently created a choke, or pulse block, that forced the current to go to the central primary circuit.

It is evident that even then, in 1919, "the powers that be" were not going to allow "free energy" to come into use.

In the magazine "Electrical Experimenter" of February, 1919, in an article titled "Famous Scientific Illusions," written by Nikola Tesla, he says regarding his transmission of power; "Some experts, whom I have credited with better knowledge, have for years contended that my proposals to transmit power without wires are sheer nonsense but I note that they are growing more cautious every day. The latest *objection to my system* is found in the *cheapness of gasoline*. These men labor under the impression that the energy flows in all directions and that, therefore, only a minute amount can be recovered in any individual receiver. But this is far from being so. The power is conveyed in only one direction, from the transmitter to the receiver, and none of it is lost anywhere. It is perfectly practicable to recover at any point of the globe energy enough for driving an airplane, or a pleasure boat or for lighting a dwelling. I am especially sanguine in regard to the lighting of isolated places and believe that a more economical and convenient method can hardly be devised. The future will show whether my foresight is as accurate now as it has proved heretofore."

ARTICLES SINCE 1973

Here in 1919 you see the greatest genius, Nikola Tesla, saying it can be done and in Seattle unknown to Tesla, Hubbard was transmitting energy to drive a *pleasure boat*. Tesla's reference to "the cheapness of gasoline" being the opposition to his principles of clean power is pos-sibly why after Tesla died, his giant energy transmission tower on Long Island was torn down and his energy transmission station at Colorado Springs was obliterated. Today Ed Gray is running into the same opposition in getting his magnetic motor into production motor cars.

Hugo Gernsback, President of the Experimenter Publishing Co., in which Tesla's articles were printed, says in the same issue; "If we were sending pure Hertzian waves, why do we connect one wire at both sending and receiving stations to the ground? Hertz never dreamt of such a thing. If you are still unconvinced that the earth is the chief medium of transmission, disconnect your ground wires entirely and try to send and receive. Now you may work with Hertz waves but the distances you can bridge will be pitifully small."

One can check the earths energy, not only as a conductor, but as an amplifier by putting a ground wire on their radio to the chassis.

A book, published in the German language, in Innsbruck, Austria in 1952, explains the findings of outstanding researchers into the earths power grid system. The title of this book is "The World of the Secret Forces." In German, "Die Welt Der Geheimen Machte."

The men involved are Dr. Willi Schlosser, Prof. Hellmut Wolff, Hans-Wilhelm Smolik, Heinrich Reblitz, Theodor Weimann, Herbert A. Lohiein, Ferdinand Reich, Univ. Prof. Dr. Hubert J. Urban, Dir. Prof. Dr. K. Sailer, Prof. Dr. Georg Anschutz, Prof. Dr. Theol and Adolf Koberle. Quite an impressive group of qualified professional people, to agree, and be involved in one book. They established that the earth is covered on the surface by a grid system of positive and negative poles in a checkerboard pattern.

ARTICLES SINCE 1973

Excerpts from the book are as follows:

"Each of the squares has a *center pole* surrounded by *8 smaller poles*. (Here again is the Chinese Cosmic Flower, the Hubbard Coils, the Tesla System of extracting energy from the earth. Ed.)

These squares vary in size from the equator, getting smaller in the direction of the earths poles. The main pole concentrates energy. At North Latitude 48° (The latitude where these men conducted their research. Ed.) the center pole has a diameter of 2.45 meters. The 8 smaller poles have a diameter of 60 c.m. Four of the 8 outer poles (alternately) send energy up toward the sky. The other four send energy outward horizontally to North, South, East and West.

The squares (48° N. Latitude) are 15.90 meters diagonally from center to center poles.

$$\frac{N}{sinus} \quad 45° = \frac{15.9}{0.707} = 22.50 \text{ meters}$$

A border field is mingled together in the Northwest and Southeast directions and in the Southwest and Northeast directions. These 4 corners of the squares seem to connect the fields of 2 of the negative smaller poles and two of the positive smaller poles.

At these points any person (or body) will receive a mixture of negative and positive energies.

The side length measurements at the equator are 32 meters long. It was found out that the earth between its North and South Poles was a "stick" magnet. On this magnetic field there are electric currents perpendicular to the "stick" magnet.

Strange to say that the Cheops pyramid on the 30° North latitude, stands on a diagonal measurement of the pole field of 30 meters on each side of the squares.

ARTICLES SINCE 1973

The main center poles of each positive square shows a direction of energy from above to below the earths surface. There a vortex is created with a pulse like the hand of a clock. The negative poles are vice versa.

Dr. Rohracher, of the University of Vienna made a very sensitive electro-magnetic tuning fork (The Hendershot device also has a magnetic tuning fork. Ed.) that showed from 7 to 18 movements per second. Prof. Dr. Regelsberger made an electrometer which showed electric impulses of 10 millionth of an amp.

Dr. Muller, from Zurich, Switzerland, measured the electric field on the human body. The body "aura" will change if you move into a different location.

This means the magnetic or electric field of the earth is different.

The 'dowsing rod' can locate the center of these positive and negative poles. These measurements should be made with different lengths of 'dowsing rods.' The length gives different wave length readings.

The point you find with the rod is a knot of a free standing wave. (We call this energy point a 'time zone' or 'this other energy.' It is not magnetic, or electric. Hieronymous calls it 'Eloptic Energy.' Ed.)

The 'aura' of the human body will be charged on all positive polarity pole centers and it will discharge the human 'aura' on all negative poles until no aura is registered. This is how one can register whether the poles are positive, or negative.

These experiments are physiologically and psychologically of the greatest importance to health. Whoever goes into the secret of the earths ray powers will know the wheel of destiny.

ARTICLES SINCE 1973

These powers are free, not the power from our power plants. These in and out powers have to do with the human organism. The trouble zones and health zones have to do with the movement of the planets and stars. In the micro-cosmos it (the earth) is the electron that is in the command of our creator. (What a statement to come from these distinguished men. Ed.).

This is the pattern of the secret of creation and this is why the Chinese speak of the secret of *the golden blossom.*

It is well known that there are rows of cancer houses in certain towns and most of these inhabitants are dying of this terrible sickness. The dowsers have proven that the bedrooms of cancer patients are on the grid crossings of the trouble zones.

Waldemar V. Jankowsky wrote about the cancer problem and said the light quantum and the Pi-electron are the cause. The dowsers proved these trouble zones are in the positive fields. Frh. V. Pohl wrote; 'earth beams are sickness exciters. We could find the positive fields by experiments.'

The places of the negative polar fields shows entirely different effects on the human organism. Now here is an entirely new field for search-ing doctors who are interested in the world of fine beams. Through *this effect* the life span of the human can be changed." (This verifies what we are trying to do with the "Integratron" machine. Ed.).

Captain Bruce Cathie's two books "Harmonic 33" and "Harmonic 695" seem to follow a pattern "township" grid composed of many of the smaller grids like "sections."

It is strange that the German material and Cathies grids coincide on the great pyramid, and other points on the earths surface. These researches conducted years apart and on opposite sides of the globe tend to verify each other.

ARTICLES SINCE 1973

The fact that microwave transmissions, and receptions, are being carried on through the earths surface by coordinating resonance at different points, is proof that secret scientific people are already aware of the great potentials of the grid system for power, navigation, and antigravity directional control.

Baxter's research with plants; the Hieronymous research with insects; research into bio-transducers by L. George Laurence; Kirlian photo-graphy; acupuncture, and numerous other aspects are verifying each other.

In the "Proceedings" of November *1953*, on page five we explained the "earths force field." Four years later science verified this and called it the "Van Allen Radiation Belt." In the 1953 article we printed: "this ring maintains balanced interchange of power through the crust and atmosphere of this planet."

In the September-October *1965* issue of the "Proceedings," on page 4, we wrote up the earth forces in an article titled, "This Amazing Armature." In the 1965 article we said, "There are other fields in the earths bulk that are not measurable with a magnetic instrument such as a compass. These fields, and currents are the carriers and distributors of what we call 'life force.' This 'life force' is only measurable and detectable through *'living'* instruments and it is also subject to *thought."*

If people knew they were living in a positive square on the earth they would move, or be subject to the physical ailments caused by it.

This article could go on indefinitely, because there is not enough research going on for the benefit of people, and too much going on for their detriment.

Mrs. Ford, the Presidents wife, and Mrs. Rockefeller, having to suffer the conditions of breast cancer surgery, is proof that the detrimental forces can affect people in the highest positions in life.

ARTICLES SINCE 1973

It looks like the government would appropriate more money to study these forces and subsidize those people who are already involved in the research into this "life force."

ARTICLES SINCE 1973

THE BERMUDA TRIANGLE

The "Bermuda Triangle," the "Devil's Triangle" and other references to the area near Bermuda is receiving much attention lately in motion pictures and national magazines.

Most of the events pictured, and written about, end up with the same old question of "what happened to the ships and planes that disappeared? Some authors assume that the U.F.O.s caused the phenomena without one iota of true evidence in that direction.

In the first place there are 12 of these areas known to exist in the world. Researching this as a hobby over the last 20 years has established several things to us.

1. The U.F.O.s have nothing to do with it.
2. The forces that cause it to occur are intermittent and unpredict-able at present.
3. The Navy Department and Advanced Military Research know more about it than anyone except us, and they are not going to tell anybody.

There are some things about this phenomena that we cannot write about; but we are going to offer you more than you have read before.

The *pure* creation of everything out of perfect Universal Mind started matter and energy, as contrasting manifestations of duality in all things. Each creation has within itself the ups and downs and the positive and negative polarities of electrical law; the north and south of magnetic laws, and the good and bad of the laws of order and conscience.

ARTICLES SINCE 1973

The earth, being a speck of matter in the universe, was once created from the primary lines of energy, in space, and established as a crystal dodecahedron with twelve facets.

The laws of perfection are *exact* in crystallography, showing the *order* of creation from intelligence beyond our human comprehension. The crystals of each chemical substance have a separate and definite set of angles. In all crystals of the same substance, the angles between corresponding faces are constant.

Twelve facets — twelve hours — twelve months — twelve disciples —all come from a system of *order.*

Since silicon is the most abundant element found in the earth (outside of oxygen which is a gas), the earth would logically have been created as a silicon crystal. Silicon in crystal form is quartz and quartz crystalizes in equal divisions of 6 sided pyramids. This is 12 facets on both ends. The six side facets are prismic connectors of the two ends due to the volume of material present.

So we have 6 facets in each hemisphere of the earth — six facets on each end of a silicon crystal and the fact that the most abundant element of the earth's composition is silicon . . . Hang on "Bermuda Triangle" lovers, we are coming to that!

Quartz, the pure crystalline form of silica, also shows other interesting potentials. Electrical currents come from a quartz crystal under pressure. This is referred to as the piezo-electric effect. Quartz crystals, sliced into thin wafers control frequency in radio and communications. Since the structure of the earth is under changing pressure, it resolves that intermittent reactions can occur with influence from the sun and other planets. Now note that the lines and the nodes of the world grid seem to manifest reactions relative to a time influence, not yet calculated; also it is obvious that atomic tests above, or below, the sur-face can have long range results in both atmospheric and geophysical happenings.

ARTICLES SINCE 1973

Years ago Dr. Kowski, and engineer Frost, demonstrated gravity nullification in the Nessertsaddin Werke (Laboratory) at Darredein, Poland. They caused a 25 kilo (57 lbs.) weight to levitate with the application of constant wavelengths over a quartz-resonator. A clear quartz crystal became cloudy and expanded in size. The quartz crystal never became clear again and remained in its expanded state. Apparently the electrons moved out of the molecule band and could not return and thus the whole structure of the crystal was changed. The question of the clear quartz crystal not being transparent anymore was explained through the expansion of the crystal. In spite of the expansion of the quartz crystal of 5.2 mm length and 1.5 mm profile to 10 cm gross, it *retained its original shape.*

The reason I am bringing out this information is to validate our conclusions that the node of the crystal structure of the earth at the point of the "Bermuda Triangle" becomes active at intervals and levitates ships and planes into space. This is why no debris has ever been found of the lost ships and planes, either in the water, or on the bottom of the ocean at this location.

The clouding in the quartz crystal, when it raised 57 lbs., could also account for the last radio message from a flight of 5 Navy aircraft that disappeared on December 5, 1945. They radioed at 3:45 P.M. that they had no idea where they were, that "everything looks strange, even the ocean. It looks like we are entering white water." What they described was a condition of molecular change in both the ocean and atmosphere. The visual ionization of the atmosphere left the pilots with no horizon, or direction, as their instruments failed to work. This foggy condition was equivalent to the cloud effect that occurred in the quartz crystal when gravity nullification effects occur where moisture is present.

Gravity holds things *together.* Antigravity *separates.* Further expansion of the quartz crystal would have caused it to disappear — or be converted from matter back into energy. This happened as

ARTICLES SINCE 1973

a side effect in a quartz crystal we were lapping to the final precision measure-ments of the square of the lines of primary energy. When the exact dimension was reached the quartz pyramid vanished suddenly. No sound — no light — no heat — no nothing, and no place for it to go. This is what occurs when ships and planes reach a resonance of the frequency of their molecules and an energy time constant.

We have recently taken part in producing a motion picture about phenomena for a German producer that, we understand, will be released in five languages. Through this association we became friends with Dr. Frank Lang of Delta Productions, Ltd., who is now planning a motion picture on the "Bermuda Triangle." They have purchased the eight-man submarine that was used in the movies made with Lloyd Bridges. Frank was here a few weeks ago and I had the opportunity of seeing many color pictures they had taken from the air over the "Bermuda Triangle." Under the clear water is a *long white line* which we believe to be one of the world grid interlace edges of a silicon earth crystal facet.

The only other place we know where the *white line* appears is on land in Ecuador in South America. Interesting — one of the 12 pentagon grid nodes is also in that area! We wrote in a past "Proceedings" about this white line, but will use the data here again to correlate the grid with the white line in the "Bermuda Triangle."

The *white line* in Ecuador causes a person to feel weightless as they come close to it. Secretly it was called "the only place of nongravity on the earth." Ecuadoran natives in the area shun it as tabu and tell of animals that run onto the white line being instantly whisked into outer space. It seems that a form of security by some authority keeps people who try to investigate this phenomena out of the area.

Dr. Lang offered your director an invitation to be one of the eight men aboard the submarine that is to explore and make a new

ARTICLES SINCE 1973

factual undersea motion picture of the "Bermuda Triangle." I turned the invitation down because of the risk involved, since our work here to finish the "Integratron" is most important. I would have enjoyed being a part of this thrilling adventure but responsibility is greater than desire.

In his book, "Harmonic 695," Captain Bruce Cathie calculated the grid harmonics for the "Bermuda Triangle" area on the date and time of the Navy plane disappearance a quarter of a century ago. His calculations relative to the sun at the latitude of 26° 20' north and longitude of 78° 25' west, established that there was an unstable set of harmonics at that point in the world grid system at the time of that particular incident. His conclusions were that, "all the aircraft involved in the disappearance were either completely disintegrated, or moved through space time."

Most disappearances, in any of the 12 known areas of the world seem to occur only at periodic intervals. In the "Bermuda Triangle" most of the ships and planes have vanished between November and February. This is the winter solstice time relative to the sun.

Evidence that a space-time continuem is involved, is the fact that airliners flying over these areas, have on several occasions arrived several hours ahead of schedule at their point of destination. The time of some of these flights, from take-off to landing exceeds the speed capability of the aircraft by several hundred miles per hour.

In our "Proceedings" issues of October and November of 1954, and January of 1955, we printed drawings showing the linear lines of energy in space causing the earth to orbit the sun, the earth to rotate on its axis, and the moon to orbit the earth.

In the December 15 issue of the "Proceedings" in 1953, we printed the data on these linear lines of energy relative to speed and density. At that time however we failed to relate that the *negative* lines of linear energy in space are *backing up* in time, or going retrograde from the present.

ARTICLES SINCE 1973

In the October 1954 "Proceedings" we explained how disintegration occurs. The article was titled "Birth and Death." Since everything from atoms, to planets, to galaxies is affected by these linear lines of force, "Birth and Death" is an interchange of matter and energy. Time, as we know it, relative to motion, is a day by day experience which seems to go faster as we get older.

If the grid output in the "Bermuda Triangle" reaches a resonance with the positive and negative linear lines of energy at the 16,000 miles per second differential, then anything at that point, and time, will either fly off the planet as gravity is nullified, or disintegrate. The sun plays an important part in this, as Hieronymous found out; that in the shadow side of the moon *emission of energy* is nullified. The negative won't work without the positive.

Creation is an act of mind. Mind is the causal excitation of the linear lines of energy in space. Atoms are formed from the induction of these linear lines. Molecules are atoms clustered in the structure of matter, people, aircraft, and ships. Creation was made to also unmake itself, like unraveling a knitted sweater.

The Creator (Infinite Mind), established laws that demonstrate to people, in many ways, that time is absolute. Atoms change in what we call the half life cycle. They produce tremendous power if this natural change is accelerated as in an atom bomb. This is a matter to energy change. The critical mass exceeds its ability to stay glued together, (like people falling down when they lose their balance).

What occurs at the nodes and edges of the world grid lattice is a refraction between two facets (like mirrors) by the linear lines of energy creating a resonance that disintegrates, or nullifies gravity.

If Kowski and Frost had increased the expansion of their quartz crystal beyond the gravity nullification and antigravity point, their quartz crystal would have disappeared.

ARTICLES SINCE 1973

This is a difficult article to write in laymans language; we are only trying to offer you a true viewpoint on the "Triangle" disappearances around the world.

We comment to those "Johnny come lately" authors and experts who write about the "Bermuda Triangle," and never had an experience with a U.F.O., "Be thankful their crews are compassionate and forgiving people."

Bruce Cathie's calculations, verifying that the "Integratron" here is centered on a grid harmonic is geophysically indicated by the silica knolls around it.

The Bible says "in the latter days all things will be revealed," so we continue to try and find the answers.

"When Stars Look Down" they see the human race going down to ruin because they do not follow the laws of nature.

www.ingramcontent.com/pod-product-compliance
Lightning Source LLC
Chambersburg PA
CBHW062005220426
43662CB00010B/1239